COMPLETE
ARABIC
THE BASICS

LIVING LANGUAGE®

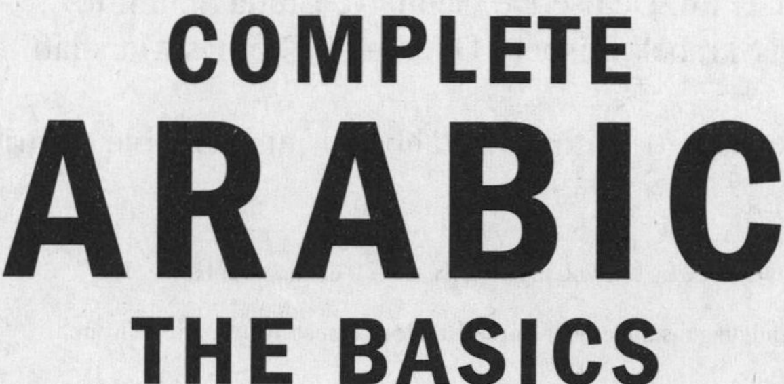

Written by
Amine Bouchentouf

Edited by
Rym Bettaieb
and
Christopher A. Warnasch

Acknowledgments

Thanks to the Living Language staff: Tom Russell, Nicole Benhabib, Christopher Warnasch, Zviezdana Verzich, Suzanne McQuade, Shaina Malkin, Elham Shabahat, Sophie Chin, Denise De Gennaro, Linda Schmidt, Alison Skrabek, Lisbeth Dyer, and Thomas Marshall.

Thanks also to Wafaa H. Wahba for his valuable contribution.

Living Language is a member of the Random House Information Group.

Published in the United States by Living Language, an imprint of Random House, Inc.

www.livinglanguage.com

Editor: Chris Warnasch
Production Editor: Lisbeth Dyer
Production Manager: Tom Marshall
Interior Design: Sophie Ye Chin

First Edition

ISBN 978-1-4000-1992-2

Library of Congress Cataloging-in-Publication Data available upon request.

PRINTED IN THE UNITED STATES OF AMERICA

10 9 8 7 6 5 4 3 2 1

TABLE OF CONTENTS

INTRODUCTION

Welcome to Living Language® *Complete Arabic: The Basics*, a beginner's course in Modern Standard Arabic developed by the experts at Living Language. The *Complete Arabic* course package includes this course book, three hours of recordings, and the *Complete Guide to Arabic Script*, which may be used with each lesson, or after you've completed the entire course. This program was designed as a simple, straightforward way to gain a strong foundation in pronunciation, vocabulary, grammar, and basic conversational skills in Modern Standard Arabic, the most widely recognized and standard form of Arabic. *Complete Arabic: The Basics* will teach you how to get by in most common and practical situations you'll encounter—traveling, shopping, eating out, talking about your family or your job, making social plans, and more. The course will provide you with a wide range of basic and useful vocabulary, and it will introduce you to all of the important grammar and structure you'll need to speak and understand Arabic. It also includes plenty of pronunciation practice and essential cultural information. If you prefer to focus on spoken Arabic, you'll find that the transcription system used in this course is intuitive and simple to master. But this program will also give you the opportunity to master reading and writing Arabic, both through short introductory sections in each lesson of this coursebook, and through the supplemental *Complete Guide to Arabic Script*. You can use the script guide along with, or after, this course book, depending on your own needs and goals.

Living Language *Complete Arabic: The Basics* is different from many of the other Arabic courses available to speakers of English. Arabic is not as commonly studied a language in the West as, for example, Spanish or French. For that reason, many of the courses available in Arabic are overly complicated because they rely on a very traditional approach, similar to the methodology used to teach native-speaking Arab children about their own language. But the Living Language *Complete Arabic: The Basics* course is designed with the same simplicity and accessibility to non-native speakers that has made the other languages in the series best sellers. Grammatical explanations are straightforward and easily understood by anyone, regardless of experience in Arabic or any other language. All potentially confusing terms are explained, whether they pertain to grammar in general or are specific to the study of Arabic. Whenever possible, clear comparisons are made to English constructions, so unfamiliar Arabic grammar is more easily grasped. Material is recycled and reviewed, making it easier to remember. There are plenty of examples, practice, and exercises to make learning Arabic an easy and enjoyable step-by-step experience. In short, this course was designed to be as uncomplicated and effective as possible, even for people who are new to studying languages.

There are fifteen lessons in *Complete Arabic: The Basics*. The first lesson is an introduction to Arabic pronunciation, and it presents each sound and its transcription, with plenty of recorded practice. Each of the following fourteen lessons focuses on a particular theme or topic, such as making introductions, eating, shopping, asking directions, talking about one's family, or making social plans. Each of these lessons includes the following components:

Dialogue

The dialogues are short and easily managed, and they include examples of vocabulary and grammar which will be covered later in the lesson. The dialogues are recorded, first completely and at slightly slower-than-normal speed, and then very slowly with pauses for repetition. The English translations of the complete dialogues are provided as well.

Language Notes

Following each dialogue is a list of language notes. They refer back to words, expressions, constructions, or bits of cultural information in the dialogue that are worthy of further discussion. A language note may clarify a point of grammar, remind you of something you learned in a previous lesson, or provide you with a cultural context for something in the dialogue.

Vocabulary

Each lesson contains a vocabulary list with words and expressions related to the topic or theme of the lesson. This list contains not just words appearing in the dialogue, but also a wide variety of items related to the lesson as a whole. Each new word is recorded so that you can model your pronunciation on that of a native speaker.

Vocabulary Practice

Following the vocabulary list is a chance to practice the material in it through a simple translation practice. The vocabulary exercises also include recycled material to help you remember words and expressions learned previously.

Grammar and Usage

Each lesson teaches three to six grammar points that were demonstrated in the dialogue. These points follow a natural progression through the course and build on one another. They are clearly explained in plain language, and there are plenty of examples of each new construction. Many of these examples are recorded to provide further practice. While new grammatical concepts and terms are explained as they appear, there is also a glossary of grammatical terms in the back of the book for reference.

Grammar and Usage Exercises

Following the presentation of new grammar and structure are several exercises for practice. They are designed to help you understand and assimilate the new information, and they also touch upon previously learned material to help you remember it.

Pronunciation

Even though the first lesson in this course presents a comprehensive overview of Arabic pronunciation, each subsequent lesson focuses on particular sounds to help your pronunciation become as close to a native speaker's as possible. The sounds are explained simply, with comparison to sounds you're already familiar with. There are also plenty of words for you to practice with on the recordings.

Arabic Script

Each lesson also focuses on a group of letters in the Arabic script. These sections serve as an introduction to written Arabic, and they are linked to specific sections in the *Complete Guide to Arabic Script* that will provide you with much more practice reading and writing. However, if you prefer to focus first on spoken Arabic, there's no need for you to refer to the material in the *Complete Guide to Arabic Script* until after you've completed this course book.

Cultural Note

The cultural note in each lesson presents important information that is not directly related to the Arabic language, but that is nonetheless essential to anyone who will interact with people from Arabic-speaking countries. These notes range from information on food and clothing to the concept of time to the place of religion in the Arab world.

Answer Key

At the end of each lesson is an answer key, containing all the answers to the vocabulary practice and the grammar and structure exercises.

How To Use This Book

The most important thing to keep in mind is that you should always proceed at your own pace. Do not feel pressured into thinking that you have one chance to digest information before moving on to new material. Read and listen to parts of lessons or entire lessons as many times as it takes to make you comfortable with the new words and the new constructions. Regular repetition is the key to learning any new language. Do not be afraid to cover material again, and again, and again!

Get yourself a notebook. Each lesson contains material that you'll learn much more quickly and effectively if you write it down, or rephrase it in your own words once you've understood it from reading it in the book. Take that notebook with you to review wherever you have time to kill—on the bus or train, waiting at the airport, while dinner is cooking, or whenever you can find the time. Remember—practice and lots of review make perfect when it comes to learning languages.

Make time for your new language. The concept of "contact hours" is another key to learning a language. It's best to set time aside regularly for yourself. Imagine that you're enrolled in a class that takes place at certain regular times during the week, and set that time aside for Arabic. It's better to spend less time several days a week than a large chunk of time once or twice a week. In other words, spending thirty or forty minutes on Monday, Tuesday, Wednesday, Friday, and Sunday will be better than spending two and a half or three hours just on Saturday. When you expose your brain to a new language frequently, it has no choice but to start picking it up. And the longer the intervals between that exposure, the more you'll forget.

Begin this course with the first lesson so that you gain a general sense of the sound system of Arabic. Part of what makes Arabic difficult for non-native speakers is that there are sounds that are, simply put, totally foreign to most other languages. But don't panic—there really are only a few of these sounds. Gaining a sense of them will make the language less daunting, and you'll be able to assimilate new words more easily if the "landscape" doesn't seem so alien. Listen to sections of the pronunciation lesson as many times as you'd like until you're familiar with all of the sounds. It's not necessary that you learn to pronounce these sounds perfectly. Good pronunciation of a foreign language comes very slowly, with a lot of practice. Be patient with yourself, don't be afraid of sounding a bit "off," and listen and repeat as many times as you'd like.

Once you've demystified the sounds of Arabic, you'll be ready to begin the actual lessons. Lesson 2 and each of the subsequent lessons can be handled in the same way.

1. **Get a sense of the lesson:** Start by reading the introduction and scanning through the entire lesson so that you have a sense of what you'll learn.

2. **Read and listen to the dialogue:** Read the dialogue through once without the recordings to give yourself a rough idea of the words and constructions you'll hear, and make sure you read the translation so that you know what's being said. Next, turn on your recordings and listen as you read. You'll first hear the dialogue through in its entirety, and then you'll hear it with pauses. Repeat in the pauses provided. Read, listen to, and repeat the dialogue a second and even a third time so that you're comfortable with it, always checking with the translation provided. Finally, it's a good idea to hear the dialogue a few times without the book, so that you can begin to build your listening comprehension.

3. **Read the language notes:** Read through the language notes so that you benefit from the explanations of particular words, expressions, constructions, or cultural information.

4. **Learn the vocabulary:** Learning new vocabulary is one of the most difficult parts of learning a language. There are several ways to go about it, and you should develop a sense of what works best for you early on.

Refer to the "Tips for Learning New Vocabulary" provided toward the end of this introduction, and try out all of the suggestions until you know which one, or which combination, works best. Use your notebook to write down the new words. You should plan on spending a good amount of time on the vocabulary list—not just reading it through once or twice. Also be sure to listen to the recording of the new words a few times. Then, see how you do with the vocabulary practice, and check your answers at the back of the lesson.

5 **Learn the grammar and listen to the examples:** Treat each grammar topic separately, and read through it and its examples a few times before moving on to the next. Look back at the dialogue, or at previous dialogues, for examples of the construction being presented, reviewed, or explained further. Use your notebook to summarize each point, and copy the examples so you can practice and review later. If there's a term that you don't understand, look it up in the glossary of grammatical terms in the back of the book. Once you've gone through all of the grammar points (and remember to take as long as you need for that!) listen to the examples that are recorded a few times. Then practice with the grammar and usage exercises and check your progress against the answer key. If you need to, go back and review again.

6 **Practice your pronunciation:** Read and listen to the pronunciation section and repeat several times so that you sound as close to the native speakers as possible. New sounds will require you to use muscles in your mouth and throat that you don't have the habit of using. You'll need to build those muscles and become familiar with using them. Apply the same principle as you would at the gym—do lots of "reps." Of course, if you have access to a native-speaking friend, ask him or her to help you out as well. If you can, listen to Arabic songs or newscasts and try to focus on the sounds you've learned. Don't be afraid to imitate—even in an exaggerated way—native speakers you hear.

7 **Learn the new letters:** Read the section on Arabic script next. This will give you a brief introduction to several Arabic letters. If you've decided to focus on spoken Arabic first, you can leave it at that. Don't worry about tackling the material in the *Complete Guide to Arabic Script* until you've completed this course book. Or, if you've decided to learn written and spoken Arabic simultaneously, each of the script sections will refer you to specific sections and practice exercises in the *Complete Guide to Arabic Script*.

8 **Learn a bit of culture:** Read the cultural note in each lesson to become familiar—in a broad sense—with some aspect of life in the Arab world. Remember that these are short, general notes, so particulars will probably vary from place to place. If you have access to people who have lived in an Arabic speaking country, whether they're Arabs or not, ask them to share their experiences. And always remember that cultural gen-

eralizations, while helpful as a starting point, are just that—generalizations.

9 **Repeat, as necessary:** Go back and repeat as much of each lesson as you need to. Don't be afraid to do the whole thing over a second or third time if you need to. Each lesson is a foundation for everything that comes after it in the course; so, the better you build that foundation, the sturdier the whole structure will be.

Tips

As you work through each lesson, here are some tips to help you get the most out of your studies:

Tips for Using the Recordings

All of the recorded material appears in print in the book—in the dialogues, the vocabulary lists, the grammar sections, and the pronunciation sections. Use the recordings along with the book at first, and then listen to them without the aid of the book to help build your listening comprehension. The recordings will also offer a great way to review older material as you progress. Take them with you on a portable player and review dialogues you've already learned. Listen in your car, on the train, while you walk, while you jog, or anywhere you have free time. Remember that the more exposure to and contact with Arabic you have, the better you'll learn.

Tips for Learning New Vocabulary

You obviously need to learn new words in order to speak a language. Even though that may seem straightforward compared with learning how to actually put those words together in sentences that mean anything, it's really not as simple as it appears. Memorizing words is difficult, even just memorizing words in the short term. But long term memorization takes a lot of practice and repetition. There are a few different ways to "lodge" a word in your memory, and some methods may work better for you than others. The best thing to do is to try a few different methods until you feel that one is right for you. Here are a few suggestions and pointers:

Spoken Repetition. Say a word several times aloud, keeping your eye on the written word as you hear yourself speak it. It's not a race—don't rush to blurt the word over and over again so fast that you're distorting its pronunciation. Just repeat it, slowly and naturally, being careful to pronounce it as well as you can. And run your eye over the shape of the word each time you say it. You'll be stimulating two of your senses at once that way—hearing and sight—so you'll double the impact on your memory.

Written Repetition. Write a word over and over again across a page, speaking it slowly and carefully each time you say it. Don't be afraid to fill up entire sheets of paper with your new vocabulary words.

Flash Cards. They may seem like child's play, but they're effective. Cut out small pieces of paper (no need to spend a lot of money on index cards) and write the English word on one side and the Arabic word on the other. Just this act alone will put a few words in your mind. Then read through your "deck" of cards. First go from Arabic into English—that's easier. Turn the Arabic side face up, read each card, and guess at its meaning. Once you've guessed, turn the card over to see if you're right. If you are, set the card aside in your "learned" pile. If you're wrong, repeat the word and its meaning and then put it at the bottom of your "to learn" pile. Continue through until you've moved all of the cards into your "learned" pile. Once you've completed the whole deck from Arabic into English, turn the deck over and try to go from English into Arabic. You'll see that this is harder, but also a better test of whether or not you've really mastered a word.

Mnemonics. A mnemonic is a device or a trick to trigger your memory, like "King Phillip Came Over From Great Spain," which you may have learned in high school biology to remember that species are classified into kingdom, phylum, class, order, family, genus, and species. They work well for vocabulary, too. When you hear and read a new word, look to see if it sounds like anything—a place, a name, a nonsense phrase. Then form an image of that place or person or even nonsense scenario in your head. Imagine it as you say and read the new word. For example, the word for book is *kitaab*. That sounds a bit like "key tab." Imagine a book with tabs in its pages and a key on the cover, or your Aunt Kay drinking a Tab and reading a book, or your friend Keith's tabby cat asleep on a book, or anything that works for you. It doesn't have to make sense to anyone else. This may sound like a round-about way to learn a word, but it will really help.

Remember that the more sense triggers you have—hearing, reading, writing, speaking, imagining a crazy image—the better you'll remember.

Groups. Vocabulary should be learned in small and logically connected groups whenever possible. Don't try to tackle a whole list at once. Choose your method—repeating a word out loud, writing it across a page, etc., and practice with a small group.

Practice. Don't just learn a word out of context and leave it hanging there. Go back and practice it in the context provided in this course. If the word appears in the dialogue, read it in the full sentence and call to mind an image of that sentence. If possible, substitute other vocabulary words into the same sentence structure ("Ahmed goes to the *library*" instead of "Ahmed goes to the *store*.") As you advance through the course, try writing your own simple examples of words in context.

Return. This is the key to learning vocabulary—not just holding it temporarily in your short term memory, but making it stick in your long-term memory. Go back over old lists, old decks of flashcards you made, or old example sentences. Listen to recorded vocabulary lists of previous lessons. Pull up crazy mnemonic devices you created at some point earlier in your studies. And always be on the lookout for old words appearing again throughout the course.

Tips for Practicing

Try to expand your experience of Arabic outside of this course. The best option, if available to you, is to practice with native speakers you may know. Even if it's just a ritualized "hello, how are you today?" it will help. As you gain more confidence and learn more, practice asking more complex questions and trying to decipher the answers. If you don't know anyone who speaks Arabic, television, radio, music, films, or the internet will help. Listen to an Arabic news channel, rent a subtitled Arabic film, listen to an interview or a song, or search the internet for words written with letters that you might recognize. You won't understand everything, of course, or even most of it, but you'll be surprised at how much you can pick up. And then there's always one of the greatest joys of learning a new language—enjoying the cuisine. Go to a Middle Eastern restaurant, and if the Arabic names are printed on the menu, try to order in Arabic, learn a few new vocabulary items, or at least sample some wonderful new food.

Now, you're ready to begin. *HaDHDHan saxiidan*! Best of luck!

LESSON 1

PRONUNCIATION AND TRANSCRIPTION

In this first lesson you're going to focus on Modern Standard Arabic pronunciation and the transcription system used in this course. The purpose of this first lesson is not to make you an expert, so don't pressure yourself to master every sound and memorize every single transcription symbol used. You don't even have to memorize the meanings of the examples now. What this lesson is meant to do is to give you a general sense of Arabic pronunciation and show you that by far the majority of sounds used in Arabic are not really so foreign. That way, when you move into the actual language lessons, you'll have something to hold on to.

Luckily most of the sounds in Arabic are pronounced exactly like sounds in English, and in these cases the transcription system in this course simply uses the letters that represent those sounds. For example, there is a sound in Arabic that is pronounced just like the sound at the beginning of the English word "big," so the transcription symbol used for that sound is *b*. Then there are other sounds that do not occur in English, but are found in other European languages, so even if you're not familiar with them, they're explained easily enough. Finally, there are a small number of sounds that are most likely very foreign to you, but still, they'll be described in detail, and you'll have plenty of opportunities to hear, repeat, and practice them. The key is to listen carefully to the recordings and mimic the native speakers as they pronounce the examples of each sound.

Before we get into the pronunciation of Arabic, let's talk very briefly about the Arabic alphabet and writing system. For a much more in-depth presentation of Arabic script, along with plenty of reading and writing practice exercises, see the *Complete Guide to Arabic Script*. Arabic is written right-to-left in a cursive script, meaning that most of the letters are joined to one another, like English handwriting as opposed to the letters you're reading right now. The letters take different shapes depending on where they appear in a word—first, in the middle, last, or in isolation. The Arabic letters you'll see in this section are the isolated forms, and they're included not so that you memorize them, but just to remind you that the transcription you'll be using is a short-cut to the "real" thing.

Another characteristic of written Arabic to keep in mind is that short vowels are not normally written, except in children's courses, the Koran, and, thankfully, in courses for students of Arabic! Normally, just the consonants, long vowels, and diphthongs are written. When the short vowels are written, they appear as small strokes or swirls above or below the consonant that is "carrying" them. In other words, *da* would be written in Arabic as the letter *d* with a small stroke written just above it. Long vowels and diphthongs are written as bona fide letters, but you don't need to concern yourself too much with this right now. All vowels are of course written in the transcription used in this course. You'll learn much more about the Arabic alphabet in the Arabic Script section of each lesson and in the supplemental *Guide to Arabic Script.*

Now we'll take a look at all of the sounds in Modern Standard Arabic so that you'll know how to pronounce each new word that you see in this course. We'll divide the sounds into groups—vowels, the many sounds that will give you no problem because they're pretty much identical to sounds in English, the fewer sounds that will give you very little trouble because they're found in other familiar languages, and finally the few difficult cases. You'll see the actual Arabic letter, its name, the transcription letter used in this course, a description of the sound, and several examples of Arabic words where the sound occurs. Don't worry if you want more practice—you'll focus on particular sounds of Arabic in each of the lessons that follow.

Vowels

There are three vowels in Modern Standard Arabic, but each one has both a long and a short variety. There are also two diphthongs, which are compound vowel sounds formed by gliding more than one simple vowel together. So, all in all, there are eight vowel sounds to focus on. Bear in mind that vowels in Arabic should always be clear and crisp, and they should never be reduced as vowels often are in English.

َ

a

The first short vowel in Arabic, called *fatHa*, is written as a short stroke on top of other letters. It can be pronounced like the *o* in *hot*, the *u* in *sun* or the *e* in *bet*, depending on the consonant before it. Consonants pronounced in the front of the mouth or with the teeth tend to make this sound more like *eh*.

wa (and) ***man*** (who)
walad (boy) ***kataba*** (he wrote)

ُ

u

The second short vowel in Arabic is *Damma*. It is written like a tiny, backwards *e* over another letter. It's pronounced like the vowel sound in *put* or *foot*.

kutub (books) ***hum*** (they)
hunna (they) ***funduq*** (hotel)

---

i

ِ

The third and last short vowel in Arabic is *kasra*, written just like the *a* sound, but below the letter that carries it instead of above it. It's pronounced like the vowel in *sit* or *fit*.

bint (girl) ***min*** (from)
'ism (name) ***rijl*** (foot)

ا **aa**

The long vowel *'alif*, which is also the first letter of the Arabic alphabet, is pronounced like the short *a*, but it's held longer. It can also sound like a long *–eh*, depending on the consonant before it.

baab (door) ***kitaab*** (book)
laa (no) ***salaam*** (peace)

و **uu**

The long vowel written with the Arabic letter *waaw* is pronounced like the vowel in *pool* or *tool*. If you pronounce the English words *look* and *Luke*, but hold the vowel in *Luke*, you're pronouncing both the short and long *u* and *uu* of Arabic.

nuur (light) ***duud*** (worms)
thuum (garlic) ***katabuu*** (they wrote)

ي **ii**

The long vowel written with the Arabic letter *yaa'* is pronounced like the vowel in *sea* or *me*. If you pronounce the English words *pit* and *Pete*, you're pronouncing the short and long Arabic *i* and *ii*.

diin (religion) ***kabiir*** (big)
qaSiir (short) ***'ismii*** (my name)

وْ **aw**

The compound sound, or diphthong, written with the letter *waaw* with a small circle over it is pronounced like the vowel in *house* or *brown*.

yawm (day) ***SawT*** (sound)
dhawq (taste) ***xawm*** (swim)

يْ **ay**

The diphthong written with the letter *yaa'* with a small circle over it is pronounced like the vowel in *bait* or *late*, or sometimes like the vowel in *my* or *buy*.

bayt (house) ***laylaa*** (Layla)
kayf (how) ***khayr*** (goodness)

Consonants

Now let's take on the consonants. Remember that we'll use the convention of dividing them into three groups—the ones that are just about identical to sounds found in English, the ones that occur in other familiar languages, and finally the really tricky ones that generally give non-native speakers the hardest time.

Before we begin to look at the consonants, though, it's important to mention one important point. There is a difference in pronunciation between single and double consonants in Arabic. A double consonant must be held longer than a single one. For example, the *n* in *'anaa* (I) is held for about half as long as the *n* in *fannaan* (artist). This is easier to do with some consonants, such as *f*, *z*, *s*, *sh*, *th*, *n*, and *m*, which are produced with a continuous flow of air. Say these consonants aloud and you'll see that you can hold them for as long as your air supply lasts. Other consonants, such as *b*, *t*, *d*, or *k*, are produced by blocking airflow, so you can't hold them as you can the others. In these cases, pronounce the double consonants with a pause in the word. For example, *shubbaak* (window) sounds almost like two words *shub* and then *baak*.

Group One

ب **b**

The letter *baa'* is pronounced just like the *b* in *boy* or *book*.

bint (girl) ***bayt*** (house)
baab (door) ***al-baSra*** (Basra)

ت ***t***

The letter *taa'* is pronounced like the *t* in *take* or *tip*.

taktub (you write) ***tazuur*** (you visit)
tilmiidh (pupil, student) ***fatHiyya*** (woman's name)

ث **th**

The letter *thaa'* is pronounced like the *th* in *thank* or *think*. Be careful not to pronounce it like the *th* in *this* or *that*; this sound is a separate letter in Arabic.

thaaniya (second) ***thalaatha*** (three)
thaa' (the letter *th*) ***thuum*** (garlic)

ج ***j***

The letter *jiim* is pronounced differently throughout the Arab world. In western and central North Africa as well as in the Levant, it is pronounced like the *s* in *measure* or *pleasure*. In Egypt and Yemen, it is pronounced like the hard *g* in *go* or *get*. And in the eastern Arab world, it is pronounced like the *j* in *jelly* or *joke*.

jariida (newspaper) ***jamiil*** (beautiful)
jaziira (island) ***jayyid*** (good)

د ***d***

The letter *daal* is pronounced like the *d* in *day* or *do*.

darasa (he studied) ***diin*** (religion)
dunyaa (world) ***dimaagh*** (brain)

ذ ***dh***

The letter *dhaal* is pronounced like the *th* in *this*, *that*, or *other*. Do not confuse it with the *th* of *thank* or *think*.

dhahab (gold) ***dhahaba*** (he went)
dhiraax (arm) ***'ustaadh*** (professor)

ز **z**

The letter *zaay* is pronounced like the *z* in *zoo* or *zipper*.

zaytuun (olives) ***zaada*** (he added)
xaziiz (man's name) ***zawj*** (husband)

س **s**

The letter *siin* is pronounced like the *s* in *so* or *sit*.

samiik (thick) ***rasm*** (painting)
'islaam (Islam) ***salaam*** (peace, hello)

ش **sh**

The letter *shiin* is pronounced like the *sh* in *shoe* or *ship*.

shukran (thank you) ***shams*** (sun)
sharibat (she drank) ***shaykh*** (sheikh)

ف **f**

The letter *faa'* is pronounced like the *f* in *far* or *feel*.

fii (in) ***faransaa*** (France)
fannaan (artist) ***fiil*** (elephant)

ك **k**

The letter *kaaf* is pronounced like the *k* in *kite* or *keep*.

kitaab (book) ***kalb*** (dog)
kayfa (how) ***kursiyy*** (chair)

ل **l**

The letter *laam* is pronounced like the *l* in *like* or *let*.

layl (night) ***laa*** (no)
laTiif (friendly) ***laysa*** (he is not)

م **m**

The letter *miim* is pronounced like the *m* in *make* or *meet*.

maa (what) ***masaa'*** (evening)
maktab (office) ***mumtaaz*** (wonderful, excellent)

ن **n**

The letter *nuun* is pronounced like the *n* in *now* or *neat*.

nuur (light) ***'anaa*** (I)
nawm (sleep) ***naxam*** (yes)

ه **h**

The letter *haa'* is pronounced like the *h* in *here* or *happy*.

hunna (they) ***huduu'*** (quiet)
haadhaa (this) ***hiya*** (she)

و **w**

The letter *waaw* is pronounced like the *w* in *we* or *wool*. (It is also used in the Arabic alphabet to represent the long vowel in *tool* or *pool* and the diphthong in *house*.)

wa (and) ***walad*** (boy)
waziir (minister) ***waSala*** (he arrived)

ي **y**

The letter *yaa'* is pronounced like the *y* in *yes* or *yellow*. (It is also used in the Arabic alphabet to represent the long vowel in *week* or *see* and the diphthong in *bait*.)

yawm (day)	***yaabaan*** (Japan)
yaktubu (he writes)	***yasmiin*** (woman's name)

Group Two

The following three consonants occur in other languages you may be familiar with.

خ **kh**

The sound of the letter *khaa'* is not found in most varieties of English, but the sound at the end of the Scottish word *loch* is very close to it. It's also similar to the German sound in *Bach* or *Buch* or the Hebrew *Baruch*. It's a deep, throaty sound like a tight, raspy *h*.

khawkh (peach)	***'akh*** (brother)
'ukht (sister)	***khamsa*** (five)

ر **r**

The sound of *raa'* is not the standard *r* of English, but rather the rolled *r* of Italian or Spanish.

rajul (man)	***rakhiiS*** (inexpensive)
rasm (painting)	***ra's*** (head)

غ **gh**

The sound of the letter *ghayn* is very similar to the gargled *r* of the French words *rue* or *rare*. It comes from the back of the throat, near where *g* or *k* are produced.

ghadan (tomorrow) | **ghariib** (strange)
ghurfa (room) | **dimaagh** (brain)

Group Three

Finally, these are the letters that are most likely to give you trouble, because they're very much unlike sounds in English or in other European languages.

ص **S**

The letter *Saad* is pronounced like an emphatic, forceful *s*. It doesn't exist in English, but it's not difficult to make if you practice. Start by saying *s* as in *saw*, but then draw your tongue back and lower your jaw slightly. If you're having trouble doing this, just pronounce the long, deep "ah" that you make when the doctor examines your throat. That will automatically put your tongue in the right position for *Saad*. *Saad* (as well as *Daad*, *Taa'* and *Dhaa'*) change the quality of the vowels near them—they make them deeper. (Be careful in the transcription system to differentiate between *s*, which is like the English *s*, and *S*.)

Siin (China) | **Saghiir** (small)
Sadiiq (friend) | **SabaaH** (morning)

ض **D**

The letter *Daad* has the same relationship to the *d* in *day* as *S* has to the *s* in *say*. Practice in the same way—say a *d*, and then draw your tongue back and lower your jaw. Make the surrounding vowels deep.

Dabaab (fog) | **Daruuriyy** (necessary)
mariiD (sick) | **Daxiif** (skinny)

ط T

The letter *Taa'* is a *t* with the tongue drawn back and the jaw lowered. Start with *t* as in *toy*, and make the same adjustments as you did for *S* and *D*.

Taqs (weather) **Tifl** (child)
Taalib (student) **Taawila** (table)

ظ DH

The letter *DHaa'* is the last of the emphatic letters. It's the *th* in *this*, but pronounced with the tongue drawn back and the jaw lowered.

DHahr (back) **DHuhr** (noon)
DHahara (he appeared) **DHalaam** (darkness)

ق q

The letter *qaaf* is similar to the sound of a *g* or a *k*, but it's produced further back in the throat, closer to where the sound of the gargled French *r* is produced. You should feel the constriction at the very back of your mouth, near the top of your throat.

qaa'id (leader) **qalb** (heart)
qaamuus (dictionary) **Sadiiq** (friend)

ء '

The sound of the letter *hamza* isn't thought of as a "standard" English sound, but if you know what to listen for, you'll hear that it's far from rare. In fact, you produce it every time you say *"uh-oh!"* It's technically called a glottal stop, because it's a quick block in the airflow through your mouth caused by closing the very top of your throat, the glottis. But you don't need to get so technical to make this sound. Think of the Cockney pronunciation of the words "bottle" or "settle," with a short, gentle coughing sound where the double *t* is written. There are also many regional American accents, particularly around New York City, that use a very similar sound to pronounce the final *t* in words like *put*, *cat*, or *sit*. Notice that this sound is transcribed by an apostrophe, and in fact it occurs in the names of many of the Arabic letters. Make sure you pronounce it when you see it.

ka's (glass) ***maa'*** (water)
qara'a (he read) ***maa'ida*** (dining room table)

You'll also see this letter at the beginning of Arabic words that start with a vowel. Don't make any special effort to pronounce the *hamza* at the beginning of words. It's natural, even in English, to automatically produce a glottal stop whenever you begin to pronounce a word that starts with a vowel.

'ayna (where) ***'adrusu*** (I study)
'awlaad (boys) ***'ibn*** (son)

 ***H***

The sound of the letter *Haa'* is perhaps the second hardest Arabic sound to make. But again, you've probably made this sound many times. Imagine that you're lowering yourself into a very hot bath. That very enthusiastic, forceful *Ha*!, with some constriction at the top of your throat, is the sound of *Haa'*. You also make this sound when you've put too much jalapeño in your chili or too much wasabi on your sushi. Or, if you prefer meat and potatoes, you make this sound when you blow on your glasses to clean them. The only difficulty in pronouncing *Haa'* probably comes from the fact that you think of it as an exclamation rather than a consonant. If you get used to that, you'll have no trouble pronouncing *Haa'*.

Haarr (hot) ***Hajar*** (stone)
masraH (theater) ***miSbaaH*** (lamp)

ع *x*

Following the tradition of leaving the best for last, the letter *xayn* is almost definitely the hardest Arabic sound to pronounce. It's similar to the very emphatic *H* of *Haa'*, but it vibrates as well, and airflow is just about choked off by constriction at the top of the throat. You use the necessary muscles when you gag, and if you put your fingers on your throat and make yourself gag slightly, you'll feel the muscles you'll need to produce *xayn*. Again, it's not that it's impossible to produce this sound, but it's hard to get used to the idea that it's a regular consonant in a language. In Arabic, it's even a common consonant!

xarabiyya (Arabic language) ***xalaykum*** (on you)
al-xiraaq (Iraq) ***faxaltu*** (I did)

LESSON 2

HELLO! *'assalaamu xalaykum!*

In this first lesson you're going to learn some basic greetings and how to ask questions such as "how are you doing?" and "what is your name?" If you need to review any of the tips for how to use each lesson and get the most out of this course, turn back to the introduction.

2A Dialogue

Listen as Kareem bumps into an old high school friend, Kamal. They haven't seen each other in a long time.

kariim	***'ahlan wa sahlan!***
kamaal	***'ahlan wa sahlan!***
kariim	***kayfa l-Haal?***
kamaal	***al-Hamdu lillaah. wa 'anta, kayfa l-Haal?***
kariim	***al-Hamdu lillaah.***

Kareem	Hi!
Kamal	Hi!
Kareem	How are you?
Kamal	I'm doing well. And you, how are you?
Kareem	I'm doing well.

That wasn't so bad, was it? Now let's let's listen as Chris, a student at Al-Azhar University in Cairo, Egypt, introduces himself to his classmate Layla on the first day of classes.

kris	***'as-salaamu xalaykum.***
laylaa	***wa xalaykum as-salaam.***
kris	***kayfa l-Haal?***
laylaa	***al-Hamdu lillaah. wa 'anta, kayfa l-Haal?***
kris	***al-Hamdu lillaah, shukran.***
laylaa	***maa 'ismuka?***
kris	***'ismii kris. wa 'anti, maa 'ismuki?***
laylaa	***'ismii laylaa.***
kris	***'ahlan wa sahlan.***
laylaa	***'ahlan wa sahlan.***

Chris	Hello.
Layla	Hello.
Chris	How are you?

Layla	I'm doing well. And you, how are you?
Chris	I'm doing well, thank you.
Layla	What's your name?
Chris	My name is Chris. And you, what's your name?
Layla	My name is Layla.
Chris	Nice to meet you.
Layla	Nice to meet you.

2B Language Notes

The most basic greeting in Arabic is the phrase *'as-salaamu xalaykum.* Literally it translates as "may peace be upon you," but it is the English equivalent of "hello." When a person says *'as-salaamu xalaykum,* the most common reply is *wa xalaykum as-salaam.* This translates as "and upon you peace," but it also simply means "hello."

Another very common greeting, a bit less formal, is *'ahlan wa sahlan.* This is the friendly greeting that Kareem and Kamal used.

In Arabic, just like in many other languages, there are certain greetings that are used at specific times of the day. For example, you can use *SabaaH al-khayr* or "good morning" to greet someone before noon. If someone says *SabaaH al-khayr* to you, you can reply by saying *SabaaH an-nuur,* which also means "good morning." As a general rule, you can use this greeting anytime between sunrise and noon.

You can use the greeting *masaa' al-khayr* and its response *masaa' an-nuur* during late afternoon, early evening, or at nighttime. As a general rule you can start using *masaa' al-khayr* and *masaa' an-nuur* an hour before the sun sets. This greeting can then be translated as "good afternoon," "good evening," or even "good night" in some circumstances.

To say good night more personally, for example to a loved one before going to bed, you might say *layla saxiida* (good night) or *TusbiH xalaa khayr* (wake up in good health).

An important and useful expression to know is, of course, "good bye." In Arabic it's literally "[go] with peace," or *maxa s-salaama.*

Did you notice in the second dialogue that when Layla speaks to Chris she says *'anta* for "you" and *maa 'ismuka* for "what is your name?" But when Chris speaks to Layla he says *'anti* and *maa 'ismuki* to mean the same things. Those aren't typos—they're feminine and masculine forms for the same expression. You'll also notice that in the first dialogue, Kamal addresses Karim with *'anta*. You'll learn much more about these forms later, but for now, just be careful to notice the differences.

2C Vocabulary

Now let's take a look at the vocabulary you saw in the dialogue as well as some other words and expressions you'll come across in this lesson. Read through the list and familiarize yourself with the new words by repeating them several times, writing them down, or even using flashcards. At the end of the lesson, you might want to come back and work with the list again. For more tips on learning new vocabulary, turn back to the introduction.

'as-salaamu xalaykum	hello, good day
wa xalaykum as-salaam	response to *'as-salamu xalaykum*
kayfa l-Haal	How are you?
al-Hamdu lillaah	I'm fine, I'm doing well.
'anta, 'anti	you (masculine, feminine)
kayfa	how
'ism	name
'ismii	my name
'ismuka, 'ismuki	your name (masculine, feminine)
wa	and
maa	what?
yawm	day
SabaaH	morning
masaa'	late afternoon, evening
layl	night
shukran	thank you
kitaab	book
Taalib	student (m.)
Taaliba	student (f.)
'ustaadh	professor (m.)
'ustaadha	professor (f.)
jaamixa	university

kulliyya	college
qaamuus	dictionary
bint	girl
walad	boy
rajul	man
'imra'a	woman
Saghiir	small, little, young (people)
kabiir	big, old (people)

2D Vocabulary Practice

Before you go further, take a moment to practice some of the new vocabulary you've just learned. Answer each of the following questions.

1. You walk into a conference room in Jeddah, Saudi Arabia. What is the first thing that you say?
2. What would be said to you in response?
3. How do you say "morning?"
4. How would you say "night?"
5. You see a friend and want to ask her how she's doing. How would you say it?
6. To tell someone your name, what would you say?
7. Translate into English: *bint, Saghiir, shukran, kitaab.*
8. Now translate into Arabic: woman, man, big, and, what?

2E Grammar and Usage

Now let's begin to take a closer look at Arabic grammar and structure. Every lesson will add on to what you've learned in previous ones, so be sure that you're comfortable with each of the following points. Go at your own pace, and don't be afraid to review.

1 "To Be" in Arabic

Take a look at the sentences *kayfa l-Haal?* and *'ismii laylaa.* You know that they mean "How are you?" and "My name is Layla," but do you notice anything missing in the Arabic? If you've guessed that there are no words for "are" and "is," you're right. In Arabic, there is no translation of "to be" in the present tense. That means that "am," "are," and "is" are understood.

'anaa Taaliba.	I [am] a student.
'ismii kamaal	My name [is] Kamal.
kayfa l-Haal	How are you? (Literally, How [is] the condition?)

2 Definite and Indefinite Articles

An article is a little word that tells you something about a noun. For example, in English, if you say "a computer," the indefinite article "a" shows that you mean any old undefined computer. But if you say "the" computer, that definite article "the" means that you have a specific, defined computer in mind.

There are no overt indefinite articles (a/an) in Arabic. For example, *SabaaH* (morning) means both "morning" and "a morning," because even though it's not there, the indefinite article is implied. Similarly, *masaa'* (evening) can mean both "evening" and "an evening." But Arabic does have a definite article (the) which can be added to the beginning of a word by attaching the prefix *al-*. For example, *al-masaa'* means "the evening." Here are a few more examples

bint	(a) girl
al-bint	the girl
kitaab	(a) book
al-kitaab	the book

Arabic uses the definite article much like English, to specify something in particular. But it also uses the definite article to make general statements. For example, while in English we'd say "chocolate is good" or "international phone calls are expensive," Arabs say "<u>the</u> chocolate is good" and "<u>the</u> international phone calls are expensive."

There is one other important rule to keep in mind when it comes to the definite article *al*. Do you remember the expression *SabaaH an-nuur*, or "good morning?" The *an* in *an-nuur* means "the," but as you can see, it's pronounced differently from *al*. That's because the *–l* in *al* will change before the letters *t–, th–, d–, dh–, r–, z–, sh–, S–, D–, T–, DH,* and finally *n–,* into that letter. You'll sometimes hear these letters called "sun letters," because the word for "sun"—*shams*—begins with one of them. The other letters, which don't force the *l* in *al* to change, are called "moon" letters, because the word for moon—*qamar*—begins with one of them. The easiest way to remember the sun letters is that they're the ones that are pronounced with the tongue very close to where it is when the *l* in *al* is pronounced.

SabaaH	(a) morning
aS-SabaaH	the morning
dhahab	gold
adh-dhahab	the gold
shams	sun
ash-shams	the sun
rajul	(a) man
ar-rajul	the man

3 Gender

Arabic, like Spanish or French or German, is a language that has gender. This mcans that every noun is either masculine or feminine. Sometimes this can be pretty obvious, if the grammatical gender of a noun is the same as its natural gender. So, an animate male noun will be masculine, and an animate female noun will be feminine.

ar-rajul	the man (masculine)
al-'imra'a	the woman (feminine)
walad	a boy (masculine)
bint	a girl (feminine)

But even nouns that do not have natural gender—inanimate objects, for example—are grammatically either masculine or feminine. Luckily, it's easy to tell whether an inanimate noun is masculine or feminine. Inanimate nouns are generally feminine if they end in *–a,* and masculine if they end in anything else, including a *hamza* (').

kitaab	(a) book (masculine)
Taawila	(a) table (feminine)
al-qaamuus	the dictionary (m.)
al-kulliyya	the college (f.)
al-masaa'	the evening (m.)

Keep in mind that not all feminine nouns end in *–a*. An animate female noun, regardless of its ending, is feminine, such as *bint* (girl) or *'ukht* (sister). There are also a few inanimate nouns which are feminine but do not end in *–a*, such as *ash-shams* (sun). This kind of irregular gender is rare, though, and it will be indicated in the vocabulary lists.

4 Nouns and Adjectives

Nouns in Arabic function the same way as they do in English—they are used to name a person, place, thing, quality, or concept. In both English and Arabic, we use adjectives to describe or modify nouns. But in Arabic, unlike in English, adjectives come after the nouns that they modify.

kitaab Saghiir	a small book
qaamuus kabiir	a big dictionary

As you can see, since there are no definite articles in the above phrases, they're translated into English as indefinite phrases—that is, phrases with "a" instead of "the." So, *kitaab Saghiir* means "a small book" and not "the small book." We'll see how to say "the small book" in the next lesson. For now, get used to the idea that whenever you see a noun followed by an adjective, and neither one has *al* (or its other forms) attached, it's translated as an indefinite phrase such as "a small book" or "a big dictionary."

2F Grammar and Usage Exercises

Are you ready to practice some of what you've learned in this lesson? If not, don't be afraid to go back and read over the Grammar and Usage section again.

Exercise 1 Change these indefinite nouns into definite nouns, making sure to use the appropriate form of the prefix *al-*. Then translate each definite noun phrase into English.

1. *shams*
2. *kitaab*
3. *qaamuus*
4. *bint*
5. *rajul*
6. *'ustaadh*
7. *Taaliba*
8. *dhahab*

Exercise 2 Give the gender of each of the following Arabic nouns.

1. rajul
2. Taawila
3. qaamuus
4. 'ustaadh
5. 'imra'a
6. kulliyya
7. kitaab
8. shams

Exercise 3 Translate the following phrases into English.

1. aT-Taawila
2. rajul kabiir
3. 'ismii laylaa.
4. wa 'anta, kayfa l-Haal?
5. kitaab Saghiir
6. maa 'ismuka?
7. al-kulliyya
8. 'ustaadh kabiir

2G **Pronunciation Practice** Vowels

In each lesson we'll focus on certain sounds in Arabic. As you know, some of them are very simple and similar, if not identical, to sounds you know from English and perhaps from other European languages. But there are a few that you've probably never heard before. Don't worry, we'll get to them slowly and steadily. For now, let's begin with some easy sounds. Listen to your recordings and repeat after the native speakers as you work through this section.

Arabic has three basic vowel sounds, *a*, *i*, and *u*. These are each short, crisp sounds.

kamaal, wa, 'ahlan, walad
'ism, bint, min, 'ibn
mudun, 'ukht, kutub, shukr

One important aspect of Arabic pronunciation is that these vowels have a range of pronunciation, especially the *-a*, which can sometimes sound like the *a* in "father" and sometimes like the *e* in "set." It all depends on the consonant before the vowel. Don't worry about any rules at this point—just be careful to listen to how the vowels are pronounced on the recordings.

Another important aspect of Arabic pronunciation is that these vowels can be either short or long. A long vowel is pronounced literally longer than a short one—hold it for a beat or two. In transcription, we'll show these vowels as *aa*, *ii*, and *uu*.

masaa', laa, 'ustaadh, Taalib
kabiir, Saghiir, diin, qariib
nuur, thuum, tuunis, suuq

2H **Arabic Script** Overview, the letters *baa'*, *taa'* and *thaa'*

The Arabic script is written and read from right to left, so if you were to pick up a book you would have to open it from the opposite side of a book written in English. Lines would also start on the right side of the page instead of on the left, and you would read the letters in individual words from right to left as well. The Arabic script consists of two kinds of letters—ones that connect to the letters after them, and others that don't.

For example, the letter *baa'* (*b*) is a connecting letter, which means that it is written differently depending on whether it is located at the beginning of a word, in the middle of a word, at the end of a word, or isolated and not part of a word. So, there are really four different forms of each connecting letter—initial, medial, final, and isolated. Non-connecting letters only have two forms. Since they do not connect to the letters after them, their isolated and initial forms will look alike, as will their final and medial ones. This may not make much sense right now, but it will become clear as you see examples of actual Arabic letters and how they're used to form words.

We'll start with the first three consonants of the Arabic alphabet—*baa'*, *taa'*, and *thaa'*. They're pronounced *b*–, *t*–, and *th*– respectively, and they're all connecting letters. This means that they have four different forms, although there is only a slight variation among those forms. The initial form is written with a "tail" that connects to the letter after it, the medial has two "tails" connecting to letters on either side of it, and the final has a "tail" connecting it to the letter before it.

	isolated	initial	medial	final
b	ب	بـ	ـبـ	ـب
t	ت	تـ	ـتـ	ـت
th	ث	ثـ	ـثـ	ـث

As you can see, these three letters are all identical, except for the number of dots that they carry. The letter *baa'* has one dot below, while *taa'* has two above and *thaa'* three above.

Try reading these example words using the letters *baa'*, *taa'*, and *thaa'*. Don't worry about the vowel sounds yet—we'll come back to them. For now, focus on picking out *baa'*, *taa'* and *thaa'*.

باب	*baab* (door)	ثبت	*thabata* (it was confirmed)

For more practice, read *The Basics*, *The Arabic Alphabet*, *Connecting and Non-Connecting Letters*, and Reading Practice 1 of *Part 2: Reading Arabic* in the *Complete Guide to Arabic Script*. Or, if you prefer to tackle Arabic script later, move right ahead to section 2I.

2I **Cultural Note** What, Exactly, is Arabic?

Generally speaking, there are three forms of Arabic found in any given place in the Arabic-speaking world. There is Modern Standard Arabic, which is the language of business, literature, education, politics, the media, and most "official" situations. There's also Koranic Arabic, which is the strict and traditional form used in religious matters, such as the Koran. These two forms of Arabic do not vary across the Arab world. But the third form does vary from place to place. It is the local colloquial (spoken) dialect, which is used in informal and familiar settings, and which is not usually written. These dialects do not necessarily split along easily identified geographical lines, but you'll often hear of such dialects as Egyptian, Saudi, Iraqi, Gulf, Levantine, and North African. These dialects are all very closely related, of course, but their differences can be either subtle or not so subtle, related to pronunciation, vocabulary, or even grammatical constructions. In other words, the Arabic spoken among men sitting at a café in Amman, Jordan, is going to be different from the Arabic spoken by a family sitting down to a meal in Bahrain. But the language that they use when reading the Koran, listening to the news, or conversing in academic or business settings will be the same for the most part.

That is the type of Arabic that we are using in this book, called Modern Standard Arabic (MSA), which is the most generic and most widely used and understood form of Arabic in the Middle East and beyond. It is more formal than some of the local dialects, but less rigid than the very strict Koranic Arabic. Most people in the Arab world understand and speak Modern Standard Arabic, and if you learn it, you can communicate with the majority of Arabic speakers.

If you would like to move on later to learn a local dialect, MSA will be an excellent foundation.

Lesson 2 Answer Key

Vocabulary Practice: 1. *'as-salaamu xalaykum.*; 2. *wa xalaykum as-salaam.*; 3. *SabaaH*; 4. *layl*; 5. *kayfa l-Haal?*; 6. *'ismii . . .* (insert your name); 7. girl, little/small/young, thank you, book; 8. *'imra'a, rajul, kabiir, wa, maa?* **Exercise 1:** 1. *ash-shams* (the sun); 2. *al-kitaab* (the book); 3. *al-qaamuus* (the dictionary); 4. *al-bint* (the girl); 5. *ar-rajul* (the man); 6. *al-'ustaadh* (the male professor); 7. *aT-Taaliba* (the female student); 8. *adh-dhahab* (the gold) **Exercise 2:** 1. masculine; 2. feminine; 3. masculine; 4 masculine; 5. feminine; 6. feminine; 7. masculine; 8. feminine **Exercise 3:** 1. the table; 2. a big (or old) man; 3. My name is Layla.; 4. And you, how are you?; 5. a small book; 6. What is your name? 7. the college; 8. a big (or old) professor

LESSON 3

WHERE ARE YOU FROM? *min 'ayna 'anta?*

In this lesson you'll learn how to talk a little bit about yourself, and you'll cover more of the basics of Arabic sentences.

3A Dialogue

Listen in as Jim Murray, an American student studying at Al-Azhar University in Cairo, Egypt, walks into a coffee shop. He strikes up a conversation with the man sitting next to him, Ahmed Ziyad, a journalist for an Egyptian newspaper.

jim	***as-salaamu xalaykum.***
'aHmad	***wa xalaykum as-salaam.***
jim	***kayfa l-Haal?***
'aHmad	***al-Hamdu lillaah. wa 'anta?***
jim	***al-Hamdu lillaah. 'ismii jim. maa 'ismuka?***
'aHmad	***'ismii 'aHmad.***
jim	***'ahlan wa sahlan yaa 'aHmad.***
'aHmad	***'ahlan wa sahlan. min 'ayna 'anta?***
jim	***'anaa min 'amriikaa, min nyuu-yuurk.***
'aHmad	***haadhaa mumtaaz! maadhaa tafxalu fii miSr?***
jim	***'anaa Taalib fii jaamixat al-'azhar. wa 'anta?***
'aHmad	***'anaa min al-maghrib. wa laakin haadhihi s-sana th-thaaniya fii miSr. 'anaa SaHaafiyy maxa jariidat al-bayaan fii l-qaahira.***
Jim	Hello.
Ahmed	Hello.
Jim	How are you doing?
Ahmed	I'm fine. And you?
Jim	I'm doing fine. My name's Jim. What's your name?
Ahmed	My name is Ahmed.
Jim	Nice to meet you, Ahmed.
Ahmed	Nice to meet you. Where are you from?
Jim	I'm from America, from New York.
Ahmed	That's wonderful! What are you doing in Egypt?
Jim	I'm a student at Al-Azhar University. And you?
Ahmed	I'm from Morocco. But this is my second year in Egypt. I'm a journalist with Al-Bayan newspaper in Cairo.

3B Language Notes

By now you should be able to recognize a lot of the dialogue from what you've seen in the previous lesson. Remember that *as-salaamu xalaykum* is the standard form of greeting somebody you do not know. If Jim and Ahmed knew each other they might have used the more familiar *'ahlan wa sahlan*. Also remember that *kayfa l-Haal* is the common way of asking people, either male or female, how they are. And *al-Hamdu lillaah* is widely used to say "I'm doing well" or "I'm fine."

To ask where someone is from, say *min 'ayna 'anta* to a man or *min 'ayna 'anti* to a woman. Word by word, that's *min* (from), *'ayna* (where), and *'anta* or *'anti* (you). Remember that Arabic doesn't express "is", "are," or "am," and that there are two forms of you, *'anta* if you're speaking to a man or *'anti* if you're speaking to a woman. There are even different forms for speaking to two people or to three or more, but don't worry about that yet!

To answer the question *min 'ayna 'anta/i*, say *'anaa min . . .*, which means "I [am] from . . ." Unlike *'anta* and *'anti* (you), *'anaa* is a gender-neutral personal pronoun that you can use whether you're a man or a woman.

The way to ask a man what he does is *maadhaa tafxalu*. To ask a woman, you'd say *maadhaa tafxaliina*. That's *maadhaa* (what) and *tafxalu* or *tafxaliina*, which are forms of the verb *faxala* (do). Don't worry about the verb forms yet—we'll come back to them later. For now just memorize the forms you see in each new expression. And notice that *maadhaa* (what) is different from the form of "what" that you learned in the last lesson, *maa*. There are rules for the different ways of asking "what" that we'll look at in more detail later.

Did you notice that when Jim says "I'm a student at Al-Azhar University"—*'anaa Taalib fii jaamixat al-'azhaar*—the word *jaamixa* became *jaamixat*? You'll see that the feminine ending *-a* becomes *-at, -atu* or even *-ati* for certain grammatical reasons. The word *jariidat* (newspaper, also *jariida*) in the last line of the dialogue is another example of this. Don't worry about the specific rules yet, but don't be surprised if you see these slight changes. Just think of the feminine ending *–a* as having a "hidden *t*" that sometimes shows itself, and sometimes brings along an *i*. You'll learn when this happens as you proceed through the course.

3C Vocabulary

Once again, let's take a look at some vocabulary. Some of it is recycled to help you remember more easily. A few entries include *(a)* after a noun; this is of course the feminine form. If you've forgotten the hints for learning new vocabulary, just turn back to the introduction. Try to form good vocabulary learning habits early!

SaHaafiyy	journalist
jariida	newspaper
Taalib(a)	student, usually a college or graduate student
tilmiidh(a)	student, pupil, generally in high school or elementary school
'ustaadh(a)	professor
Sadiiq(a)	friend
'ab	father
'umm	mother
'ibn	son
bint	daughter, girl
walad	boy
'akh	brother
'ukht	sister
kulliyya	college
jaamixa	university
maktab	office
thaaniya	second, both unit of time and number
'anaa	I
mumtaaz	wonderful, amazing, excellent
'azraq	blue
jamiil	pretty, beautiful
laTiif	nice, friendly
Tawiil	tall
qaSiir	short
xaDHiim	great, powerful
min	from

'ayna	where
fii	in
maxa	with
al-maghrib	Morocco
al-jazaa'ir	Algeria
tuunis	Tunisia
miSr	Egypt
al-xiraaq	Iraq
as-saxuudiyya	Saudi Arabia
'amriikaa	America (popular name for the U.S.)
al-wilaayaat al-muttaHida	The United States (formal, proper name)
'injiltraa	England
faransaa	France
al-yaabaan	Japan

3D Vocabulary Practice

1. What does a *SaHaafiyy* work for?
2. Where would you find a *Taalib* or a *Taaliba*?
3. Who teaches them?
4. Where are Mecca, Medina, and Riyadh?
5. Translate the following words into English: *tilmiidh*, *thaaniyya*, *Sadiiq*.
6. Now translate the following words into Arabic: journalist, I, Tunisia.

3E Grammar and Usage

1 Subject Pronouns

Pronouns, in both English and Arabic, are the words that stand in for nouns. For example, instead of saying "Ahmed," you can say "he," and instead of saying "Mary and Layla" you can say "they." Subject pronouns just mean the pronouns that can be used as the subject of a sentence (I, he, we) as opposed to object pronouns (me, him, us). Here are the subject pronouns in Arabic.

'anaa	I
'anta	you (m.)
'anti	you (f.)
huwa	he, it

hiya	she, it
naHnu	we
'antum	you (m. or mixed plural)
'antunna	you (f. plural)
hum	they (m. or mixed)
hunna	they (f.)

You already know that *'anaa* (I) can be used by both men and women, but *'anta* (you) is masculine and *'anti* (you) is feminine. The pronouns *huwa* (he) and *hiya* (she) are self explanatory, except that they can also be used to mean "it." Remember that Arabic is a language with grammatical gender, so you use *huwa* (he) to refer to masculine nouns and *hiya* (she) to refer to feminine nouns.

(aT-Taawila)	*hiya Saghiira.*
(the table)	It is small.
(al-maktab)	*huwa kabiir.*
(the office)	It is big.

The equivalents of the English plural pronouns "you" (when talking to more than one person) and "they" are a bit trickier. If you're addressing a group of men, you will use the masculine plural pronoun *'antum*. Similarly, if you're addressing a group of women, you're going to use the feminine plural pronoun *'antunna*. That's straightforward. But, if you're addressing a mixed group, use the masculine plural pronoun *'antum*, no matter what the ratio of men to women may be.

The same is true of the forms meaning "they." Use *hum* to talk about men, *hunna* to talk about women, and *hum* again for mixed groups, no matter what the ratio of male to female. "They" referring to non-human nouns (tables, offices, computers, cities, mountains, animals, etc.) may be a bit surprising. In Arabic, it's *hiya*, or "she/it (f.)." You'll learn more about that when you learn plurals, but for now just keep in mind that *hum* and *hunna* are used only for people.

There is also a special set of "dual" pronouns in Arabic used to talk to or about two people. The pronoun *'antumaa* means "you two" or "both of you" and is used when you're addressing two people, either men or women. And the pronoun *humaa* means "they two" or "the two of them" and is used to talk about two people, either men or women.

2 Gender in Animate Nouns

In the last lesson you learned that all Arabic nouns have gender. Animate nouns—nouns that refer to people and animals—follow their natural gender. But inanimate nouns—nouns that refer to things we normally think of as neuter—also have gender. There are a few irregular nouns you have to memorize, but for the most part inanimate nouns are feminine if they end in *-a*, and masculine otherwise.

That feminine *-a* ending also allows us to change a masculine noun into a feminine noun, as you saw in the vocabulary list. This can be done to many animate nouns that refer to people, such as professions or nationalities, as well as some animate nouns that refer to animals. It's similar to the relationship between "actor" and "actress," "waiter" and "waitress," and "bull" and "cow" in English.

tilmiidh	student, m.
tilmiidha	student, f.
'ustaadh	professor, m.
'ustaadha	professor, f.
Sadiiq	friend, m.
Sadiiqa	friend, f.
SaHaafiyy	journalist, m.
SaHaafiyya	journalist, f.
mudarris	teacher, m.
mudarrisa	teacher, f.

It's important to note that this rule does not apply to all nouns. For example, you can't change the words *'ab* (father) or *'akh* (brother) into the words for "mother" or "sister" by adding an *-a*. "Mother" and "sister" have their own forms, which are *'umm* and *'ukht*.

❸ Definite Noun/Adjective Phrases

In the last lesson you learned that the phrase *kitaab Saghiir* is an indefinite phrase that can be translated as "a small book." You also learned that *kitaab* on its own means "book" or "a book," and that the definite equivalent of that is *al-kitaab*, meaning "the book." Now let's look at how to combine all of this and say "the small book." The only thing to remember is that if you make the noun definite by adding *al*, you have to do the same thing to the adjective: *al-kitaab aS-Saghiir*. Here are a few more examples:

ar-rajul al-xaDHiim	the great man
al-maktab al-kabiir	the big office
al-qaamuus aS-Saghiir	the small dictionary

Don't forget that *Saghiir* starts with a "sun" letter, so the definite equivalent is *aS-Saghiir*. Also, this rule of adding the definite article to adjectives applies even if more than one adjective modifies the noun.

al-qaamuus al-kabiir al-'azraq	the big blue dictionary

❹ Adjective Agreement

You've just learned one form of adjective agreement, that adjectives have to agree with the nouns they modify in definiteness, meaning that if the noun is definite, then the adjective has to be as well. Take a look at these examples:

Sadiiq laTiif	a nice male friend
aS-Sadiiq al-laTiif	the nice male friend
Sadiiqa laTiifa	a nice female friend
aS-Sadiiqa l-laTiifa	the nice female friend

Can you see the differences? Notice that after the noun *Sadiiqa*, *laTiif* changes to *laTiifa*. That's because *Sadiiqa* is feminine, so the adjective *laTiif* has to agree with it by taking on that familiar feminine ending *-a*. The noun *Sadiiq* is masculine, so the masculine form *laTiif* is used instead. So, now you know that adjectives have to agree with the nouns that they modify in both gender and definiteness. Here are a few more examples:

al-kitaab aS-Saghiir	the small book
al-bint aS-Saghiira	the little girl
al-maktab al-'azraq	the blue office

ash-shams al-jamiila	the beautiful sun
al-mudarris aT-Tawiil	the tall (male) teacher
al-mudarrisa l-qaSiira	the short (female) teacher

3F Grammar and Usage Exercises

Exercise 1 Make these masculine nouns and adjectives feminine. Then translate each of the answers.

1. *at-tilmiidh*
2. *Sadiiq*
3. *Saghiir*
4. *kabiir*
5. *laTiif*
6. *jamiil*
7. *mumtaaz*
8. *al-'ustaadh*

Exercise 2 Now turn these masculine phrases into feminine phrases, and then translate each one.

1. *SaHaafiyy Tawiil*
2. *Taalib laTiif*
3. *al-mudarris aT-Tawiil*
4. *aS-Sadiiq al-laTiif*
5. *al-'ustaadh al-qaSiir*
6. *tilmiidh laTiif*

Exercise 3 Match the person or people in the left column with the correct pronoun in the right column.

1. Myriam	a. *'anti*
2. A group of eight girls and three boys	b. *huwa*
3. Hassan	c. *hunna*
4. You and a group of your friends	d. *'antum*
5. Your friend Yasmine, to whom you're speaking	e. *hiya*
6. Four girls	f. *hum*
7. A group of three women and three men to whom you're talking	g. *naHnu*
8. Your friend Kamal, to whom you're speaking	h. *'anta*
9. Your two friends, Mahmood and Ahmed, to whom you're speaking	i. *humaa*
10. Two men	j. *'antumaa*

3G Pronunciation Practice –*ay* and –*aw*

Now let's focus on the diphthongs –*ay* and –*aw*. Remember that a diphthong is a combination of two vowels. For example, the vowel in the word "cow" is actually a combination of "ah" and "oo." That's a diphthong, and it's in fact the same sound as the Arabic diphthong that we're transcribing as *-aw*. It rhymes with the vowels in "hour," "town," and "house"—not "raw" or "saw." The diphthong *-ay* sounds like the English vowel in "late" or "day," or sometimes like the English "bite" or "night." Listen and repeat after these examples:

yawm, khawkh, dhawq, 'awlaad, zawj, shawka
bayt, kayfa, laylaa, 'ayna, xayn, Haythu

3H Arabic Script *Vowels*

Remember that there are two kinds of vowels in Arabic—long and short. Long vowels, which we're transcribing as *aa*, *ii*, and *uu*, are literally held longer than their short counterparts. This is very important, because the meaning of a word may be very different depending on whether it's pronounced with a long or short vowel. (Think of the English "sit" vs. "seat" or "pull" vs. "pool," which have similar distinctions.)

Another important thing to keep in mind about vowels is that normally only the long ones are written in Arabic. The short vowels—*a*, *i*, and *u*—are not written except in children's books, the Koran, and Arabic language courses for people like you. When they are written, they appear not as regular letters on the same level as the consonants, but instead as blips or dashes written above or below consonants. In other words, the word *walad* (boy) would be written *wld*, with a dash for *a* above the *w*, another one above the *l*, and nothing above the *d*. (But don't forget that the order would be reversed, so it would actually be *dlw*.) Long vowels, on the other hand, do appear in all writing, on the same level as consonants. So the word for door, *baab*, would be three letters long, the first (furthest to the right) *b*, the long *aa*, and then the second *b*. This isn't as hard to get used to as it may sound.

First let's look at the long vowels, which appear in all writing as their own bona fide letters. The names of the long vowels are *'alif* (*aa*), *yaa'* (*ii*), and *waaw* (*uu*).

long vowel	isolated	initial	medial	final
aa	ا	ا	ـا	ـا
ii	ي	يـ	ـيـ	ـي
uu	و	و	ـو	ـو

The letters *'alif* and *waaw* are the first two non-connecting letters you've come across. That means that they'll connect only to the letters before them, and then there will be a break in the script after them. This is also why the isolated and initial forms are identical, as well as why the medial and final forms are identical. Take a look at these examples:

باب	*baab* (door)	توت	*tuut* (a berry)

Now let's look at the short vowels, which appear as small symbols above or below the consonant that they follow. In this case you'll see the short vowels written after the three letters you learned in the last lesson, *baa'*, *taa'*, and *thaa'*. So, reading across the rows, you have *ba*, *bi*, *bu*, and then *ta*, *ti*, *tu*, and finally *tha*, *thi*, and *thu*.

consonant	+ *a*	+ *i*	+ *u*
b	بَ	بِ	بُ
t	تَ	تِ	تُ
th	ثَ	ثِ	ثُ

Notice that short *a* is a dash above the consonant, short *i* is the same dash below the consonant, and short *u* looks just like *waaw*, but much smaller and above the consonant.

ثَبَتَ	*thabata* (he stood firm, stable; it was established)	ثُبُوت	*thubuut* (permanence)
بِنْت	*bint* (girl)	تَابُوت	*taabuut* (box)

For more practice, read *Group 1: Long Vowels*, *Group 2: Short Vowels and Diphthongs*, *Group 3:* ب *b,* ت *t, and* ث *th* and reading practices 2 through 4 of *Part 2 Reading Arabic* in the *Complete Guide to Arabic Script*. You can also practice writing with Groups 1–3 and writing practices 1–7 of *Part 3: Writing Arabic.*

31 **Cultural Note *Religion in the Arab World***

In order to understand the Arab world and the Middle East, you need look no further than the Arabic language to see that religion plays a major role in the culture. Religion is woven into the daily fabric of Middle Eastern society on both a personal and a public level, and this fact is reflected in the Arabic language. Many of the simplest greetings are related in some way to God. Most official state events begin with a reference to God of some sort. Most boardroom meetings begin with a short prayer. At first glance this may seem strange, especially to people who are not particularly religious. But don't interpret the frequent references to God as religious fanaticism. Instead, for most Arabs, they simply reflect a broad cultural awareness of Islam, which literally means to surrender to something greater than oneself. Mainstream Islam, like the mainstream varieties of other religions, is peaceful and tolerant, and references to God have developed in the Arabic language to remind religious people of humility before something greater than any one person. But of course Arabic speakers, like any other people, are not all religious; so, for many people these expressions can be thought of as similar to exclaiming "God bless you!" after someone has sneezed. They are simply a fixed part of the language.

Lesson 3 Answer Key

Vocabulary Practice: 1. *jariida;* 2. *kulliyya/jaamixa;* 3. *'ustaadh/'ustaadha;* 4. *as-saxu-udiyya;* 5. student/pupil, second, friend; 6. *SaHaafiyy, 'anaa, tuunis* **Exercise 1:** 1. *at-tilmi-idha* (the pupil/student, female); 2. *Sadiiqa* (friend, female); 3. *Saghiira* (little, small); 4. *kabiira* (big, old); 5. *laTiifa* (nice, friendly); 6. *jamiila* (pretty, beautiful); 7. *mumtaaza* (wonderful, amazing, excellent); 8. *al-'ustaadha* (the professor, female) **Exercise 2:** 1. *SaHaafiyya Tawiila* (a tall journalist); 2. *Taaliba laTiifa* (a friendly student); 3. *al-mudarrisa T-Tawiila* (the tall teacher); 4. *aS-Sadiiqa l-laTiifa* (the kind/nice friend); 5. *al-'ustaadha l-qaSiira* (the short professor); 6. *tilmiidha laTiifa* (a friendly student) **Exercise 3:** 1. *e/hiya;* 2. *f/hum;* 3. *b/huwa;* 4. *g/naHnu;* 5. *a/'anti;* 6. *c/hunna;* 7. *d/'antum;* 8. *h/'anta;* 9. *j/'antumaa;* 10. *i/humaa*

LESSON 4

IS KAREEM HOME? *hal kariim fii l-bayt?*

Lesson 4 focuses on the home, and in it you'll learn some more basic vocabulary and structure. You'll learn more courtesy expressions and take a closer look at prepositions and question formation.

4A Dialogue

Mahmood has decided to visit his friend Kareem at home. Kareem's mother answers the door.

maHmuud	***xafwan, hal kariim hunaaka?***
al-'umm	***laa. kariim dhahaba 'ilaa s-suuq.***
maHmuud	***mataa sa-yakuunu fii l-bayt?***
al-'umm	***dhahaba likay yashriya al-Haliib. sa yarjixu 'ay daqiiqa.***
maHmuud	***hal 'astaTiixu 'an 'atruka lahu khabaran?***
al-'umm	***tafaDDal 'ilaa l-manzil wa 'intaDHir kariim.***
maHmuud	***shukran.***
al-'umm	***haadhihi hiya ghurfat al-juluus. wa 'anaa sa-'akuunu fii l-maTbakh.***
maHmuud	***shukran jaziilan.***
al-'umm	***marHaban bika!***
Mahmood	Excuse me, is Kareem here?
Mother	No, Kareem went to the market.
Mahmood	When is he coming home?
Mother	He went to buy milk. He should be here any minute.
Mahmood	Can I leave him a message?
Mother	Come inside the house and wait for Kareem.
Mahmood	Thank you.
Mother	This is the living room. And I'll be in the kitchen.
Mahmood	Thank you very much.
Mother	You're welcome!

4B Language Notes

The expression *xafwan* is the English equivalent of "excuse me" or "I'm sorry". In the dialogue it is used as an introduction, a way of asking somebody a question. In this context it most resembles the English phrase "pardon/excuse me." It can also be used literally to excuse oneself, as when leaving a room. For example, *xafwan, yajibu 'an 'adhhaba* means "I'm sorry, but I have to go." It can also be used as an apology, as in *xafwan, lam 'axnii shay'an*, "I apologize, I didn't mean anything by it."

Any time someone says *tafaDDal* (masc.) or *tafaDDalii* (fem.) it means that they're welcoming you, literally, into their lives, their space, their home, etc. This expression is commonly used when a host wants to welcome a guest into his or her house, as if to say "come on in." It is a gesture of respect and a sign of warmth. It can also be used when someone is walking with another person into a room and pauses to allow that person to go first, meaning "please, after you."

The more generic way to say "welcome" is *marHaban bika* (masc.) or *marHaban biki* (fem.) While *tafaDDal* is a literal invitation to "come in", *marHaban* is used more broadly. It is used to greet someone that you haven't seen in a long time. It would be something that you would say if a relative just got out of a bus, a train, or an airplane, for example.

As you can see in the dialogue, the Arabic word for no is *laa*, with a long "ah" sound. The word for yes is *naxam*.

In the very first line of the dialogue, Mahmood asks "is Kareem here?" The Arabic is *hal kariim hunaaka*? This question consists of a question particle, which we'll come back to in the Grammar and Usage section, followed by the name Kareem, and finally the word *hunaaka*, which means "there." Since you already know that Arabic doesn't express "is" and "are," the word *hunaaka* can mean both "there" and "there is/are."

The word *dhahaba* is a past tense verb form meaning "he went." The words *sa-yakuunu* (he will be) and *sa-'akuunu* (I will be) are also verbs. You'll learn more about them later.

Mahmood asks *mataa sa-yakuunu fii l-bayt?* "When will he be home?" The word *mataa* means "when," *sa-yakuunu*, again, means "he will be" and *fii l-bayt* means "in the house," or "at home."

4C Vocabulary

manzil	home, residence
bayt	house
daar	house (feminine)
shuqqa	apartment
ghurfa	room
maTbakh	kitchen
Hammaam	bathroom
ghurfat an-nawm	bedroom
ghurfat al-juluus	livingroom, sitting room
kursiyy	chair
sariir	bed
ma'waa s-sayyaara	garage
karaaj	garage (more colloquial)
baab	door
shubbaak	window
bustaan	garden
warda	rose
zahra	flower
sayyaara	car
madiina	city
shaarix	avenue
nahj	street
funduq, nuzul	hotel
maHall	store
suuq	market, marketplace
Haliib	milk
maa'	water
khubz	bread
jubn	cheese
jayyid	good
radii'	bad
samiin	fat
naHiif	thin, slim

4D Vocabulary Practice

1. Where would you find a *warda*?
2. Where do you park a *sayyaara* at night?
3. How do you say house, as opposed to home?
4. What do you sleep on?

5. Which room would you find it in?
6. Name two things you can drink.
7. Translate into English: *suuq, ghurfa, kursiyy, Hammaam*
8. Translate into Arabic: street, door, window, hotel.

4E Grammar and Usage

1 Forming Questions in Arabic

In English, questions are formed by reversing the order of words in a statement ("she has gone" becomes "has she gone?") or by inserting a new "helping" verb ("he spoke" becomes "did he speak?") Thankfully, Arabic questions are much more straightforward. A question can look just like a statement, with of course a question mark and raised intonation.

kariim dhahaba 'ilaa s-suuq.
Kareem went to the market.
kariim dhahaba 'ilaa s-suuq?
Did Kareem go to the market?

Note though that this is common in informal Arabic or in dialects. In more formal Modern Standard Arabic, a question is formed by the addition of the question particle, *hal*, at the beginnig of a statement, as you saw in the dialogue.

hal kariim hunaa?	Is Kareem here?
hal laylaa fii l-ghurfa?	Is Layla in the room?

Of course, questions can also be formed with question words, like who, what, where, when, and how. But we'll come back to that later.

2 Common Prepositions

A preposition is a little word that indicates things like location, direction, time, etc. You've already seen a few prepositions in Arabic: *min* (from), *fii* (in), and *maxa* (with). Here are some other common prepositions:

xalaa	on
al-kitaab xalaa T-Taawila.	The book is on the table.
'ilaa	to
kariim dhahaba 'ilaa s-suuq.	Kareem went to the market.

qariib min	near, close to
al-Haliib qariib min al-khubz.	The milk is near the bread.
taHta	under
al-maa' taHta T-Taawila.	The water is under the table.
bijaanibi	next to
al-kursiyy bijaanibi s-sariir.	The chair is next to the bed.
waraa'a	behind
al-bustaan waraa'a l-bayt.	The garden is behind the house.

3 Linking Sounds

You know that the definite article in Arabic is *al*, but that it can be pronounced *an, aDH, aT, aD, aS, ash*, and so on before the "sun" letters *n, DH, T, D, S, sh, s, z, r, dh, d, th*, and *t*. That's not the only pronunciation change that can take place in Arabic. Look at this phrase taken from the example of the question particle *hal* that you read:

fii l-ghurfa	in the room

Notice that the vowel in *al* was dropped altogether, leaving *l-ghurfa*. This is called "elision," which means dropping a sound when you link words together. If you've studied French or Italian, for example, you're familiar with this concept. Because the word before the definite article ends in a vowel, the *a-* in *al* disappears to avoid a choppy, clunky pronunciation. Look back at the examples of prepositions. How many cases of elision can you find? You'll notice that this happens a lot with prepositions, many of which end in vowels and tend to be followed by the definite article.

xalaa T-Taawila	on the table
maxaa r-rajul	with the man
taHta s-sariir	under the bed
'ilaa s-suuq	to the market

There is another minor change that takes place in a prepositional phrase as well. If the preposition ends in a long vowel (*aa*, *ii*, or *uu*) that vowel will shorten before *al*. So the preposition *fii* will be pronounced like *fi* in the phrase *fii l-ghurfa*. You'll see it transcribed as *fii* in all cases, though, to avoid too much complication. But listen to the pronunciation on the recordings to hear the difference.

❹ There is / There are

As you saw in the dialogue, the word *hunaaka* means "there" and can also be used to mean "there is" or "there are" before indefinite nouns. Notice that in English, it's correct to use "there is" before singulars and "there are" before plurals. In Arabic, *hunaaka* is used in both cases. We'll stick to singulars for now, though.

hunaaka kursiyy fii l-ghurfa.	There is a chair in the room.
hunaaka zahra jamiila fii l-bustaan.	There is a pretty flower in the garden.
hunaaka sayyaara fii ma'waa s-sayyaara.	There is a car in the garage.

To ask the question "is there . . . ?" you simply add *hal*, "is there/are there".

hal hunaaka sayyaara fii ma'waa s-sayyaara?	Is there a car in the garage?

❺ Basic Sentence Structure

You already know that there is no equivalent of the verb "to be" in Arabic, and this can sometimes make it difficult to distinguish between a phrase and a sentence. Take a look at the following examples:

1. *bint jamiila* (a beautiful girl)
2. *al-bint al-jamiila* (the beautiful girl)
3. *al-bint jamiila*. (The girl is beautiful.)
4. *hiya Saghiira*. (She is young.)
5. *naHnu min al-maghrib*. (We are from Morocco.)
6. *al-'ustaadh fii l-kulliyya*. (The professor is at the college.)

The first two examples are phrases rather than sentences. You already know that an indefinite noun (a noun without *al*, as in *bint*) followed by an indefinite adjective gives you a phrase that begins in English with "a" or "an:" *bayt kabiir* (a big house), *Taalib Tawiil* (a tall student), etc. To make these phrases definite, you know that you have to add the article *al* to both the noun and the adjective, *al-bint al-jamiila* (the beautiful girl), *al-bayt al-kabiir* (the big house), *aT-Taalib aT-Tawiil* (the tall student).

But in the third example, *al-bint jamiila*, a definite noun is followed by an indefinite adjective. This construction is translated as a sentence, "the girl is beautiful." Keep in mind this distinction between *al-bint jamiila* (the girl is beautiful) and *al-bint al-jamiila* (the beautiful girl). And don't forget that "am," "are," and "is" are understood in Arabic.

The fourth, fifth, and sixth examples are very similar to English sentence construction, with the obvious exception that there is no form of "to be." Also notice that the name of the country Morocco in Arabic has a definite article—*al-maghrib*. You've also learned that *al-jazaa'ir* (Algeria), *al-xiraaq* (Iraq), and *al-yaabaan* (Japan) also take articles. But not all countries do. To say, "We are from America" you'd say *naHnu min 'amriikaa.*

4F Grammar and Usage Exercises

Exercise 1 Change the following phrases into questions using the question phrase ***hal hunaaka.*** Translate your answers.

1. *sariir fii ghurfati n-nawm**
2. *zahra jamiila fii l-bustaan*
3. *sayyaara fii ma'waa s-sayyaara*

Exercise 2 Combine the elements in each of the following groups to form a complete sentence. Then translate the new sentence.

Example *kitaab / xalaa / Taawila*

Answer *al-kitaab xalaa T-Taawila.* (The book is on the table.)

1. *Haliib / fii / maTbakh*
2. *sariir / fii / ghurfati n-nawm*
3. *sayyaara / bijaanibi / daar*
4. *warda / fii / bustaan*
5. *qaamuus / xalaa / Taawila*
6. *rajul / fii / maktab*

*Notice the *–i* in *ghurfati n-nawm*. Following prepositions such as *fii*, Arabic adds an *–i* after the "hidden t" of feminine nouns in certain grammatical circumstances that you'll learn more about later. Don't worry too much about that yet–just notice it when it occurs.

Exercise 3 Change each of the following indefinite noun/adjective phrases into definite noun/adjective phrases. For example, *qaa'id xaDHiim* (a great leader) would become *al-qaa'id al-xaDHiim* (the great leader). This is also a good opportunity to pick up some new vocabulary.

1. great leader (*qaa'id xaDHiim*) ___________
2. new house (*manzil jadiid*) ___________
3. happy worker (*xaamila saxiida*) ___________
4. great soldier (*jundiyy xaDHiim*) ___________
5. lazy student (*tilmiidha kasuula*) ___________
6. blue pen (*qalam 'azraq*) ___________
7. small girl (*bint Saghiira*) ___________
8. sad dog (*kalb Haziin*) ___________

Exercise 4 Now change the phrases from exercise 3 into is/are sentences. For example, *'ustaadh xaDHiim* (great professor) would become *al-'ustaadh xaDHiim* (the professor is great).

Exercise 5 Translate the following sentences into English.

1. *aT-Taawila Saghiira.*
2. *al-qaamuus fii l-maktab.*
3. *ad-daar kabiira.*
4. *ash-shams jamiila.*
5. *hunaaka bint fii l-bustaan.*
6. *hal laylaa hunaaka?*
7. *ar-rajul min al-maghrib.*
8. *naHnu min 'amriikaa.*

4G Pronunciation Practice Familiar Sounds

In this lesson you'll take a close look at all of the sounds in Arabic that are identical, or at least very close, to sounds you know in English. Keep in mind that this group includes most of the sounds of Arabic: *b, t, th, j, d, dh, z, s, sh, f, k, l, m, n, h, w,* and *y*.

Let's start with *th* and *dh*. Remember that these are two different sounds, and both exist in English. The trouble is that in English they're spelled the same way –th. In Arabic, they're two separate letters. In our transcription, we're spelling the "th" in "think" or "thorough" with *th*, but the "th" in "these" or "other" with *dh*. Can you hear the difference?

thaaniya, thalaatha, thaa', thuum, 'ithnayn, thubuut, thaabit
dhahab, dhahaba, dhiraax, 'ustaadh, dhaal, 'abuu DHaby

Now let's look at *j*, which has three common pronunciations. In much of North Africa and the Levant, it has the "zh" sound you hear in "pleasure," "measure", or "treasure." In Egypt and Yemen, it's pronounced as the "g" in "go." And in the Gulf and the Arabian Peninsula, it has the sound of "j" in "jam."

jariida, jamiil, jaziira, jayyid

All of the others are self explanatory: *b, t, d, z, s, sh, f, k, l, m, h, w, y*. Just keep in mind that *s* is always pronounced like the *ss* in "kiss," and *z* is always pronounced like the *zz* in "buzz." The sound *h* is just like the sound in "house" or "here," but it can show up anywhere in a word, even at the end. The sound we're transcribing as *H* is different, and we'll come back to that later.

bayt, kamaal, kayfa, 'ismuki, shams, sahlan, kitaab, maktaba, yawm, shukran, walad, mumtaaz, faransaa, hunaak, zahra

Also, don't forget to pronounce double consonants as double consonants. This means that you should hold the consonant literally for twice as long as a single consonant.

as-salaam, sayyaara, shubbaak, Hammaam, jayyid

4H Arabic Script *jiim, Haa', khaa'*

In Lesson 4 we're going to take a look at another trio of consonants that are all very similar, except for the presence or placement of a dot: *j, H, kh*. Remember that *jiim* is pronounced like the *s* in "pleasure," or the *g* in "get," or the *j* in "jam" depending on the region. *H* is pronounced like a strong, forceful *h!*, almost like when you blow on your glasses to clean them. And *kh* is pronounced like the *ch* in the German *Bach* or Scottish *loch*.

	isolated	initial	medial	final
j	ج	جـ	ـجـ	ـج
H	ح	حـ	ـحـ	ـح
kh	خ	خـ	ـخـ	ـخ

See if you can recognize these letters in the following words. Again, don't worry about the letters you haven't seen; just focus on being able to pick out the ones that have been introduced.

حُبّ	*Hubb* (love)	خُبز	*khubz* (bread)
بَخت	*bakht* (luck)	جَبَل	*jabal* (mountain)

For more practice, read *Group 4:* ج *j,* ح *H,* خ *kh* and reading practice 6 of *Part 2: Reading Arabic* in the *Complete Guide to Arabic Script*. You can also practice writing Group 4 with writing practices 8–10 of *Part 3: Writing Arabic*.

41 **Cultural Note** *The Arab World at a Glance*

Naturally, even though the Arab world is united by language and, for the most part, religion, there are distinct characteristics among the many different Arab countries. These may be in the areas of food, politics, social and cultural trends, economics, local dialects, and more. As you learn more about the region and its people, this richness will become clearer. In the meantime, here is a very broad overview of the Arab world.

Country	Captial	Major Cities	Population	Major Industries
Morocco	Rabat	Casablanca, Marrakesh, Tangier	31,700,000	phosphate mining, leather, textiles, tourism
Algeria	Algiers	Oran, Annaba, Constantine	32,800,000	petroleum and natural gas, mining
Tunisia	Tunis	Sfax, Sousse Gabes	10,000,000	petroleum, mining, tourism, textiles
Libya	Tripoli	Banghazi, Misurata, Tobruq	5,500,000	petroleum, food processing, textiles
Egypt	Cairo	Alexandria, Al-Jizah, Port Said	74,800,000	textiles, food processing, tourism, chemicals
Saudi Arabia	Riyadh	Mecca, Medina, Jiddah	24,300,000	oil, petroleum
Yemen	Sanaa	Aden	19,400,000	oil and petroleum processing, cotton textiles, leather
Oman	Muscat	Salaalah	2,800,000	oil refining, gas production
United Arab Emirates	Abu Dhabi	Dubai	2,500,000	petroleum, fishing, pearls
Qatar	Doha	Ar-Rayyaan	820,000	oil production and refining, fertilizers
Bahrain	Manama	Al-Muharraq	670,000	petroleum processing and production, aluminum smelting. banking
Kuwait	Kuwait City	Al-Jahra, Hawallii	2,200,000	petroluem, desalination, food processing
Iraq	Baghdad	Basrah, Mosul, Irbiil	24,700,000	petroleum, chemicals, textiles
Jordan	Amman	Az-Zarqaa, Irbid	5,500,000	phosphate mining, pharmaceuticals, petroleum refining, tourism
Syria	Damascus	Aleppo, Hims	17,600,000	petroleum, textiles, food processing, tobacco
Lebanon	Beirut	Sidon, Tripoli	3,800,000	banking, food processing, jewelry, cement, wood
Palestine*	East Jerusalem*	Ramallah, Gaza, Nablus	3,000,000	agriculture, construction, manufacturing

* Although there is currently no official Palestinian state, the Palestinian territories cover the West Bank and Gaza. Most Palestinians who support independence from Israel express a desire that the capital of any future state be East Jerusalem.

Lesson 4 Answer Key

Vocabulary Practice: 1. *bustaan;* 2. *ma'waa s-sayyaara / karaaj;* 3. *bayt / daar;* 4. *sariir;* 5. *ghurfat an-nawm;* 6. *Haliib, maa';* 7. market, room, chair, bathroom; 8. *nahj, baab, shubbaak, funduq / nuzul* **Exercise 1:** 1. *hal hunaaka sariir fii ghurfati an-nawm?* (Is there a bed in the bedroom?) 2. *hal hunaaka zahra jamiila fii l-bustaan?* (Is there a pretty flower in the garden?) 3. *hal hunaaka sayyaara fii ma'waa s-sayyaara?* (Is there a car in the garage?) **Exercise 2:** 1. *al-Haliib fii l-maTbakh.* (The milk is in the kitchen.) 2. *as-sariir fii ghurfati an-nawm.* (The bed is in the bedroom.) 3. *as-sayyaara bijaanibi d-daar.* (The car is next to the house.) 4. *al-warda fii l-bustaan.* (The rose is in the garden.) 5. *al-qaamuus xalaa T-Taawila.* (The dictionary is on the table.) 6. *ar-rajul fii l-maktab.* (The man is in the office.) **Exercise 3:** 1. *al-qaa'id al-xaDHiim;* 2. *al-manzil al-jadiid;* 3. *al-xaamila s-saxiida;* 4. *al-jundiyy al-xaDHiim;* 5. *at-tilmiidha l-kasuula;* 6. *al-qalam al-'azraq;* 7. *al-bint aS-Saghiira;* 8. *al-kalb al-Haziin* **Exercise 4:** 1. *al-qaa'id xaDHiim.* 2. *al-manzil jadiid.* 3. *al-xaamila saxiida.* 4. *al-jundiyy xaDHiim.* 5. *at-tilmiidha kasuula.* 6. *al-qalam 'azraq.* 7. *al-bint Saghiira.* 8. *al-kalb Haziin.* **Exercise 5:** 1. The table is small. 2. The dictionary is in the office. 3. The house is big. 4. The sun is beautiful. 5. There is a girl in the garden. 6. Is Layla there? 7. The man is from Morocco. 8. We are from America.

LESSON 5

AT THE AIRPORT *fii l-maTaar*

In Lesson 5 you'll learn some very practical vocabulary for getting around an airport and taking public transportation. You'll also focus on numbers, telling time, asking questions, and making negative statements.

5A Dialogue

Abdallah's flight has just arrived in Cairo, and he's trying to get from the airport to his hotel. Let's listen in as he asks directions at the information desk.

xabdallah	***xafwan. 'ayna funduq ruuyal?***
al-muDHiifa	***al-funduq fii l-madiina. 'innahu qariib min maHaTTati l-qiTaar.***
xabdallah	***wa hal al-funduq qariib 'aw baxiid min hunaa?***
al-muDHiifa	***al-funduq laysa qariib min hunaa—'innahu baxiid. wa lakin hunaaka Haafila 'ilaa maHaTTatl l-qiTaar, wa l-funduq bijaanibi al-maHaTTa.***
xabdallah	***'ayna maHaTTat al-Haafila?***
al-muDHiifa	***maHaTTat al-Haafila hunaaka, baxda l-'abwaab xalaa l-yamiin, bijaanibi at-taksiyaat. al-Haafila raqm sabxata xashara tadh-habu 'ilaa maHaTTati l-qiTaar.***
xabdallah	***mataa tadh-habu l-Haafila?***
al-muDHiifa	***tadh-habu xalaa l-waaHida wa n-niSf. wa taSil xalaa s-saaxa th-thaaniyya wa n-niSf.***
xabdallah	***shukran jaziilan!***
al-muDHiifa	***laa shukra xalaa waajib. maxa s-salaama, wa yawman saxiidan.***
xabdallah	***maxa s-salaama.***
Abdallah:	Excuse me. Where is the Hotel Royal?
Attendant	The hotel is in the city. It's close to the train station.
Abdallah:	And is the hotel close or far from here?
Attendant	The hotel isn't nearby–it's far. But there's a bus that goes to the train station, and the hotel is next to the station.
Abdallah:	Where's the bus stop?
Attendant	The bus stop is there, through the doors on the right, next to the taxis. Bus 17 goes to the train station.

Abdallah:	When does the bus leave?
Attendant	It leaves at 1:30. And it arrives at the train station at 2:30.
Abdallah:	Thank you very much!
Attendant	You're welcome. Good bye, and have a good day.
Abdallah:	Good bye.

5B Language Notes

Notice that the adjectives *qariib* (near) and *baxiid* (far) are followed by *min* (from). So, *baxiid min maHaTTati l-qiTaar* means "far from the train station."

Take a closer look at the expressions for "train station" and "bus stop." They're *maHaTTat al-qiTaar* and *maHaTTat al-Haafila*. Literally, they mean "stopping place [of] the bus" and "stopping place [of] the train." In Arabic, when you put two nouns right next to each other, and if only the second one takes *al-*, this forms a possessive construction, A of B or X of Y. You just have to imagine that there's an invisible *of* between the two nouns. You'll learn more about these constructions later, but keep an eye out for them, since they're very common.

You may also have noticed that in the phrase *l-funduq bijaanibi al maHaTTa* (the hotel is close to the station) the word appears as *maHaTTa*, without the *-t*. That's the feminine ending *-a*, which in certain circumstances shows its "hidden *t*." The possessive noun construction described in the last note is one of those cases. It's in fact the same thing that you saw in Lesson 3, with the phrases *jaamixat al-'azHar* ("University of Al-Azhar) and *jariidat al-bayaan* ("newspaper of Al-Bayaan").

Note that the word for "station" or "stop"—*maHaTTa*—often appears in the dialogue as *maHaTTati,* with both its hidden *t* and an extra *i*. This happens after prepositions such as *min* or *'ilaa*. You saw this added *-i* in the last lesson in the expression *fii ghurfati an-nawm*, in the bedroom. You'll learn more about that later.

In the second line of the dialogue the attendant says: *'innahu qariib min maHaTTati l-qiTaar*, or "it is close to the train station." The word *'inna* is often used in Arabic "to be" sentences. It takes certain endings to show the subject. In this case *-hu* means "it" or "him," referring to *funduq*, the hotel. So, think of *'innahu* as simply another way of expressing *huwa*, or "he/it."

Notice the spelling of the verb *tadh-habu* ("she, it goes.") The hyphen is inserted to make it clear that the sounds of *dh* and *h* are separate and should both be pronounced in the transcription. The word *tadh-habu* is a present tense form of the verb *dhahaba* (go), which you saw in the dialogue in lesson 4: *kariim dhahaba 'ilaa s-suuq* (Kareem went to the market). You'll learn much more about verbs later.

Abdallah also used this verb to mean "leave," as in *mataa tadh-habu l-Haafila?* (When does the bus leave/go?)

Notice that the polite response to *shukran* (thank you) or *shukran jaziilan* (thank you very much) is *laa shukra xalaa waajib* ("you're welcome" or "don't mention it.")

5C Vocabulary

Taa'ira	airplane
Taa'iraat	airplanes
maTaar	airport
wuSuul	arrival
'inTilaaq	departure, take-off
'amtixa	baggage
tasliim al-'amtixa	baggage claim area
biTaaqat ar-rukuub	boarding pass
tadhkira	ticket
maktab	counter
riHla	flight
muDHiif, muDHiifa	(flight) attendant
riHla dawliyya	international flight
raakib	passenger
Hammaal	porter/baggage handler
mawxid al-wuSuul	time of arrival
diiwaana, jumruk	customs

jawaaz as-safar	passport
Haafila	bus
maHaTTat al-Haafila	bus station
taaksii	taxi
qiTaar	train
maHaTTat al-qiTaar	train station
madiina	city
jadwal	schedule
qariib	near(by)
baxiid	far
baahiDH	expensive
rakhiiS	cheap, inexpensive
sariix	fast
baTii'	slow
jadiid	new
qadiim	old (things)
hunaa	here
hunaaka	there
yamiin	right
yasaar	left
bijaanibi	next to

5D Vocabulary Practice

Translate each of the following.

1. the flight attendant
2. the airport
3. a big airplane
4. the big airplane
5. the bus
6. The bus is cheap.
7. The train is small.
8. Is the train small?
9. The hotel is next to the train station. (Use the –*ti* ending after the preposition.)
10. The city is far away.

5E Grammar and Usage

1 Numbers 1–100

Using numbers in Arabic can get a bit complicated, so we're going to keep it as simple as possible for now and give you the most common forms that you'll find practical for telling time, talking about dates, and understanding prices. As you can guess, numbers are written differently in Arabic from the way numbers are written in English. But don't worry—they're not that hard, and you'll become aquainted with them in the Arabic script section. Now let's start with 0–10.

0	*Sifr*
1	*waaHid*
2	*'ithnayn*
3	*thalaatha*
4	*'arbaxa*
5	*khamsa*
6	*sitta*
7	*sabxa*
8	*thamaaniya*
9	*tisxa*
10	*xashara*

Notice that the word *xashar* (a slight modification of *xashara*) is important for the numbers 11 through 19. The numbers 1 and 2 undergo changes in 11 and 12, and 3 through 9 just add *–ta* when combined with *xashar* in 13 through 19.

11	*'aHada xashar*
12	*'ithnaa xashar*
13	*thalaathata xashar*
14	*'arbaxata xashar*
15	*khamsata xashar*
16	*sittata xashar*
17	*sabxata xashar*
18	*thamaaniyata xashar*
19	*tisxata xashar*

Here are 20 through 23. As you can see, the simple numbers are added to the word for twenty, *xishruun*, connected with the word *wa*, and. So twenty one is "one and twenty."

20	*xishruun*
21	*waaHid wa xishruun*
22	*'ithnayn wa xishruun*
23	*thalaatha wa xishruun*

Now, let's cover 30 through 100. Notice that just as in English, where –ty marks twenty, thirty, etc., the endings *–iin* and *–uun* are important in Arabic, simply added to the basic numbers. The difference is a grammatical one, but just be aware of both forms for now. One hundred is a special case, also just like in English.

30	*thalaathiin / thalaathuun*
40	*'arbaxiin / 'arbaxuun*
50	*khamsiin / khamsuun*
60	*sittiin / sittuun*
70	*sabxiin / sabxuun*
80	*thamaaniin / thamaanuun*
90	*tisxiin / tisxuun*
100	*mi'a*

There's one other set of important numbers to learn—the ordinal (first, second, third, etc.) numbers. We'll only cover first through twelfth, though, since those are needed to tell the time. Ordinal numbers are adjectives, so they have to agree with the noun they're describing. The two forms given below are the masculine and then the feminine, with that familiar *–a* ending.

first	*'awwal, 'uulaa*
second	*thaanii, thaaniya*
third	*thaalith, thaalitha*
fourth	*raabix, raabixa*
fifth	*khaamis, khaamisa*
sixth	*saadis, saadisa*
seventh	*saabix, saabixa*

eighth	*thaamin, thaamina*
ninth	*taasix, taasixa*
tenth	*xaashir, xaashira*
eleventh	*Haadii xashar, Haadiia xashra*
twelfth	*thaanii xashar, thaaniia xashra*

Did you notice a pattern in the vowels in each of the ordinal numbers? The consonants are for the most part the same as in the cardinal numbers ("sixth" is an exception), but the pattern of vowels for each one is consonant—*aa*—consonant—*i*—consonant. Arabic has a lot of patterns like this—it's always helpful to keep an eye out for them.

2 Telling Time

First, here is some basic vocabulary related to time.

saaxa	hour, clock
daqiiqa	minute
thaaniya	second
al-yawm	today
al-ghad, ghadan	tomorrow
'ams, al-baariHa	yesterday
baxda l-ghad	the day after tomorrow
'ams al-'awwal	the day before yesterday
baxda	after
qabla	before

Now let's look at telling time. Notice that the simple hour, such as 1:00 or 2:00, uses the word *as-saaxa* and an ordinal number, both in the definite form, meaning "the first hour, the second hour," and so on. Since *saaxa* is feminine, the ordinal number with take an *-a* on the end. Don't forget your "sun" letters, though! And instead of using *'awwal* (first) for 1:00, use *waaHida*.

What time is it?	*kam as-saaxa*?
It's 1:00.	*as-saaxa l-waaHida.*
It's 2:00	*as-saaxa th-thaaniya*
It's 3:00.	*as-saaxa th-thaalitha.*
It's 7:00.	*as-saaxa s-saabixa.*

To say half past an hour, you need to use the phrase wa *n-niSf* ("and the half.")

It's 10:30. *as-saaxa l-xaashira wa n-niSf.*
It's 7:30. *as-saaxa s-saabixa wa n-niSf.*

To say that it's quarter past an hour, use the phrase *wa r-rubux* ("and the quarter.")

It's 5:15. *as-saaxa l-khaamisa wa r-rubux.*
It's 8:15. *as-saaxa th-thaamina wa r-rubux.*

The word *'illaa* (minus) can also be used to tell the time.

It's 5:45. *as-saaxa s-saadisa 'illaa r-rubux.* (It's six o'clock minus a quarter.)
It's 8:45. *as-saaxa t-taasixa 'illaa r-rubux.* (It's nine o'clock minus a quarter.)
It's 3:50. *as-saaxa r-raabixa 'illaa xashara.* (It's four o'clock minus ten.)

Of course, you can also use the hour + *wa* + a number of minutes.

It's 9:35. *as saaxa t-taasixa wa khamsa wa thalaathuun.*
It's 3:50. *as saaxa th-thaalitha wa khamsuun.*

If it's not clear from the context whether the time referred to is AM or PM, there are certain key words that will help you determine that.

aS-SabaaH, aS-SubH	morning
aDH-DHuhr	noon
baxda DH-DHuhr	afternoon
al-xasr	late afternoon
al-masaa'	evening
al-layl	night

Notice that you can use the preposition *fii* with these expressions.

It's 10:00 in the morning.	*as-saaxa l-xaashira fii S-SubH.*
It's 7:00 in the evening.	*as-saaxa s-saabixa fii l-masaa'.*

To say that something happens at a certain time, use the prepositions *xalaa* (at/on).

al-Haafila taSilu xalaa s-saaxa l-waaHida.	The bus arrives at 1:00.
al-qiTaar yaSilu xaala s-saaxa thaamina.	The train arrives at 8:00.

3 Question Words

In lesson 4 you learned how to form questions by raising your intonation or by using the question word *hal*. Now let's look at questions with question words such as "who," "what," "where," etc.

maa	what? (used with nouns and pronouns)
maa haadhaa?	What is this?
maa 'ismuki?	What is your name?
maadha	what? (used with verbs)
maadha kataba?	What did he write?
maadha tafxal?	What are you doing?
man	who?
man hum?	Who are they?
man ar-rajul?	Who is the man?
'ayna	where?
min 'ayna 'anta?	Where are you from?
'ayna l-kitaab?	Where is the book?
mataa	when?
mataa dhahabat 'ilaa s-suuq?	When did she go to the market?
mataa kataba l-kitaab?	When did he write the book?
kayfa	how?
kayfa l-Haal?	How are you? (How's the health?)
kayfa dhahaba 'ilaa l-maTaar?	How did he go to the airport?
kam (min) (Used with singular nouns)	how much (of)? / how many (of)?
kam min kitaab qara'a?	How many books did he read?
kam min khubz hunaak?	How much bread is there?

4 Negative "To Be" Sentences

If you've studied other languages, you've most likely had to memorize terribly irregular forms of the verb "to be." If so, you may have been very happy to learn that there is no such verb in Arabic. Unfortunately, that's only true if you want to say "am," "is," or "are." If you want to say "am not," "is not," or "are not," there are special—and yes, irregular—forms to learn.

'anaa lastu	I am not
'anta lasta	you are not (masculine)
'anti lasti	you are not (feminine)
huwa laysa	he is not, it is not

hiya laysat	she is not, it is not, they (non-human) are not
naHnu lasnaa	we are not
'antum lastum	(all of) you are not (masculine or mixed)
'antunna lastunna	(all of) you are not (feminine)
hum laysuu	they are not (masculine or mixed)
hunna lasna	they are not (feminine)
'antumaa lastumaa	the two of you are not
humaa laysaa	the two of them (m.) are not
humaa laysataa	the two of them (f.) are not

al bint laysat fii l-bustaan.	The girl is not in the garden.
'anaa lastu min al-yaabaan.	I am not from Japan.
naHnu lasnaa fii l-maTaar.	We are not at the airport.

5F Grammar and Usage Exercises

Exercise 1 Write out each of the following numbers in Arabic.

1. 4
2. 6
3. 9
4. 0
5. 10
6. 17
7. 24
8. 40
9. 55
10. 97

Exercise 2 Write out each of the following times in Arabic.

1. 4:00
2. 8:00
3. 3:30
4. 5:15
5. 9:30
6. 11:55
7. 7:20
8. 1:15

Exercise 3 Translate each of these words and phrases related to time.

1. half
2. quarter
3. the day
4. the morning
5. the evening
6. the night
7. today
8. tomorrow
9. yesterday
10. the day after tomorrow

Exercise 4 Complete each of the following questions with the question word given in parentheses. Then translate each sentence.

1. __________ *haadhaa?* (what)
2. __________ *al-maTaar?* (where)
3. __________ *dhahaba 'ilaa l-maTaar?* (when) (*dhahaba* means "he went")
4. __________ *ar-rajul?* (who)
5. *min* __________ *hum?* (where)
6. __________ *'ismuki?* (what)
7. __________ *katabat al-kitaab?* (when) (*katabat* means "she wrote")
8. __________ *min kursiyy hunaaka fii ghurfati l-juluus?* (how many?)
9. __________ *al-'ustaadh?* (how)
10. __________ *tafxalu?* (what)
11. __________ *al-jaamixa?* (where)
12. __________ *min sayyaara hunaaka fii ma'waa s-sayyaara?* (how many?)

Exercise 5 Make each of the following "to be" sentences negative, and then translate the answers.

1. *ar-rajul fii l-ghurfa.*
2. *'anta min miSr.*
3. *'anaa fii l-maTaar.*
4. *al kitaab xalaa T-Taawila.*
5. *hunna fii s-suuq.*
6. *'anaa fii l-maktab.*
7. *hiya Taaliba fii jaamixat nyuu yuurk.*
8. *naHnu fii l-maTbakh.*

5G Pronunciation Practice *kh, r, gh, q*

In this lesson we're going to take a close look at the three Arabic sounds that do not exist in English, but that do exist in other languages you may be familiar with. We'll also review the sound of *q*.

Let's start with *kh*, which is the same sound that you hear in the Scottish pronunciation of "loch." The sound also exists in German, Dutch, Hebrew and Slavic languages. It's a deep, raspy sound that comes from the top of your throat. Listen and repeat:

khamsa, khawkh, 'ukht, 'akh, rakhiiS, khaala, khafiif

The Arabic *r* is a rolled or trilled r, just as you'd hear in Spanish, Italian, or many other languages. Start by putting your tongue on the ridge just behind your upper teeth, and then let it vibrate as the air passes through.

rajul, raakib, safar, rakhiiS, ra's, khariiTa, ghurfa, bardaan

You're familiar with the sound of *gh* if you speak French, or even if you can just think of what French sounds like. The French *r*, in words like *rare* or *riche*, comes from the throat, very close to where the *kh* is pronounced. That is the sound of the Arabic *gh*. Be careful to distinguish between *gh* and *kh*.

ghurfa, ghanam, al-ghad, Saghiir, baghdaad, maghrib, dimaagh, ghaalii

Finally, the sound of the transcribed letter *q* is also a sound that does not exist in English. It is similar to the k sound of "cat," but it is produced further back in the throat, in fact in the same place where *kh* and *gh* are produced. Start by saying the *kh* sound of the word *loch*, as in Loch Ness. Now, instead of letting the air roll out continuously, stop it, as if you were saying a "k." You should feel a restriction, and then a release of air like a cork popping in your throat as the very deep *q* sound is made. Practice with these examples:

qaamuus, qalb, qalam, 'aqlaam, Sadiiq, qariib, qiTaar, Taabiq, muqliq

5H Arabic Script *daal, dhaal, numbers*

The next two letters in the Arabic alphabet are *daal* and *dhaal*, which both look like small hooks that sit on the line. Notice that *dhaal* has a dot, though. And don't forget that *dhaal* is pronounced like the th in "this," unlike *thaa'*, which is pronounced like the th in "think." Both *daal* and *dhaal* are non-connectors, meaning that they cannot be connected to the letters that come after them, so their initial and isolated forms are the same, as are their medial and final ones.

	isolated	initial	medial	final
d	د	د	ـد	ـد
dh	ذ	ذ	ـذ	ـذ

دِين	*diin* (religion)	دَرْس	*dars* (lesson)
ذَهَب	*dhahab* (gold)	ذِرَاع	*dhiraax* (arm)

For more practice, begin *Group 5:* د *d,* ذ *dh,* ر *r,* ز *z* and reading practice 6 of *Part 2: Reading Arabic* in the *Complete Guide to Arabic Script.*

Since you learned how to say the numbers in Arabic in this lesson, let's take a look at how they're written. As you can see, they're not so hard.

0	٠	This is just a dot, not a full open circle as in English.
1	١	This is easy enough, just a stroke similar to 1.
2	٢	This looks like a 2 on its side.
3	٣	This looks like a 3 on its side, but with a long tail.
4	٤	This looks a bit like a backwards 3.
5	٥	Be careful. This is a 5, not a 0.

6	٦	Be careful. This may look like 7, but it's 6!
7	٧	Think of the "v" in the word "seven."
8	٨	This looks like a tee-pee.
9	٩	Easy enough, just like a 9.
10	١٠	A 1 followed by a 0, just like in English.

Keep in mind that even though Arabic words are written right-to-left, Arabic numbers are written left-to-right.

45	٤٥
210	٢١٠
367	٣٦٧

51 **Cultural Note** *Getting Around in the Arab World*
In the metropolitan areas, such as Dubai, Cairo, or Amman, many people get around in cars. However, taxis are a very common means of transportation for tourists, who of course

do not have cars and who are visiting a Middle Eastern city for a short period of time. There are also buses used for public transportation within cities, and charter buses are common for sightseeing excursions organized for tourists. Train travel between cities is also a possibility, but train travel between countries is less practical due to geography and the lack of interconnected railways. Generally speaking, the plane is the preferred method of travel between countries in the Middle East.

Lesson 5 Answer Key

Vocabulary Practice: 1. *al-muDHiif/al-muDHiifa*; 2. *al-maTaar*; 3. *Taa'ira kabiira*; 4. *aT-Taa'ira l-kabiira*; 5. *al-Haafila*; 6. *al-Haafila rakhiiSa*; 7. *al-qiTaar Saghiir*. 8. *hal al-qiTaar Saghiir?* 9. *al-funduq bijaanibi maHaTTati l-qiTaar;* 10. *al-madiina baxiida*. **Exercise 1:** 1. *'arbaxa*; 2. *sitta*; 3. *tisxa*; 4. *Sifr*; 5. *xashara*; 6. *sabxata xashar*; 7. *'arbaxa wa xishruun/-iin*; 8. *'arbaxuun/-iin*; 9. *khamsa wa khamsuun/-iin*; 10. *sabxa wa tisxuun/-iin* **Exercise 2:** 1. *as-saaxa r-raabixa*. 2. *as-saaxa th-thaamina*. 3. *as-saaxa th-thaalitha wa n-niSf*. 4. *as-saaxa l-khaamisa wa r-rubux*. 5. *as-saaxa t-taasixa wa n-niSf*. 6. *as-saaxa l-Haadiia xashar wa khamsa wa khamsuun*. 7. *as-saaxa s-saabixa wa xishruun*. 8. *as-saaxa l-waaHida wa r-rubux*. **Exercise 3:** 1. *niSf*; 2. *rubux*; 3. *al-yawm*; 4. *aS-SabaaH/aS-SubH*; 5. *al-masaa'*; 6. *al-layl*; 7. *al-yawm*; 8. *al-ghad/ghadan;* 9. *'ams/al-baariHa;* 10. *baxda l-ghad* **Exercise 4:** 1. *maa* / What is this? 2. *'ayna* / Where is the airport? 3. *mataa* / When did he go to the airport? 4. *man* / Who is the man? 5. *'ayna* / Where are they from? 6. *maa* / What is your name? 7. *mataa* / When did she write the book? 8. *kam* / How many chairs are there in the living room? 9. *kayfa* / How is the professor? 10. *maadha* / What do you do? 11. 'ayna / Where is the university? 12. kam / How many cars are there in the garage? **Exercise 5:** 1. *ar-rajul laysa fii l-ghurfa*. (The man is not in the room.) 2. *'anta lasta min miSr*. (You are not from Egypt.) 3. *'ana lastu fii l-maTaar*. (I am not at the airport.) 4. *al-kitaab laysa xalaa T-Taawila*. (The book is not on the table.) 5. *hunna lasna fii s-suuq*. (They (f.) are not at the market.) 6. *'anaa lastu fii l-maktab*. (I am not in/at the office.) 7. *hiya laysat Taaliba fii jaamixat nyuu yuurk*. (She is not a student at New York University.) 8. *naHnu lasnaa fii l-maTbakh*. (We are not in the kitchen.)

LESSON 6

AT THE HOTEL *fii l-funduq*

Lesson 6 focuses on hotels, so you'll learn some very important and practical vocabulary. You'll also learn about plurals, professions, and nationalities.

6A Dialogue

Julie Wells has just arrived at the Hotel Sphinx in Cairo. Let's listen in as she checks in.

muwaDHDHaf al-'istiqbaal ***SabaaH al-khayr, wa marHaban biki 'ilaa funduq sfinks.***

julii ***SabaaH an-nuur. shukran. hal ladaykum ghurfa?***

muwaDHDHaf al-'istiqbaal ***naxam, ya sayyidatii. hal turiidiina ghurfa li shakhS waaHid 'aw ghurfa li shakhSayni?***

julii ***ghurfa li shakhS, shukran.***

muwaDHDHaf al-'istiqbaal ***li kam min layla?***

julii ***li 'arbaxat layaali, min faDlika.***

muwaDHDHaf al-'istiqbaal ***ghurfa bi Hammaam? bi dush? 'aw biduuni Hammaam?***

julii ***bi Hammaam wa dush, min faDlika. hal xindakum fuTuur?***

muwaDHDHaf al-'istiqbaal ***naxam, ya sayyidatii. wa xindanaa khidma li l-ghurfa wa maTxam li l-ghadaa' wa l-xashaa'. xindaki ghurfa raqm thalaatha mi'a wa 'arbaxata xashar, fii T-Taabiq ath-thaalith. al-ghurfa kabiira wa mushmisa.***

julii ***hal al-ghurfa haadi'a?***

muwaDHDHaf al-'istiqbaal ***naxam, ya sayyidatii. al-ghurfa haadi'a.***

julii ***haadhaa mumtaaz. 'anaa taxbaana jiddan.***

muwaDHDHaf al-'istiqbaal ***hal kaana s-safar Tawiilan?***

julii ***naxam. min nyuu yuurk.***

muwaDHDHaf al-'istiqbaal ***'anti 'amriikiyya. tatakallamiina xarabiyya mumtaaza.***

julii ***'anaa min kanadaa, wa laakin ji'tu min nuu yuurk. wa shukran. al-xarabiyya lugha Saxba wa laakin jadiira bi l-'ihtimaam.***

Clerk Good Morning, and welcome to the Hotel Sphinx.

Julie Good Morning. Thank you. Do you have a room?

Clerk Yes, ma'am. Would you like a single or a double?

Julie	A single room, thank you.
Clerk	For how many nights?
Julie	For four nights, please.
Clerk	With a bathroom? With a shower? Or without a bathroom?
Julie	With a bathroom and shower, please. And do you have breakfast?
Clerk	Yes, ma'am. There is also room service and a restaurant for lunch and dinner. You'll be in room 314, on the third floor. It's big and sunny.
Julie	Is the room quiet?
Clerk	Yes, ma'am. The room is very quiet.
Julie	That's wonderful. I'm very tired.
Clerk	Was your trip long?
Julie	Yes. From New York.
Clerk	You're American. You speak excellent Arabic.
Julie	I'm from Canada, but I came from New York. And thank you. Arabic is a hard language, but very interesting.

6B Language Notes

Notice that the clerk says *marHaban biki* to Julie. Remember that this is the feminine form of the expression "welcome." If Julie were a man, the clerk would say *marHaban bika*.

Note that the expression *min faDlik* translates as "please." In proper Modern Standard Arabic, the expression is *min faDlika* to a man and *min faDliki* to a woman. However, you will very often hear a simple *min faDlik* used in all cases.

The polite word for "ma'am" is *sayyida*, or *sayyid* for "sir." In this case the ending *–tii* is a possessive meaning "my," which is a courteous form of address.

Notice that the word for person is *shakhS*. To say two people, the clerk uses the form *shakhSayni*. This is the dual form of the noun, and you'll learn about it in this lesson.

Notice the ending on *Tawiil* in the question *hal kaana s-safar Tawiilan*? The *–n* ending serves a grammatical function in Arabic, and you can see it on several common expressions such as *shukran* (thank you), *'ahlan wa sahlan* (hello), *xafwan* (you're welcome), *Tabxan* (of course) *jiddan* (very), and *'abadan* (never). You don't need to worry too much about this point of grammar, though. It will be enough simply to remember the common expressions that use it.

The clerk says to Julie *tatakallamiina xarabiyya mumtaaza*, "you speak excellent Arabic." Other forms of this verb are *'atakallamu* (I speak) and *tatakallamu* (you speak, m.). To ask someone if they speak English, ask *hal tatakallamu l-'injliiziyya* or *hal tatakallamiina l-'injliiziyya?*

Notice in the vocabulary list below that the word for lobby is transcribed as *rad-ha*. That is because the *d* and *h* are separate sounds, not to be pronounced as the "th" in "this."

6C Vocabulary

funduq	hotel
rad-ha	lobby
maktab al-'istiqbaal	reception desk
muwaDHDHaf al-'istiqbaal	desk clerk
bawwaab	concierge
Hajz	reservation
xindii Hajz	I have a reservation.
miftaaH	key
ghurfa	room
Taabiq	floor
aT-Taabiq al-'awwal	first floor
miSxad	elevator
mushrifat al-ghurfa	cleaning woman
qaaxat aT-Taxaam	dining room
maTxam	restaurant
ghurfa li-waaHid	single room
ghurfa li-ithnayn	double room
Hammaam	bathroom
banyuu	bathtub
sariir	bed
dush	shower
maghsala	sink
mirHaaD	toilet
fuuTa	towel
baTTaniyya	blanket

mikwaa	clothes iron
miSbaaH	lamp
miftaaH an-nuur	light switch
mir'aat	mirror
wisaada	pillow
raadyuu	radio
tilifizyuun	television
haatif	telephone
khizaana	safe
shubbaak	window
'iDaafiyya	extra
kabiir	big
Saghiir	small
rakhiiS	cheap
ghaalii	expensive
xaalii	loud
haadi'	quiet
naDHiif	clean
wasikh	dirty
thaqiil	heavy
khafiif	light
li	for
bi	with
biduuni	without

6D Vocabulary Practice

Translate each of the following words, phrases, and sentences into Arabic.

1. lobby
2. key
3. reception desk
4. a small room
5. the quiet room
6. the sink and the toilet
7. a towel and a blanket
8. I have a reservation.
9. The hotel is big.

10. The room is expensive.
11. I am in the lobby.
12. Is there a television in the room?

6E Grammar and Usage

1 Nationalities

In Lesson 2 you learned how to say the names of several countries. Now let's add to that list, and also learn nationalities. First you'll see the name of the country (*al-maghrib*, for example) and then the masculine adjective (*maghribiyy*, for a man from Morocco) and finally the feminine adjective (*maghribiyya*, for a woman from Morocco). Notice that a lot of the names of countries are cognates—words that sound similar in different languages. Also notice that the masculine adjective ending is *–iyy*, which is an "ee" sound followed by a long "y" as in "yes," and the feminine is *–iyya*. This should remind you of the typical feminine ending *–a*, which you learned in lesson 2. If the name of the country ends in *–aa*, as in *amriikaa*, that *–aa* is dropped before the endings. If the name of the country ends in a consonant, *–i* is inserted, and if the country begins with *al-*, that is dropped.

al-maghrib, maghribiyy, maghribiyya	Morocco, Morrocan
al-jazaa'ir, jazaa'iriyy, jazaa'iriyya	Algeria, Algerian
tuunis, tuunisiyy, tuunisiyya	Tunisia, Tunisian
liibyaa, liibiyy, liibiyya	Libya, Libyan
miSr, miSriyy, miSriyya	Egypt, Egyptian
as-saxuudiyya, saxuudiyy, saxuudiyya	Saudi Arabia, Saudi
filiSTiin, filiSTiiniyy, filiSTiiniyya	Palestine, Palestinian
lubnaan, lubnaaniyy, lubnaaniyya	Lebanon, Lebanese
suuriyaa, suuriyy, suuriyya	Syria, Syrian
al-'urdun, 'urduniyy, 'urduniyya	Jordan, Jordanian
al-xiraaq, xiraaqiyy, xiraaqiyya	Iraq, Iraqi
al-kuwayt, kuwaytiyy, kuwaytiyya	Kuwait, Kuwaiti
al-baHrayn, baHrayniyy, baHrayniyya	Bahrain, Bahraini
qaTar, qaTariyy, qaTariyya	Qatar, Qatari
al-yaman, yamaniyy, yamaniyya	Yemen, Yemeni
xumaan, xumaaniyy, xumaaniyya	Oman, Omani
'amriikaa, 'amriikiyy, 'amriikiyya	The US, American
kanadaa, kanadiyy, kanadiyya	Canada, Canadian

'injiltiraa, 'injliiziyy, 'injliiziyya	England, English
faransaa, faransiyy, faransiyya	France, French
'almaanyaa, 'almaaniyy, 'almaaniyya	Germany, German
'iTaliaa, 'iTaaliyy, 'iTaaliyya	Italy, Italian
'isbaaniyaa, 'isbaaniyy, 'isbaaniyya	Spain, Spanish
al-yaabaan, yaabaaniyy, yaabaaniyya	Japan, Japanese
aS-Siin, Siiniyy, Siiniyya	China, Chinese
kuuriyaa, kuuriyy, kuuriyya	Korea, Korean
tayland, taylandiyy, taylandiyya	Thailand, Thai
al-hind, hindiyy, hindiyya	India, Indian
'afghaanistaan, 'afghaaniyy, 'afghaaniyya	Afghanistan, Afghani
as-suudaan, suudaaniyy, suudaaniyya	Sudan, Sudanese
as-sinighaal, sinighaaliyy, sinighaaliyya	Senegal, Senegalese
kiinyaa, kiiniyy, kiiniyya	Kenya, Kenyan

2 Gender Endings in Human Nouns

In Lesson 2 you learned that all nouns in Arabic have gender, whether they refer to humans, animals, or inanimate objects. With nouns that have natural gender, such as *bint* (girl) or *walad* (boy), the gender is always logical. With inanimate nouns, the typical feminine ending is *–a*, so with just a few exceptions that you have to memorize, such as the feminine *shams* (sun) or *daar* (house), an inanimate noun is masculine if it ends in something other than *-a*.

In the case of many human nouns, especially nouns referring to professions and the like, you can change the gender from masculine to feminine simply by adding the *-a* ending. You saw this in the last section with nationalities. Let's take a look at some examples using professions.

SaHaafiyy, SaHaafiyya	journalist
Taalib, Taaliba	college or graduate student
tilmiidh, tilmiidha	high school student
mudarris, mudarrisa	teacher
'ustaadh, 'ustaadha	professor
Tabiib, Tabiiba	doctor
Tabiib al-'asnaan, Tabiibat al-'asnaan	dentist
muHaamii, muHaamiya	lawyer
muhandis, muhandisa	engineer
mumaththil, mumaththila	actor
mughannii, mughanniya	singer

kaatib, kaatiba	writer
kahrabaa'iyy, kahrabaa'iyya	electrician
saa'iq, saa'iqa	driver
shurTiyy, shurTiyya	policeman/woman
najjaar, najjaara	carpenter
muusiiqiyy, muusiiqiyya	musician

faaTima Tabiiba.	Fatima is a doctor.
hal 'anta kahrabaa'iyy?	Are you an electrician?

3 "Sound" Plurals

Now that you've learned several nouns denoting human beings—nationalities, professions, etc.—it's time to learn how to form the plurals of these words. Take a look at a few examples.

miSriyy	Egyptian man
miSriyyuun	Egyptian men
miSriyya	Egyptian woman
miSriyyaat	Egyptian women
'amriikiyy	American man
'amriikiyyuun	American men
'amriikiyya	American woman
'amriikiyyaat	American women
mudarris	male teacher
mudarrisuun	male teachers
mudarrisa	female teacher
mudarrisaat	female teachers
SaHaafiyy	male journalist
SaHaafiyyuun	male journalists
SaHaafiyya	female journalist
SaHaafiyyaat	female journalists

As you can see, forming the plural of most human nouns denoting professions and nationalities is quite easy. You simply add the ending *-uun* to singular masculine human nouns, and the ending *-at* to singular feminine human nouns.

(Remember to keep the final *–a* of the feminine singular, so that you have a long *–aat* in the plural.) You'll also see that the masculine ending *–uun* changes to *–iin* in certain grammatical instances, but don't worry too much about that now.

This type of plural is often called a "sound plural." It's important to keep in mind that it's limited mainly to human nouns denoting professions and nationalities. It can be used with a few other nouns, especially long nouns of several syllables, but it is not the most common type of plural in Arabic. For example, you cannot form the plural of words like *bint* (girl), *rajul* (man), *yawm* (day), *bayt* (house), or *kitaab* (book) with these endings. Those nouns, and for that matter most Arabic nouns, take what's often called a "broken" plural, and we'll come back to that later.

It's also important to keep in mind that not all professions or nationalities take sound plurals. For example, *Tabiib* (doctor) has the plural form *'aTibbaa'*, but the feminine *Tabiiba* has the sound plural *Tabiibaat*. And the word *xarabiyy* (Arab, masculine) has the plural *xarab*, while *xarabiyya* (Arab, feminine) has the sound plural *xarabiyyaat*.

4 The Dual Form

As you saw with the pronouns *'antumaa* (you two) and *humaa* (the two of them), the dual form is a special way to talk about two things or a pair of things that is different from both the singular and plural forms in Arabic. Thankfully, it's like the sound plurals in that it's a simple ending: *–aani,* or especially in the spoken language, *–ayni*. Even better, it can be used with all nouns. Learn to recognize both endings in the dual.

kitaab	a book
kitaabaani/kitaabayni	two books, a pair of books
bint	a girl
bintaani/bintayni	two girls, a pair of girls
haatif	a phone
haatifaani/haatifayni	a pair of phones

mudarris	a male teacher
mudarrisaani/mudarrisayni	two male teachers

If a singular noun ends in the feminine ending *–a*, the dual ending is *–taani/-tayni* instead of *–aani/-ayni*. Remember that *–a* has a "hidden t," and this is one of the instances where it comes out of hiding.

ghurfa	a room
ghurfataani/ghurfatayni	a pair of rooms
madiina	a city
madiinataani/madiinatayni	two cities
miSriyya	an Egyptian woman
miSriyyataani/miSriyyatayni	two Egyptian women

6F Grammar and Usage Exercises

Exercise 1 Give both the masculine and feminine nationalities for each of the following countries:

1. *'amriikaa*
2. *miSr*
3. *tuunis*
4. *lubnaan*
5. *faransaa*
6. *al-yaabaan*
7. *as-sinighaal*
8. *kiinyaa*
9. *'almaanyaa*
10. *aS-Siin*
11. *kanadaa*
12. *al-xiraaq*

Exercise 2 Change the gender of each of the following nouns. If you see a masculine form, give the feminine, and if you see a feminine form, give the masculine.

1. *SaHaafiyya*
2. *mudarris*
3. *'ustaadh*
4. *Taaliba*
5. *muhandis*
6. *muHaamiya*
7. *Tabiiba*
8. *mughannii*
9. *kaatiba*
10. *mumaththila*

Exercise 3 Now give both the masculine and feminine plural forms of these professions.

1. journalists
2. teachers
3. engineers
4. singers
5. actors

Exercise 4 Give the dual form of each noun. For now, use the *–aan*i form.

1. *kitaab*
2. *haatif*
3. *bint*
4. *ghurfa*
5. *walad*
6. *rajul*
7. *mudarrisa*
8. *funduq*
9. *madiina*
10. *qaamuus*
11. *SaHaafiyya*
12. *amriikiyya*

6G Pronunciation Practice *S, D, T,* and *DH*

The consonants *S*, *D*, *T*, and *DH* are basically deeper, more open varieties of *s*, *d*, *t*, and *dh*. Although the same distinction doesn't exist in English, it's not hard to make these sounds. Start with the sound *s-s-s* as in "hiss" and notice the position of the tip of your tongue, pressed gently above and behind your upper teeth. As you pronounce *s-s-s-s-s*, there's just enough space between your tongue and your teeth to make a hissing sound. Now, move the tip of your tongue back slightly in your mouth, so that it's resting right behind the bony ridge behind your upper teeth. The body of your tongue will drop down, lower in your mouth, similar to the position your tongue has when the doctor tells you to open wide and say *ahhhhh*. With your tongue tip against the bony ridge and the body of your tongue drawn back and low in your mouth, say *Sa*. Can you hear how deep the *ah* sound is? That's the easiest way to notice the difference between *s* and *S*, *d* and *D*, *t* and *T*, and *dh* and *DH*—the vowels around these consonants will be much deeper. Listen to the recordings and practice these examples of *S*, *D*, *T*, and *DH*.

SabaaH, Saabuun, miSr, Sadiiq
Didd, Dayyiq, 'arD, Dakhm
Tibb, baTal, Tawiila, nafT
'abuu DHabi, DHuhr, DHafr, DHilaal

6H Arabic Script The letters *raa'* and *zaay*

The letters *raa'* and *zaay*, pronounced *r* (rolled) and *z*, are both written like large commas which extend below the line. The only difference is that *zaay* is dotted, while *raa'* is not. Notice that both of these letters are non-connectors, so there are only two forms for them.

	isolated	initial	medial	final
r	ر	ر	ـر	ـر
z	ز	ز	ـز	ـز

بَار	*baar* (bar)	دَرْس	*dars* (lesson)
زَيْتُون	*zaytuun* (olive)	عَزِيز	*xaziiz* (man's name)

For more practice, continue reading *Group 5:* د *d,* ذ *dh,* ر *r,* ز *z* and reading practice 6 of *Part 2: Reading Arabic* in the *Complete Guide to Arabic Script*. You can also practice writing with Group 5 and writing practices 11–14 of *Part 3: Writing Arabic.*

61 **Culture Note** *Living in the Arab World*

As you might expect, there are some stark differences between life in cities and life in the country in the Arab world. Major Arab metropolitan areas—Cairo, Tunis, Baghdad, Casablanca, Amman, Dubai, Riyadh—are densely populated and have a lot in common with any major city throughout the world. There are downtown business areas, high rise apartment complexes, schools, universities, shopping centers, mosques, and traditional marketplaces. There are parks and gardens, streets and avenues, and of course traffic and noise, like in any other city. Stretching around cities are suburbans areas, which naturally become thinner and thinner as the city center falls further into the distance. The large middle class of Arab cities and suburbs lives in either apartment complexes or individual houses, where the living room is the center of gravity for the family. It can serve as TV room, dining room, family room, and sometimes prayer room.

Far away from urban and suburban areas, the rural regions of the Arab world tend to be dotted with small villages, if indeed there are any people at all. Tribal ties, similar to clan ties, are very strong in some areas of the Arab countryside, and some groups, called bedouins, even lead nomadic or semi-nomadic lives. Most rural people in the Arab world depend on agriculture to make a living. Types of houses vary greatly depending on local customs, geography, and building materials, and they may include mud brick huts or houses and tents.

Lesson 6 Answer Key

Vocabulary Practice: 1. *rad-ha*; 2. *miftaaH*; 3. *maktab al-'istiqbaal*; 4. *ghurfa Saghiira*; 5. *al-ghurfa l-haadi'a*; 6. *al-maghsala wa l-mirHaaD*; 7. *fuuTa wa baTTaniyya*; 8. *xindii Hajz*. 9. *al-funduq kabiir*. 10. *al-ghurfa ghaaliya*. 11. *'anaa fii r-rad-ha*. 12. *hal hunaaka tilifizyuun fii l-ghurfa*? **Exercise 1** 1. *'amriikiyy, 'amriikiyya*; 2. *miSriyy, miSriyya*; 3. *tuunisiyy, tuunisiyya*; 4. *lubnaaniyy, lubnaaniyya*; 5. *faransiyy, faransiyya*; 6. *yaabaaniyy, yaabaaniyya*; 7. *sinighaaliyy, sinighaaliyya*; 8. *kiiniyy, kiiniyya*; 9. *'almaaniyy, 'almaaniyya*; 10. *Siiniyy, Siiniyya* 11. *kanadiyy, kanadiyya*; 12. *xiraaqiyy, xiraaqiyya*; **Exercise 2** 1. *SaHaafiyy*; 2. *mudarrisa*; 3. *'ustaadha*; 4. *Taalib*; 5. *muhandisa*; 6. *muHaamii*; 7. *Tabiib*; 8. *mughanniya*; 9. *kaatib*; 10. *mumaththil* **Exercise 3** 1. *SaHaafiyyuun, SaHaafiyyaat*; 2. *mudarrisuun, mudarrisaat*; 3. *muhandisuun, muhandisaat*; 4. *mughanniyuun, mughanniyaat*; 5. *mumaththiluun, mumaththilaat*; **Exercise 4** 1. *kitaabaani*; 2. *haatifaani*; 3. *bintaani*; 4. *ghurfataani*; 5. *waladaani*; 6. *rajulaani*; 7. *mudarrisataani*; 8. *funduqaani*; 9. *madiinataani*; 10. *qaamuusaani*; 11. *SaHafiyyataani*; 12. *'amriikiyyataani*

LESSON 7

AROUND TOWN *fii l-madiina*

In Lesson 7 you'll learn how to ask directions and talk about places in a typical city. You'll also learn the second and far more common type of plurals in Arabic, along with one of the most important concepts in Arabic grammar.

7A Dialogue

Keith Poole is looking for an art museum, but he is a bit lost. Listen in as he asks Adel, a passer-by, for directions.

kiith	***xafwan, hal matHaf al-funuun fii haadhaa n-nahj?***
xaadil	***laa, haadhaa laysa an-nahj aS-SaHiiH. al-matHaf fii nahj al-'andalus.***
kiith	***'anaa Daa'ix 'idhan. 'ayna nahj al-'andalus?***
xaadil	***ruuH 'ilaa s-saaHa wa liff xalaa l-yamiin. thumma 'imshii nahjayn 'ilaa l-masjid. liff xalaa sh-shimaal, wa dhaaka huwa an-nahj. matHaf al-funuun bijaanibi al-masjid.***
kiith	***shukran. shukran jaziilan.***
xaadil	***laa shukra xalaa waajib.***
kiith	***hal mumkin 'an 'as'alaka su'aalan 'aakhar?***
xaadil	***tabxan.***
kiith	***'ayna yumkin 'an 'ashtaria khariiTat al-madiina?***
xaadil	***hmmmm . . . . hunaaka maktaba fii s-saaHa, fii maqTax haadhaa n-nahj. hunaaka maktab as-siyaaHa qariib min funduq al-Hayaat. mumkin 'an tajida khariiTa hunaaka.***
kiith	***funduq al-Hayaat . . . huwa bijaanibi al-Hadiiqa?***
xaadil	***naxam. haadhaa SaHiiH.***
kiith	***shukran. nahaaruka saxiid.***
xaadil	***nahaaruka saxiid wa riHla saxiida.***
Keith	Excuse me, is the art museum on this street?
Adel	No, this isn't the right street. It's on Andalus Street.
Keith	I'm lost then. Where is Andalus Street?
Adel	Go to the square and turn right. Then walk two blocks to the mosque. Turn left at the mosque,

	and that's the street. The art museum is next to the mosque.
Keith	Thank you. Thank you very much.
Adel	You're welcome.
Keith	Can I ask you another question?
Adel	Of course.
Keith	Where can I buy a map of the city?
Adel	Hmmm . . . Well, there's a bookstore on the square, on the corner of this street. There's a tourism office near the Hyatt Hotel. It's possible to find maps there.
Adel	The Hotel Hyatt . . . that's next to the park?
Adel	Yes, that's right.
Keith	Thank you. Have a good day.
Adel	Have a good day, and enjoy your trip.

7B Language Notes

Notice that the phrase *haadhaa n-nahj* means "this street." Literally, that phrase translates as "this-the-street." You'll learn more about using demonstratives, such as "this" or "that," in Arabic in the next lesson, but for now be aware that you'll often see them used with the definite article, unlike in English.

In Arabic, as in many languages, the word used in place of the American expression "block" is simply "street," in Arabic *nahj*.

Did you recognize the dual form of *nahj—nahjayn—*in the expression meaning "walk two blocks/streets?"

Notice the useful expression *hal mumkin/yumkin 'an . . . or 'ayna mumkin/yumkin 'an . . .*, which mean "Is it possible to . . . " or "Where is it possible to . . . " The forms *mumkin* and *yumkin* are interchangeable, and they can often be translated as as "Can I . . . " or "Where can I . . . " as is the case in this dialogue. The verb that follows this phrase is in a special form, which you'll learn about later in this course. Another very useful word that is used in a similar way is *yajib*. This word can be translated as "it is necessary" and is used in expressions that use "have to," "need to" or "must" in English. For example, *hal yajib 'an tadrusa?* means "Do you have to study?" or "Is it necessary for you to study?"

7C Vocabulary

Starting with this vocabulary list, you'll see the plural forms of nouns next to their singular forms. For example, *madiina* means "city" and *mudun* means "cities." Try to learn each plural form that is given, as some are the more regular "sound" plurals, while most are the unpredictable "broken" plurals that you'll learn about in this lesson.

madiina / mudun	city
qarya / quraa	village
nahj / 'anhuj	street
zanqa / zanqaat	little street, especially in older part of town
khariiTa / kharaa'iT	map
shaarix / shawaarix	avenue
Tariiq / Turuq	main street
jisr / jusuur	bridge
timthaal / tamaathiil	statue
muntazah / muntazahaat	park
mujaawara / mujaawaraat	neighborhood
binaaya / binaayaat	building
binaayat al-xamal	office building
binaayat as-sakan	apartment building
matHaf / mataaHif	museum
fann / funuun	art
masjid / masaajid	mosque
jaamix / jawaamix	mosque
kaniisa / kanaa'is	church, synagogue
maktaba / maktabaat	library / bookstore
madrasa / madaaris	school
mustashfaa / mustashfayaat	hospital
suuq / 'aswaaq	market
makhbaz / makhaabiz	bakery
jazzaar / jazzaaruun	butcher shop
maTxam / maTaaxim	restaurant
masraH / masaariH	theater
baar / baaraat	bar
malhaa / malaahii	discotheque
haram / 'ahraam	pyramid
saa'iH / suwwaaH	tourist
su'aal / 'as'ila	question
qariib	near

baxiid	far
SaHiiH	right, correct
khata'	wrong
'anaa Daa'ix(a)	I'm lost
yasaar, shimaal	left
liff xalaa sh-shimaal	turn left
yamiin	right
liff xalaa l-yamiin	turn right

7D Vocabulary Practice

Translate each of the following words, phrases, and sentences into Arabic.

1. city
2. question
3. museum
4. building
5. the map
6. the little village
7. the mosque and the church
8. a big library
9. the big library
10. I am lost.
11. There is a museum in the city.
12. There is a beautiful statue in the park.
13. The bookstore is next to the bakery.
14. The park is big and beautiful.

7E Grammar and Usage

❶ Introduction to the Consonant Root System

Take a look at the following words, all of which you've already seen in this course.

kitaab	book
maktab	office
kataba	he wrote
maktaba	library, bookstore
kaatib	writer

First consider the meanings of these words. What common theme do they share? If you've guessed that they all have some kind of connection to writing or written things, you're correct. Now take a look at the shapes of the words themselves. Do you see any common thread running through all of them? If your answer is that they all have the consonants *k-t-b*, in that order, then you're right on track.

Arabic makes use of a system of consonant roots, meaning that many of its words—verbs, nouns, adjectives, plurals, etc.—are formed by taking a basic word shape or skeleton, which usually consists of three consonants, and manipulating it by interspersing vowels, or adding prefixes or suffixes. Each different type of manipulation forms a variation on the basic theme of that root.

So, from *k-t-b*, if you add an *-a* after each consonant, you get *kataba* meaning "he wrote." But if you add the prefix *ma-* and an *-a* between the second and third consonants, you get *maktab*, which is "office," or a place of writing. To test this on other roots, take a look at the word for school, *madrasa*, which is a place of studying. Can you see what the three roots are? If you took off the *ma-* "place-of" prefix and guessed *d-r-s*, then you're right. So, if *kataba*, from *k-t-b*, means "he wrote," how do you think you say "he studied?" You've got it pretty much figured out if you guessed *darasa*.

This is of course different from anything you're familiar with in English. But it's not completely alien. English manipulates basic roots, too. Think about *place*, *placed*, *replace*, *placement*, *replacement*, *displace*, *displaced*, *displacement*, etc. Each one of those meanings is a variation on a basic theme, with certain changes made to that theme. You expect these changes and know how to decipher them because you know English. The idea of taking a root of three consonants and adding vowels before, after, and in between just takes some getting used to, and some practice, but it's only another way of doing something that you already do in English (or in many other languages for that matter). And if you've ever spoken *ig-pay atin-lay*, you know how quickly you can train yourself to "play" with the shapes of words!

So, what does this mean for Arabic? Consonant roots—and the many changes made to them—show up just about everywhere in the language. Most plurals (the "broken" ones) are formed this way, as are verb tenses, words derived from verbs, different forms of adjectives, and a lot more. It's a pretty useful system, actually. And, you'll be happy to know, it's the most complicated thing you'll ever have to learn about Arabic. After this, it's all easy.

2 "Broken" Plurals

Now that you know what the consonant root system is, you're ready to take on the so-called broken plurals, which are the most common forms of plurals. Let's start with one example, *walad* (boy), which becomes *'awlaad* (boys) in the plural. Can you see what the root consonants are? The "skeleton" of the word *walad* is *w-l-d*, and to form its plural, *'awlaad*, you can see that you add an *a–* before the first consonant, and then a long *–aa–* between the second and third. This is one of a few common patterns for forming broken plurals in Arabic. Below you'll see a list of the most common patterns, but do not try to memorize them now. Instead, you should learn each new plural along with its singular, and from this point forward you'll see plural forms as well as singular ones in the vocabulary lists. There is, unfortunately, no way of knowing which pattern a singular will follow to transform into the plural—you just have to memorize them, or of course look them up in a dictionary. One last note—since we're working with a transcription system, don't forget that certain sounds, which are transcribed with two letters such as *gh*, *sh*, or *kh*, are still just one sound. So, even though there are four written consonants in *ghurfa* or *shams*, there are just three sounds in their roots—*gh-r-f* and *sh-m-s*.

Pattern 1 *'a//aa/* *walad–'awlaad* (boy/boys)

Nouns that follow pattern 1 add *'a–* before the first root consonant, and insert *–aa–* between the second and third. Another example is *waqt* / *'awqaat* (time/times).

Pattern 2 */u/uu/* *fann–funuun* (art/arts)

Nouns that follow pattern 2 insert *–u–* between the first and second root consonants, and then *–uu–* between the second and third. Another example is *malik* / *muluuk* (king/kings).

Pattern 3 */i/aa/* *kalb–kilaab* (dog/dogs)

Nouns that follow pattern 3 insert *–i–* between the first two root consonants and *–aa–* between the last two. Another example is *rajul* / *rijaal* (man/men).

Pattern 4 */u/u/* *kitaab–kutub* (book/books)

Nouns that follow pattern 4 insert *–u–* between both the first two root consonants and the last two as well. Another example is *madiina / mudun* (city/cities).

Pattern 5 */u/a/* *dawla–duwal* (country/countries)

Nouns that follow pattern 5 add a *–u–* between their first two root consonants and an *–a–* between their last two root consonants. Another example is *ghurfa / ghuraf* (room/rooms).

Pattern 6 *a//u/* *shahr–'ashhur* (month/months)

Nouns that follow pattern 6 add *a–* before the the first root consonant and *–u–* between the last two. Another example is *nahr* / *'anhur* (river/rivers).

Pattern 7 */u/a/aa'* *xaalim–xulamaa'* (scholar/scholars)

Nouns that follow pattern 7 add *–u–* between the the first and second root consonants and *–a–* between the last two. They also add *–aa'* after the third root consonant. Another example is *waziir* / *wuzaraa'* (minister/ministers).

Pattern 8 *'a//i/aa'* *Sadiiq–'aSdiqaa'* (friend/friends)

Nouns that follow pattern 8 add *a–* before the first root consonant, *–i–* between the last two, and*–aa'* after the third root consonant. Another example is *qariib / 'aqribaa'* (relative/relatives).

As you can see, there are a few patterns that you can look for in plurals. But, the best way to handle plurals is to memorize each one as you learn a new word. The following is a list of the plurals of some of the most important nouns you've learned so far. Practice each one until it becomes familiar to you, and look for more examples of some of the more common patterns listed above.

'ism / 'asmaa'	name
yawm / 'ayyaam	day
kitaab / kutub	book

Taalib / Tullaab	student
'ustadh / 'asaatidha	professor
bint / banaat	girl, daughter
walad / 'awlaad	boy
rajul / rijaal	man
'imra'a / nisaa'	woman
'ab / 'aabaa'	father
'umm / 'ummahaat	mother
'ibn / 'abnaa'	son
'akh / 'ikhwa	brother
'ukht / 'akhawaat	sister
Sadiiq / 'aSdiqaa'	friend
maktab / makaatib	office
bayt / buyuut	house
baab / 'abwaab	door
madiina / mudun	city
haatif / hawaatif	telephone

Notice that a lot of nouns that have the feminine *–a* ending have the sound plural ending *–aat*, but not all.

jaamixa / jaamixaat	university
kulliyya / kulliyyaat	school, college
Hafla / Hafalaat	party
sharika / sharikaat	company
'ustaadha / 'ustaadhaat	professor (f.)
Sadiiqa / Sadiiqaat	friend (f.)
Taaliba / Taalibaat	student (f.)

But not all feminine nouns ending in *–a* form their plural with *–aat*. Some have broken plurals:

Suura / Suwar	photograph
madiina / mudun	city
risaala / rasaa'il	letter
waraqa / 'awraaq	sheet of paper

3 Sound Plurals vs. Broken Plurals and Plurals of Complex Nouns

Now that you've seen both types of plurals in Arabic, this is a good time to review sound plurals and to compare them to broken plurals. Sound plurals, as you recall, are very easy to form—simply add *–uun* (or *–iin*) for the masculine plural and *–at* for the feminine forms, keeping the *–a* of the feminine singular for a long *–aat* ending. Broken plurals are formed by manipulating the (usually) three root consonants of a word in certain ways, many of which follow patterns.

So, which words take sound plurals, and which words take broken plurals? You learned in the last lesson that sound plurals, *-uun/-iin* and *-at*, are used mostly with human nouns, such as the ones that denote professions or nationalities. If you look back at the list of professions and nationalities, you can see that these words are for the most part long and complex compared to the words listed above that take broken plurals. Obviously, if a broken plural is formed by manipulating root consonants in a certain way, the root consonants must allow this kind of manipulation easily. Roots like *k-t-b* (from *kitaab*), *w-l-d* (from *walad*), and *sh-h-r* (from *shahr*) all work quite well. But take the consonants in *mudarris* (*m-d-r-r-s*) or *'amriikiyya* (*m-r-k-y-y*). These words are too "clunky" for broken plurals, so they take the easier sound plurals, simply added to their singular forms.

There are also many nouns that refer to inanimate objects that are too long and complex for Arabic broken plurals. Take for example the word *tilifizyuun*, "television." It's not a human noun, it doesn't refer to a profession or a nationality, but it clearly is far too complex for any kind of broken plural. It includes the consonants *t-l-f-z-y-n*, double the length of most Arabic roots. So, it must take a sound plural, and complex words denoting "neuter" things take the feminine sound plural ending, *-aat*.

tilifizyuun	television
tilifizyuunaat	televisions
'ijtimaax	meeting
'ijtimaaxaat	meetings
munaaqasha	discussion
munaaqashaat	discussions
kuumbyuutar	computer
kuumbyuutaraat	computers

❹ Adjective Agreement with Non-Human Plurals

You've already learned how to make feminine singular adjectives agree with feminine singular nouns, simply by adding *–a*. So, *walad Tawiil* (a tall boy) becomes *bint Tawiila* (a tall girl). And you also know that adjectives must agree with the nouns they modify in definiteness, so "the tall boy" is *al-walad aT-Tawiil*, and "the tall girl" is *al-bint aT-Tawiila.* You can probably guess that if adjectives have to agree in gender and definiteness, they also have to agree in number—singular, dual or plural.

That's partially correct. Arabic makes a very important distinction in the plural between humans and non-humans. While human plurals—women, boys, doctors, students—take plural forms of adjectives, non-human plurals take the feminine singular forms. So, the adjective *Tawiila* can be used to describe one girl, one woman, or one female teacher, but it can also be used in the exact same form to describe trees, mountains, or buildings. Just remember that adjectives that describe non-human plurals will look like the feminine singular form, with an *–a* ending.

mudun kabiira — big cities
al-kutub aS-Saghiira — the small books
aS-Suwar al-jamiila — the pretty photos
Hafalaat nashiiTa — lively parties

❺ Adjective Agreement with Human Plurals

Adjective agreement with human plurals is a bit different. Let's start with feminine plurals. If an adjective describes a female human plural, it will take the feminine sound plural ending *–aat*.

bint Tawiila — a tall girl
banaat Tawiilaat — tall girls
al-mudarrisa l-jadiida — the new (female) teacher
al-mudarrisaat al-jadiidaat — the new (female) teachers
aS-SaHaafiyya l-qaSiira — the short (female) journalist
aS-SaHaafiyyaat al-qaSiiraat — the short (female) journalists

However, if an adjective describes a male human plural, it has a choice between a sound plural and a broken plural. Which type depends on the adjective itself; if it's a complex word, it will take the sound plural ending *–uun*, but if it's closer to the typical three-consonant root system, it will probably take a broken plural. But not all shorter adjectives have broken plurals. Just as with nouns, the best way to learn the plurals of adjectives—broken or sound—is to memorize each new one. Here is a list of the broken plurals of some of the more common adjectives that you've seen so far. Can you see any of the patterns that nouns follow to form their plurals?

kabiir / kibaar	big, old
Saghiir / Sighaar	small, young
xaDHiim / xuDHamaa'	great, powerful
jadiid / judud	new
qaSiir / qiSaar	short
Tawiil / Tiwaal	tall
qawiyy / 'aqwiyaa'	strong
Daxiif / Duxafaa'	weak
qadiim / qudamaa'	ancient
samiin / simaan	fat
faqiir / fuqaraa'	poor
naDHiif / niDHaaf	clean

Remember that these plural forms will only be used with masculine human plurals. Feminine human plurals will take the sound ending *–aat*, and non-human plurals will take the feminine singular ending *–a*. So, that means that with certain adjectives that you'd almost never use to describe people, you don't have to worry about memorizing a plural form. Just add *–a* to describe plural things.

rajul samiin	a fat man
rijaal simaan	fat men (male human plural)
'imra'a samiina	a fat woman
nisaa' samiinaat	fat women (female human plural)
kalb samiin	a fat dog
kilaab samiina	fat dogs (non-human plural)
al-walad aT-Tawiil	the tall boy
al-'awlaad aT-Tiwaal	the tall boys (male human plural)
al-bint aT-Tawiila	the tall girl
al-banaat aT-Tawiilaat	the tall girls (female human plural)
al-binaaya T-Tawiila	the tall building
al-binaayaat aT-Tawiila	the tall buildings (non-human plural)

6 Adjective Agreement with the Dual Form

An adjective that modifies a noun in the dual form must also take the dual form. Just like dual form nouns, all dual form adjectives take a simple ending, *–aani*, or *–taani* if the singular adjective ends in *–a*, as in the case of feminine forms.

malik xaDHiim	a great king
malikaani xaDHiimaani	two great kings
al-haatif al-jadiid	the new phone
al-haatifaani l-jadiidaani	the pair of new phones
bint Saghiira	a small girl
bintaani Saghiirataani	a pair of small girls
miSriyya laTiifa	a friendly Egyptian woman
miSriyyataani laTiifataani	two friendly Egyptian women

7F Grammar and Usage Exercises

Exercise 1 Write out the consonant roots for each of the following nouns and adjectives. For example, if you see *walad*, you'd write *w-l-d*. List double consonants just once.

1. *bint* (girl)
2. *Sadiiq* (friend)
3. *laTiif* (kind, friendly)
4. *qaSiir* (short)
5. *qaamuus* (dictionary)
6. *ghurfa* (room)
7. *shubbaak* (window)
8. *maHall* (store)
9. *bayt* (house)
10. *raakib* (passenger)
11. *riHla* (flight)
12. *jisr* (bridge)
13. *kalb* (dog)
14. *'azraq* (blue)

Exercise 2 Give the plural forms of each of the following words. A singular and plural example of the pattern they follow is given to help. For example, if you see *waqt* (time) (*walad-'awlaad*) you know that the root of *waqt* is *w-q-t* and the plural is *'awqaat*, based on the model of *'awlaad*.

1. *qalam* (pen) (*walad–'awlaad*)
2. *bayt* (house) (*fann–funuun*)
3. *maTar* (rain) (*walad-'awlaad*)
4. *kabiir* (big) (*kalb–kilaab*)
5. *jabal* (mountain) (*kalb–kilaab*)

6. *dars* (lesson) (*fann–funuun*)
7. *rijl* (foot) (*shahr–'ashhur*)
8. *SaaHib* (friend) (*walad–'awlaad*)
9. *jadiid* (new) (*kitaab–kutub*)
10. *Dayf* (guest) (*fann–funuun*)
11. *safiina* (ship) (*kitaab–kutub*)
12. *xayn* (eye) (*fann–funuun*)

Exercise 3 The following list contains some nouns that you've never seen before, as well as a few that you have. For each noun, see if you can guess whether it will take a sound plural or a broken plural. Write "S" for sound and "B" for broken.

1. *raqm* (number)
2. *muhandis* (architect)
3. *tilifizyuun* (television)
4. *yawm* (day)
5. *kitaab* (book)
6. *sariir* (bed)
7. *rassaama* (painter)
8. *naqd*(coin)
9. *mutarjim* (translator)
10. *laqab* (nickname)
11. *muSawwir* (photographer)
12. *muHaamii* (lawyer)
13. *dhiraax* (arm)
14. *Tabbaakha* (cook)

Exercise 4 Give the correct form of the adjectives in parentheses for the following nouns.

1. *muSawwiruun* (*Tawiil*)
2. *sufun* (*jadiid*)
3. *'awlaad* (*Daxiif*)
4. *banaat* (*laTiif*)
5. *sikritiiraat* (*jadiid*)
6. *duruus* (*Tawiil*)
7. *'amriikiyyaat* (*Saghiir*)
8. *kutub* (*rakhiiS*)
9. *tilifizyuunaat* (*jadiid*)
10. *jibaal* (*kabiir*)

Exercise 5 Now give the correct form of the adjectives in parentheses, this time describing the dual forms of the same nouns.

1. *muSawwiraani* (*Tawiil*)
2. *waladaani* (*Daxiif*)
3. *bintaani* (*laTiif*)
4. *sikritiirataani* (*jadiid*)
5. *'amriikiyyataani* (*Saghiir*)
6. *kitaabaani* (*rakhiiS*)

7. *tilifizyuunaani* (*jadiid*)
8. *jabalaani* (*kabiir*)

7G Pronunciation Practice *H*

In lesson 7 we'll focus on the strong, emphatic sound transcribed in this course as *H*. Remember that it is not the same sound as *h*, which is the consonant at the beginning of the English words "house" or "have." The more emphatic *H*, by contrast, is similar to the sound made when breathing on a pair of glasses to clean them. It is produced further back in the mouth, and you should feel a constriction at the top of your throat when you pronounce it. Try these examples:

Haarr, Hariir , Hadiid, Hidhaa', Haalii, Hayyaa, miSbaaH, masraH

7H Arabic Script The letters *siin* and *shiin*

Now let's focus on the Arabic letters *siin* and *shiin*, pronounced s as in "see" and sh as in "she" respectively. Notice that they are similar in shape—essentially three peaks that almost look like a "w." The only difference is that *shiin* has three dots above it, while *siin* has none.

	isolated	initial	medial	final
s	س	سـ	ـسـ	ـس
sh	ش	شـ	ـشـ	ـش

سَمِيك	*samiik* (thick)	دَرْس	*dars* (lesson)
شَمْس	*shams* (sun)	شَرِبَ	*shariba* (he drank)

For more practice, read *Group 6:* س *s, and* ش *sh* and reading practice 7 of *Part 2: Reading Arabic* in the *Complete Guide to Arabic Script*. You can also practice writing with Group 6 and writing practices 15–16 of *Part 3: Writing Arabic*.

7I Cultural Note The Golden Age of Islam

The Middle East is complex and varied, and there are many differences among the countries that comprise the region. But there is also a great sense of unity, and undoubtedly the most important elements that bind Middle Eastern countries are the Arabic language and the Islamic religion. Islam plays an important role in shaping Arab identity, both of individual people and of states, and the history of Islam is a source of pride throughout the Arab world. It is helpful then to take even a superficial look at the history of the Islamic faith and the role that it has played in forming the Arab world.

The expansion of Islam began more than fourteen centuries ago, with the prophet Muhammad on the Arabian peninsula. The Islamic religion spread in the same ways that many other religions have spread, through conquest, social and political forces, and missionaries. This created a vast empire, at one point covering Spain, the expanse of North Africa, the Arabian peninsula, Mesopotamia, southeastern Europe, and Southeast Asia. This was the Golden Age of the Islamic Empire. While the caliphs ruled the empire with great discipline, respect for minorities was also a priority, as was the pursuit of art, science and literature. Muslim scholars in fact translated from Greek and Latin a majority of the works from Greek philosophers, and it is thanks to these Muslim scholars that we have today some of Plato's works. Certain sciences, such as mathematics and astronomy, were pursued with vigor during the Islamic Golden Age while Europe was in the grips of the Dark Ages. This history is a source of pride among many in the Arab world today, and the population has a deep desire to emulate the accomplishments of their ancestors.

Lesson 7 Answer Key

Vocabulary Practice: 1. *madiina*; 2. *su'aal*; 3. *matHaf*; 4. *binaaya*; 5. *al-khariiTa*; 6. *al-qarya aS-Saghiira*; 7. *al-masjid wa l-kaniisa*; 8. *maktaba kabiira*; 9. *al-maktaba l-kabiira*; 10. *'anaa Daa'ix(a)*; 11. *hunaaka matHaf fii l-madiina*. 12. *hunaaka timthaal jamiil fii l-muntazah*. 13. *al-maktaba bijaanibi al-makhbaz*. 14. *al-muntazah kabiir wa jamiil*. **Exercise 1:** 1. b-n-t; 2. S-d-q; 3. l-T-f; 4. q-S-r; 5. q-m-s; 6. gh-r-f; 7. sh-b-k; 8. m-H-l-l; 9. b-y-t; 10. r-k-b; 11. r-H-l; 12. j-s-r; 13. k-l-b; 14. z-r-q **Exercise 2:** 1. *'aqlaam*; 2. *buyuut*; 3. *'amTaar*; 4. *kibaar*; 5. *jibaal*; 6. *duruus*; 7. *'arjul*; 8. *'aSHaab*; 9. *judud*; 10. *Duyuuf*; 11. *sufun*; 12. *xuyuun* **Exercise 3:** 1. B; 2. S; 3. S; 4. B; 5. B; 6. B; 7. S; 8. B; 9. S; 10. B; 11. S; 12. S; 13; B; 14. S **Exercise 4:** 1. *Tiwaal*; 2. *jadiida*; 3. *Duxafaa'*; 4. *laTiifaat*; 5. *jadiidaat*; 6. *Tawiila*; 7. *Saghiiraat*; 8. *rakhiiSa*; 9. *jadiida*; 10. *kabiira* **Exercise 5:** 1. *Tawiilaani*; 2. *Daxiifaani*; 3. *laTiifataani*; 4. *jadiidataani*; 5. *Saghiirataani*; 6. *rakhiiSaani*; 7. *jadiidaani*; 8. *kabiiraani*

LESSON 8

THIS IS DELICIOUS! *haadhaa ladhiidh!*

In this lesson you'll learn some very important vocabulary for ordering in a restaurant and for talking about food in general. You'll also learn about Arabic demonstratives, such as "this" or "that" as well as verbs and the past tense.

8A Dialogue

Jane has been spending the afternoon sightseeing in Kuwait City, so she's worked up an appetite. Listen in as she orders a meal in a restaurant.

jayn	***Taawila li waaHid min faDlika.***
xaamil bi l-maTxam	***tafaDDalii. maadhaa turiidiina 'an tashrubii?***
jayn	***maa' shukran. yaa sayyid, qaa'imat aT-Taxaam. bi maadhaa tanSaHunii?***
al-xaamil	***laHm al-baqar ladhiidh. wa l-kuskus ladhiidh kadhaalika.***
jayn	***sa-'aakhudhu laHm al-baqar. 'akaltu kuskus al-'ams. hal xindakum khubz?***
al-xaamil	***naxam. hal turiidiinaa shay'an 'aakhara?***
jayn	***laa. shukran.***

baxda l-wajba . . .

al-xaamil	***hal kaana T-Taxaam tayyiban?***
jayn	***kaana T-Taxaamu mumtaazan!***
al-xaamil	***hal turiidiina shay'an 'aakhara?***
jayn	***naxam. shaay, min faDlika.***
al-xaamil	***tabxan. shaay bi s-sukkar aw biduuni sukkar?***
jayn	***shaay bi s-sukkar. wa l-Hisaab 'ayDan min faDlika.***
al-xaamil	***tabxan.***
Jane	A table for one please.
Waiter	Have a seat. What would you like to drink?
Jane	Water, thank you. Sir, the menu please. What would you recommend to me?
Waiter	The beef is delicious. And the couscous is delicious, as well.

Jane	I'll have the beef. I ate couscous yesterday. Do you have bread?
Waiter	Yes. Would you like anything else?
Jane	No. Thank you.

After the meal . . .

Waiter	Was the food good?
Jane	The food was excellent!
Waiter	Would you like anything else?
Jane	Yes. Tea, please.
Waiter	Of course. Tea with sugar, or without sugar?
Jane	Tea with sugar, and the check, too, please.
Waiter	Of course.

8B Language Notes

You already know the expression *min faDlika* , "please." It literally means "from your kindness" or "from your favor." It comes from the noun *faDl*, meaning "kindness," "graciousness," "favor," etc. The ending *-ka* (your) becomes *-ki* when addressing a woman, *-kum* when addressing a group of men or mixed men and women, and finally *-kunna* when addressing a group of women. But, while all of these endings are "proper" Modern Standard Arabic, you'll often simply hear *min faDlik* in the singular forms.

The waiter responds *tafaDDalii*, which is the feminine form of *tafaDDal* and can be translated as "if you please" or "right this way."

As you saw in lesson 6, the term *sayyid* (or *sayyida* for a woman) is a polite term of address, translating as "sir" or "ma'am." When addressing a person directly, it is preceded by *yaa* as in the dialogue. You would also use *yaa* to address your professor (*yaa 'ustaadh(a)*) or anyone else whose attention you'd like to get politely.

Notice that Jane uses the future particle *sa* in the expression *sa-'aakhudhu laHm al-baqar*, "I'll take the beef."

Did you recognize *laHm al-baqar* as another one of those possessive noun constructions? It literally means "meat of the cattle." Even though there is no *al* in front of *laHm al-baqar*, the phrase is still definite—"the beef." This is because in possessive phrases, two nouns are linked, and only the second one is marked as definite. You'll learn more about possessive constructions in lesson 11.

Notice the verb *kaana* in the first two sentences after the meal. It's a form of the verb "to be" in the past tense, meaning "was." You'll learn more about this verb later.

Finally, notice the word order in the sentence, *kaana T-Taxaamu mumtaazan*, "the food was excellent." It's very common for Arabic sentences to have verb-first word order, even in statements. Both word orders mean the same thing, though, so you can use the English-type subject-first word order.

8C Vocabulary

Taxaam / 'aTxima	food
sharaab / mashruubaat	drink, beverage
xashaa' / xashaa'aat	dinner
ghadaa' / 'aghdia	lunch
fuTuur / fuTuuraat	breakfast
muqabbilaat	appetizers
kuskus	couscous
khubz	bread
'aruzz	rice
zubda	butter
milH	salt
fulful	pepper
sukkar	sugar
shawka / shawkaat	fork
milxaqa / malaaxiq	spoon
Tabaq / 'aTbaaq	plate
ka's / ku'uus	glass, cup (feminine)
kuub / 'akwaab	glass
sikkiin / sakaakiin	knife
mandiil / manaadiil	napkin
laHm al-baqar	beef
dajaaj	chicken
khinziir	pork
bayDa / bayDaat, bayD	egg

fuul	beans
baSala / baSalaat	onion
thuum	garlic
khuDar	vegetable
khiyaar	cucumber
TamaaTima / TamaaTim	tomato
faakiha / fawaakih	fruit
tuffaaHa / tuffaH	apple
tamra / tamr	date
burtuqaala / burtuqaal	orange
mawza / mawz	banana
samaka / samak	fish
Hasaa'	soup
khamr	wine
birra	beer
xaSiir	juice
Haliib	milk
shaay	tea
qahwa	coffee
Tabbaakh	cook
xaamil	worker
xaamil bi l-maTxam	waiter ("worker in the restaurant")
Hisaab	bill, check
baqshiish	tip
ladhiidh	delicious
jaa'ix / jaa'ixuun	hungry
xaTshaan / xaTishuun	thirsty
Haarr	hot
baarid	cold
Taazij	fresh
Taabiliyy	spicy
kadhaalika	as well, also, equally
baxda	after
qabla	before

8D Vocabulary Practice

Translate each of the following words, phrases, and sentences into Arabic.

1. salt and pepper
2. a fork and a spoon

3. the plate and the glass
4. the lunch and the dinner
5. We are hungry!
6. The soup is delicious.
7. The plate is on the table.
8. The sugar is next to the milk.
9. The worker is in the restaurant.
10. The cook is in the kitchen.
11. Is the food spicy?
12. Is the beer cold?

8E Grammar and Usage

1 Demonstratives

Demonstratives are words that "point" to something, such as "this," "that," "these," and "those" in English. Arabic demonstratives have different forms for masculine and feminine in the singular, but not in the plural.

Singular	Plural
haadhaa - this (masculine) *haadhihi* - this (feminine)	*haa'ulaa'i* - these (gender neutral)
dhaalika - that (masculine) *tilka* - that (feminine)	*ulaa'ika* - those (gender neutral)

If a demonstrative is used right before a definite noun, it refers directly to that noun, just as in the English constructions "this book" or "those buildings."

haadhaa l-walad	this boy
haadhihi l-bint	this girl
dhaalika l-kitaab	that book
tilka sh-shawka	that fork
haa'ulaa'i l-'aTfaal	these children
'uulaa'ika n-nisaa'	those women

But if the noun after the demonstrative is indefinite, then the construction is an "is/are" sentence.

haadhaa walad.	This is a boy.
haadhihi bint.	This is a girl.
dhaalika kitaab.	That is a book.
tilka shawka.	That is a fork.
haa'ulaa'i 'aTfaal.	These are children.
'uulaa'ika nisaa'.	Those are women.

To say "this is the . . . " you must use either *huwa* or *hiya* after the demonstrative.

haadhaa huwa l-'ustaadh al-jadiid.	This is the new professor.
haadhihi hiya s-sayyaara l-Hamraa'.	This is the red car.

And don't forget that non-human plurals will take feminine singular demonstratives.

haadhihi l-kutub	these books
haadhihi hiya l-buyuut.	These are the houses.

2 Introduction to Arabic Verbs

If you've studied other languages, you probably expect verbs to be difficult, with several tenses and forms and endings to memorize. This is not the case in Arabic. Arabic has two basic tenses, the past and the present. As you can probably guess, the three-consonant root system comes into play here, serving as the basic frame onto which you'll hang certain vowels, prefixes, or suffixes in order to specify who does what, and when they do it.

Let's go back to the example of *k-t-b* to demonstrate. You remember that this basic root conveys the idea of writing. If you add *–a* after each of the consonants in that root (we'll show that as */a/a/a*), you have *kataba*, "he wrote." But if you use the pattern */a/a/tu*, you have *katabtu*, or "I wrote." And if you use the pattern *ta//u/u,* meaning a prefix of *ta–*, nothing after the first consonant, *–u–* between the last two, and *–u* at the end, you get *taktubu*, or "she writes/she is writing" in the present tense. If you apply these same patterns to the verb root *d-r-s*, which conveys the idea of learning, you'll have *darasa* (he learned), *darastu* (I learned), and *tadrusu* (she learns/she is learning).

Don't worry about memorizing these forms yet; these examples should just give you a general sense of how Arabic verbs work. When you see a new verb, you'll see its "he" form in the past tense, since that is the most basic form—the root consonants, each followed by *–a*. Later, when you know the present tense, you'll see the present tense "he" form as well, because it will give you important information about the present tense conjugation. Here are a few examples of the verbs that you've seen so far in this course, along with their root consonants. Notice that ' (*hamza*) can be a root consonant!

kataba	he wrote	root *k-t-b*
darasa	he studied	root *d-r-s*
'akala	he ate	root *'-k-l*
faxala	he did	root *f-x-l*
dhahaba	he went	root *dh-h-b*
sa'ala	he asked	root *s-'-l*
waSala	he arrived	root *w-S-l*

3 The Past Tense

Arabic verbs are conjugated in both basic tenses. Remember that a verb conjugation is simply a pattern of matching certain verb forms with certain subjects, or doers of the action. In English, for example, the correct form of the verb "to speak" is "speak" with the subjects "the men" or "you," but "speaks" with the subjects "she" or "Richard" or "the director." Arabic conjugations are richer, with more forms, but the same basic principle is at work. A certain form matches a certain subject.

It's easier to start with the past tense in Arabic then the present tense, because its conjugation is simpler. You already know the "he" form, since it's the most basic form. Let's take a look at the full past tense conjugations of *faxala* (do) and *'akala* (eat). Don't forget the meanings of the personal pronouns: *'anaa* (I), *'anta* (you, masculine), *'anti* (you, feminine), *huwa* (he, it), *hiya* (she, it, non-human they), *naHnu* (we), *'antum* (you, plural masculine or mixed), *'antunna* (you, plural feminine), *hum* (they, masculine or mixed), *hunna* (they, feminine), *'antumaa* (you two), and *humaa* (the two of them). Notice that even though there is just one pronoun *humaa* for "the two of them," there are actually two verb forms, one for masculine, and one for feminine.

faxala—do		***'akala—eat***	
'anaa faxaltu	*naHnu faxalnaa*	*'anaa 'akaltu*	*naHnu 'akalnaa*
'anta faxalta	*'antum faxaltum*	*'anta 'akalta*	*'antum 'akaltum*
'anti faxalti	*'antunna faxaltunna*	*'anti 'akalti*	*'antunna 'akaltunna*
huwa faxala	*hum faxaluu*	*huwa 'akala*	*hum 'akaluu*
hiya faxalat	*hunna faxalna*	*hiya 'akalat*	*hunna 'akalna*
	humaa (m.) faxalaa		*humaa (m.) 'akalaa*
'antumaa faxaltumaa	*humaa (f.) faxalataa*	*'antumaa 'akaltumaa*	*humaa (f.) 'akalataa*

As you can see, the vowel *–a* is added after the first and second root consonants, and these endings are added after the third root consonant:

'anaa	*–tu*	*naHnu*	*–naa*
'anta	*–ta*	*'antum*	*–tum*
'anti	*–ti*	*'antunna*	*–tunna*
huwa	*–a*	*hum*	*–uu*
hiya	*–at*	*hunna*	*–na*
		humaa (m.)	*–aa*
'antumaa	*–tumaa*	*humaa (f.)*	*–ataa*

Notice that in several cases, the verb ending is the same or very similar to the pronoun. It's also important to point out that in some cases the middle root consonant will be followed by the vowel *–i,* as in *shariba* (he drank), *xamila* (he worked), and *fahima* (he understood). There are not many of these verbs, though, and you'll always be able to recognize them because you'll see the *–i* in the basic *huwa* form.

❹ Review of Agreement

In order to conjugate a verb correctly, you have to choose the form that "agrees" with your subject, just like you have to choose the form of an adjective that agrees with the noun it modifies. For example, you know that *laTiif* (friendly) agrees with *'ustaadh* (male professor) but *laTiifa* agrees with *'ustaadha* (female professor). Let's take a closer look at agreement in both adjectives and verbs. We'll start by reviewing adjectives once again.

ADJECTIVES MODIFYING HUMAN NOUNS

walad Tawiil	masculine singular noun with masculine singular adjective
waladaani Tawiilaani	masculine dual noun with dual *–aani* ending on adjective
'awlaad Tiwaal	masculine plural noun with broken plural form (if there is one)
'awlaad lubnaaniyyuun/-iin	masculine plural noun with sound plural (if there is no broken form) adjective
bint Tawiila	feminine singular noun with feminine singular adjective
bintaani Tawiilataani	feminine dual noun with dual *–taani* ending on the singular *–a* ending
banaat Tawiilaat	feminine plural noun with feminine sound plural *–aat* on adjective

ADJECTIVES MODIFYING NON-HUMAN NOUNS

kitaab kabiir	masculine singular noun with masculine singular adjective
shams kabiira	feminine singular noun with feminine singular adjective
kitaabaani kabiiraani	dual noun with dual *–aani* ending
kutub kabiira	plural noun with feminine singular ending

As you can see, the distinction between masculine and feminine is important for both human and non-human nouns. In the singular, all adjectives that modify feminine nouns, whether they're human or non-human, receive the feminine *–a* ending. In the plural, though, masculine human adjectives take a broken plural if there is one, or the sound plural *–uun/-iin* if there isn't. Feminine human adjectives all take *–aat*, and non-human plurals take the feminine singular ending *–a*. So, if an adjective is unlikely to be used to describe people, don't worry about its plural form.

It's important to remember that in Arabic, non-human plurals are treated as feminine singulars, not just in adjective agreement, but also in verb agreement. In other words, the masculine and feminine plural verb forms are used only for human plurals; non-human plurals take the feminine singular form. Take a look at these examples:

al-'ustaadh al-jadiid waSala.	The new professor arrived.

The noun *'ustaadh* is masculine singular, so it takes the masculine singular adjective *jadiid* and the masculine singular verb *waSala*.

al-'ustaadha al-jadiida waSalat.	The new professor arrived.

The noun *'ustaadha* is feminine singular, so it takes the feminine singular adjective *jadiida* and the feminine singular verb *waSalat.*

aD-Duyuuf al-liTaaf waSaluu.	The friendly guests arrived.

The noun *Duyuuf* is masculine plural and human, so it takes the masculine plural adjective *liTaaf* and the masculine plural verb *waSaluu.* Notice that *Duyuuf* is a broken plural (from *Dayf*), and *liTaaf* is a broken plural of *laTiif.* Again, it's best to memorize whether individual nouns and adjectives have broken or sound plurals; you cannot always predict this.

aT-Taalibaat al-'amriikiyyaat waSalna.	The American students arrived.

The noun *Taalibaat* is feminine plural and human, so it takes the feminine plural adjective *'amriikiyyaat* and the feminine plural verb *waSalna.*

at-tilifizyuunaat al-jadiida waSalat.	The new televisions arrived.

The noun *tilifizyuunaat* is non-human plural, so it takes the feminine singular adjective *jadiida* and the feminine singular verb *waSalat.*

8F Grammar and Usage Exercises

Exercise 1 Choose the correct demonstrative for each of the following, using the clues about location. Then translate, paying attention to whether the correct translation is a phrase or a sentence with is/are. And don't forget to drop the vowel in the article after another vowel.

1. __________ *ash-shawka* (here)
2. __________ *ash-shawkaat* (here)
3. __________ *al-ka's* (here)
4. __________ *khubz* (over there)
5. __________ *'aSdiqaa'* (over there)
6. __________ *buyuut* (over there)
7. __________ *as-suuq* (over there)
8. __________ *xuyuun* (here)

9. __________ *al-baqshiish* (here)
10. __________ *al-fulful* (over there)

Exercise 2 Connect the conjugated form of *dhahaba* (go) to the correct subject.

1. *dhahabta*	*'antum*
2. *dhahabtunna*	*'anta*
3. *dhahabnaa*	*'antunna*
4. *dhahabat*	*hunna*
5. *dhahabuu*	*hiya*
6. *dhahabtu*	*'anti*
7. *dhahabti*	*hum*
8. *dhahabtum*	*'anaa*
9. *dhahabna*	*huwa*
10. *dhahaba*	*naHnu*
11. *dhahabtumaa*	*humaa*
12. *dhahabaa*	*'antumaa*

Exercise 3 Give the full past tense conjugation of each of the following verbs.

1. *darasa* (study)
2. *DaHika* (laugh) (Notice the past tense *i*!)
3. *kataba* (write)
4. *sa'ala* (ask)

Exercise 4 Supply the correct forms of the adjectives and verbs in parentheses.

1. *ar-rajul (qaSiir) (waSala).*
2. *al-mudarris (xaDHiim) (dhahaba).*
3. *aD-Duyuuf (amriikiyy) (waSala).*
4. *al-kitaab (Saghiir) (waSala).*
5. *aT-Taaliba (jadiid) (darasa).*
6. *al-banaat (laTiif) ('akala).*

7. *at-tilifizyuunaat (jadiid) (waSala).*
8. *al-kilaab (kabiir) ('akala).*
9. *ar-rajul (Tawiil) (sa'ala).*
10. *al-'aqlaam (jadiid) (waSala).*
11. *ar-rijaal (Tawiil) (sa'ala).*
12. *aS-SaHaafiyya (lubnaaniyy) (kataba).*

8G Pronunciation Practice *x*

In lesson 8 we're going to focus on the pronunciation of one of the most difficult and unique consonants in the Arabic language, *xayn*, which is transcribed in this course as *x*. You've heard it throughout the course, since it is a common sound in Arabic. By now you know that the sound comes from a very tight constriction and flow of air at the back of the throat. Put your fingers on your windpipe and exercise your gag reflex slightly -you'll feel the muscles at the back of your throat tighten just a bit. That is where you should feel movement when pronouncing *x*. Tighten those muscles and let the air "scrape" through the constriction. It takes practice!

xalaykum, xarabiyy, xiraaq, naxam, faxala, xaamil, miSxad, xindii, maTxam, xaalii, xaDHiim, maxa, saaxa, sabxa, xashra, sariix, xayn

8H Arabic Script The letters *Saad* and *Daad*

Now let's focus on the first two emphatic consonants *Saad* and *Daad* in Arabic script. Notice that they have similar shapes—a flattened oval loop and a hook—but that *Daad* has a dot.

	isolated	initial	medial	final
S	ص	صـ	ـصـ	ـص
D	ض	ضـ	ـضـ	ـض

صَبَاح	*SabaaH* (morning)	مِصْعَد	*miSxad* (elevator)
ضَعِيف	*Daxiif* (thin)	مَرِيض	*mariiD* (sick)

For more practice, start *Group 7:* ص *S,* ض *D,* ط *T, and* ظ *DH* and reading practice 8 of *Part 2: Reading Arabic* in the *Complete Guide to Arabic Script.*

81 **Cultural Note** Middle Eastern Cuisine

Middle Eastern cuisine is known throughout the world for its delicious flavors and spicy aromas. Some of the most popular dishes are roasted lamb and roasted chicken. For vegetarians there is also couscous, which is made of crushed and steamed semolina, as well as stuffed grape leaves, and of course the favorite of many people, hummus, made from chick peas, garlic, olive oil, and tahini, or sesame paste. Hummus is normally eaten with small round loaves of pita bread. Babaghanoush, a creamy and smokey eggplant paste, is also a favorite of many people.

Mealtime is a special time for most Middle Eastern families. Meals are central during holidays such as *al- xiid al-kabiir.* Families gather around the table, and it is not uncommon for meals to be served out of one big plate. Smaller plates may also be used.

Most Arabs have a different approach to their food than some Westerners. The concept of micro-waving a dinner and eating in front of the TV is unknown to most people in the Middle East. Instead, mealtime is a time when family members and friends come together and enjoy one another's company or discuss current events. Meals serve far more than only a nutritional need—they are time to socialize and to come together as families or groups of friends.

Meals are usually very long, consisting of starters, two or three main dishes such as roasted lamb, steamed chicken, or fish, followed by a dessert of fruits, cakes, or other sweets. Tea and coffee are served at the end of the meal, and are usually drunk very sweet. It is not uncommon for a lunch or dinner to last longer than two hours. During Ramadan, the holy month of daytime fasting, the importance of the meal is of course magnified. The breaking of the fast can last anywhere from three to six hours, depending on the country. But of course all that time is not spent at the table!

Lesson 8 Answer Key

Vocabulary Practice 1. *milH wa fulful*; 2. *shawka wa milxaqa*; 3. *aT-Tabaq wa l-ka's*; 4. *al-ghadaa' wa l-xashaa'* 5. *naHnu jaa'ixuun/jaa'ixaat*! 6. *al-Hasaa' ladhiidh*. 7. *aT-Tabaq xalaa T-Taawila* 8. *as-sukkar bijaanibi l-Haliib*. 9. *al-xaamil fii l-maTxam*. 10. *aT-Tabbaakh fii l-maT-bakh*. 11. *hal aT-Taxaam taabiliyy*? 12. *hal al-birra baarida*? **Exercise 1:** 1. *haadhihi sh-shawka* (this fork); 2. *haadhihi sh-shawkaat* (these forks); 3. *haadhaa l-ka's* (this glass); 4. *dhaalika khubz* (That is bread.); 5. *'uulaa'ika 'aSdiqaa'* (Those are friends.); 6. *tilka buyuut* (Those are houses.); 7. *dhaalika s-suuq* (that market); 8. *haadhihi xuyuun* (These are eyes.); 9. *haadha l-baqshiish* (This tip); 10. *dhaalika l-fulful* (that pepper) **Exercise 2:** 1. *'anta dha-habta*; 2. *'antunna dhahabtunna*; 3. *naHnu dhahabnaa*; 4. *hiya dhahabat*; 5. *hum dha-habuu*; 6. *'anaa dhahabtu*; 7. *'anti dhahabti*; 8. *'antum dhahabtum*; 9. *hunna dhahabna*; 10. *huwa dhahaba*. 11. *'antumaa dhahabtumaa*. 12. *humaa dhahabaa* **Exercise 3:** 1. *'anaa darastu, 'anta darasta, 'anti darasti, huwa darasa, hiya darasat, naHnu darasnaa, 'antum darastum, 'antunna darastunna, hum darasuu, hunna darasna, 'antumaa darastumaa, humaa (m.) darasaa, humaa (f.) darasataa*; 2. *'anaa DaHiktu, 'anta DaHikta, 'anti DaHikti, huwa DaHika, hiya DaHikat, naHnu DaHiknaa, 'antum DaHiktum, 'antunna DaHiktunna, hum DaHikuu, hunna DaHikna, 'antumaa DaHiktumaa, humaa (m.) DaHikaa, humaa (f.) DaHikataa*; 3. *'anaa katabtu, 'anta katabta, 'anti katabti, huwa kataba, hiya katabat, naHnu katabnaa, 'antum katabtum, 'antunna katabtunna, hum katabuu, hunna katabna, 'antumaa katabtumaa, humaa (m.) katabaa, humaa (f.) katabataa*; 4. *'anaa sa'altu, 'anta sa'alta, 'anti sa'alti, huwa sa'ala, hiya sa'alat, naHnu sa'alnaa, 'antum sa'altum, 'antunna sa'al-tunna, hum sa'aluu, hunna sa'alna, 'antumaa sa'altumaa, humaa (m.) sa'alaa, humaa (f.) sa'alataa*. **Exercise 4:** 1. *ar-rajul al-qaSiir waSala*. 2. *al-mudarris al-xaDHiim dhahaba*. 3. *aD-Duyuuf al-'amriikiyyuun waSaluu*. 4. *al-kitaab aS-Saghiir waSala*. 5. *aT-Taaliba al-jadiida darasat*. 6. *al-banaat al-laTiifaat 'akalna*. 7. *at-tilifizyuunaat al-jadiida waSalat*. 8. *al-kilaab al-kabiira 'akalat*. 9. *ar-rajul aT-Tawiil sa'ala*. 10. *al-'aqlaam al-jadiida waSalat*. 11. *ar-rijaal aT-Tiwaal sa'aluu*. 12. *aS-SiHaafiyya al-lubnaaniyya katabat*.

LESSON 9

HOW MUCH IS THIS? *bikam haadhaa?*

In Lesson 9 you'll learn important vocabulary and constructions for shopping. You'll also expand your knowledge of Arabic grammar by learning about irregular adjectives, direct object pronouns, and more.

9A Dialogue

Like many tourists, Jack Simons is taking time to do some shopping. Let's listen in.

al-baa'ix	***hal yusaaxiduka 'aHad?***
jaak	***shukran. bikam haadhaa l-qamiiS?***
al-baa'ix	***haadhaa bi-xashrat daraahim.***
jaak	***hal ladaykum shay'an arkhaS?***
al-baa'ix	***naxam. maadhaa turiidu?***
jaak	***'arinii min faDlika dhaalika l-qamiiS.***
al-baa'ix	***tabxan.***
jaak	***haadhaa yuxjibunii. sa-'aakhudhuhu.***
al-baa'ix	***dhaalika jamiil jiddan.***
jaak	***hal yumkin 'an turiinii shay'an 'aakhara min faDlika?***
al-baa'ix	***haadhaa l-Hizaam jamiil.***
jaak	***hal yumkin 'an taluffahu?***
Salesperson	Is someone helping you?
Jack	Thank you. How much does this shirt cost?
Salesperson	This is ten dirhams.
Jack	Do you have something cheaper?
Salesperson	Yes. What would you like?
Jack	Please show me that shirt.
Salesperson	Sure.
Jack	I like this one. I'll take it.
Salesperson	That is very nice.
Jack	Can you please show me something else?
Salesperson	This belt is nice.
Jack	Can you wrap it up?

9B Language Notes

The salesperson asks Jack *hal yusaaxiduka 'aHad*, or "is someone helping you?" Another typical expression that you'll hear when you walk into a shop is *hal turiidu 'an 'usaaxidaka*, meaning "do you want me to help you?" or "can I help you?" The suffix *-ka* on *yusaaxiduka* and *'usaaxidaka* is a direct object pronoun meaning "you," which you'll learn more about in this lesson.

Remember that the question word *kam* means "how much" or "how many," and *bikam* means "how much" in the sense of price. So, to ask "how much is this?" simply ask *bikam haadhaa*? The price itself is also given with *bi–*, as in the dialogue—*bi-xashrat daraahim.*

The *dirham* is the unit of currency in Morocco and the United Arab Emirates. Notice that it has a four-consonant root, *d-r-h-m*, and its plural is *daraahim*. Don't confuse the *dirham* with the *diinar*, which is the currency of Algeria, Kuwait, Bahrain, Tunisia, Libya, Jordan, and Iraq, and is also used in Palestine. You'll learn more about the currencies in different Arab countries in lesson 14.

You already know that the adjective *rakhiiS* means "cheap." The form *arkhaS*, which is of course a manipulation of the root *r-kh-S*, means "cheaper." We'll cover these forms of adjectives in lesson 15.

Since it's such a useful verb, let's look at the full conjugation of "buy" in the past tense: *'anaa 'ishtaraytu, 'anta 'ishtarayta, 'anti 'ishtarayti, huwa 'ishtaraa, hiya 'ishtarat, 'antumaa 'ishtaraytumaa, naHnu 'ishtaraynaa, 'antum 'ishtaraytum, 'antunna 'ishtaraytunna, hum 'ishtaraw, hunna 'ishtarayna, humaa* (m.) *'ishtarayaa, humaa* (f.) *'ishtarataa.* Notice that there are some slight irregularities in this verb that we'll come back to later in the course.

9C Vocabulary

dukkaan / dakaakiin	store
matjar kabiir	department store, mall
makhbaz / makhaabiz	bakery
dukkaan al-Halwaani	pastry shop
Hallaaq / Hallaaquun	barber
maktaba / maktabaat	library/bookstore
dukkaan al-'iliktruuniyaat	electronics store
kuumbyuutar, Haasuub	computer
laaxib as-siidii / laaxibuu as-siidii	CD player

laaxib ad-diiviidii / laaxibuu ad-diiviidii	DVD player
siidii / siidiiyaat	CD
diiviidii / diiviidiiyaat	DVD
muSawwira / muSawwiraat	camera
maktab as-siyaaHa	travel agency
dukkaan as-samak	fish store
dukkaan al-fawaakih	fruit store
dukkaan al-baqqaal	grocery store
jawharii / jawhariyuun	jeweler
saaxa / saaxaat	watch
khaatim / khawaatim	ring
qilaada / qilaadaat	necklace
dukkaan al-malaabis	clothing store
mixTaf / maxaaTif	coat
lawn / 'alwaan	color
qamiiS / 'aqmiSa	shirt
sirwaal / saraawiil	pants
Hizaam / 'aHzima	belt
djiinz / djiinzaat	jeans
fustaan / fasaatiin	dress
qubbaxa / qubbaxaat	hat
jawaarib	socks
jallaabiyya / jallaabiyyaat	traditional Arab robe
Hariir	silk
qutn	cotton
jild	leather
dukkaan al-'aHdhia	shoe store
Hidhaa' / 'aHdhia	shoe, pair of shoes/shoes
balgha / balghaat	slippers
'ishtaraa	he bought
yashtarii	he buys
kallafa	cost
haadhaa yukallifu	this costs
khallaSa	pay
'ukhalliSu	I pay
kathiir, kathiiran	a lot, much
qaliil	a little
'aHad	someone
baahiDH	expensive
rakhiiS	inexpensive, cheap

9D Vocabulary Practice

Translate each of the following words, phrases, and sentences into Arabic.

1. a shirt and a belt
2. pants and jeans (each singular)
3. the dress and the shoe
4. expensive shirts
5. a cheap CD player
6. new computer
7. the old cameras
8. The watch is big, and the ring is small.
9. He bought a new shirt.
10. She bought a new dress.
11. The student (m.) bought a new computer.
12. How much is this camera?

9E Grammar and Usage

1 Irregular Adjectives

You've already seen that most masculine adjectives can be made feminine simply by adding the feminine ending *-a*, as in *kabiir—kabiira* or *Tawiil—Tawiila*. There is a small group of irregular adjectives, though, which are colors. The forms given are the masculine singular, feminine singular, and the plural. Non-human plurals will take the feminine singular form, which you'll have more use for.

white	*'abyaD*	*bayDaa'*	*biiD*
black	*'aswad*	*sawdaa'*	*suud*
red	*'aHmar*	*Hamraa'*	*Humr*
green	*'akhDar*	*khaDraa'*	*khuDr*
yellow	*'aSfar*	*Safraa'*	*Sufr*
blue	*'azraq*	*zarqaa'*	*zurq*
brown (skin)	*'asmar*	*samraa'*	*sumr*

al-qamiiS 'abyaD.	The shirt is white.
al-jallaabiyya bayDaa'.	The robe is white.
al-balghaat zarqaa'.	The slippers are blue.
al-kutub Hamraa'.	The books are red.

2 Nouns and Pronouns in "To Be" Sentences

As you know, there is no equivalent of the verb "to be" in Arabic, so it is possible to have a complete sentence in Arabic without any verb. In these cases, a noun or pronoun subject is paired with another noun or phrase in an $x = y$ relationship.

'anaa mudarris.	I am a teacher.
Hasan SaHaafiyy.	Hassan is a journalist.
'anti l-mudiira.	You are the director.
naHnu fii l-ghurfa.	We are in the room.

But it is also possible to have an Arabic sentence with both a subject noun and a subject pronoun in the first half of the equation.

Hasan huwa S-SaHaafiyy.	Hassan is the journalist. (literally, Hassan he [is] the journalist.)
maryam hiya l-mudiira	Miriam is the director. (literally, Miriam she [is] the director.)

Notice that these sentences link subjects to definite nouns (*aS-SaHaafiyy* and *al-mudiira*). They also emphasize the subjects *Hasan* and *maryam*, meaning Hassan (and not someone else) is the journalist in question, and Miriam (and not someone else) is the director. These are similar constructions to the demonstrative sentences that follow the pattern "this is the . . . " which you learned in lesson 8.

haadhaa huwa S-SaHaafiyy.	This is the journalist.

Of course, it is possible to have only pronouns in sentences with third person subjects.

huwa S-SaHaafiyy.	He is the journalist.
hiya l-mudiira.	She is the director.

3 Direct Object Pronouns

A direct object is the noun or pronoun that "receives" the action of the verb. For example, in the following sentences "book" is the direct object: I read the book. She bought a book. The children took the book. I gave the book to my brother.

Direct object pronouns are the pronouns that replace direct object nouns. In English, they are: me, you, him, her, it, us, and them. In Arabic, direct object pronouns are attached to the end of the verb as suffixes. Take a look at these examples:

'anaa katabtu l-kitaab.	I wrote the book.
'anaa katabtuhu.	I wrote it.
al-bint sharibat al-Haliib.	The girl drank the milk.
al-bint sharibat-hu.	The girl drank it.
naHnu 'akalnaa t-tuffaHaat.	We ate the apples.
naHnu 'akalnaahaa.	We ate them.

Every subject pronoun has a corresponding direct object pronoun suffix:

'anaa (I)	*–nii* (me)	*naHnu* (we)	*–naa* (us)
'anta (you, m.)	*–ka* (you)	*'antum* (you, m.)	*–kum* (you)
'anti (you, f.)	*–ki* (you)	*'antunna* (you, f.)	*–kunna* (you)
huwa (he, it)	*–hu* (him, it)	*hum* (they, m.)	*–hum* (them)
hiya (she, it)	*–haa* (her, it, them*)	*hunna* (they, f.)	*–hunna* (them)
'antumaa (you two)	*–kumaa* (you two)	*humaa* (the two of them, m. or f.)	*–humaa* (the two of them)

4 Omission of Subject Pronouns

In the last lesson you learned that the past tense in Arabic is shown by a pattern of endings added to the basic root of a verb. For example, *dhahaba* means "he went," *dhahabnaa* means "we went," and *dhahabtu* means "I went." As you can see, the endings are generally enough to specify the subject. For that reason, the subject of a sentence can often be omitted, because either the ending or the context will make it clear who or what is doing the action.

katabtu r-risaala.	I wrote the letter.
darasaa fii haadhihi l-jaamixa.	The two of them studied at this university.

In sentences with different subjects doing different actions, though, it's necessary to use the pronouns to avoid misunderstanding.

'anti 'akalti wa huwa shariba. You ate and he drank.

*Remember that *–haa* can also mean "them" in the case of non-human plurals.

9F Grammar and Usage Exercises

Exercise 1 Fill in the blanks in the following sentences with the correct form of the adjective given in parentheses. Then translate the sentences. Don't forget to add definite articles if necessary.

1. *al-kitaab __________ ('azraq) xalaa T-Taawila.*
2. *aT-Taa'ira __________ (kabiir) wa __________ ('abyaD).*
3. *al-warda __________ ('aHmar) wa __________ (jamiil).*
4. *al-funduq __________ ('abyaD) wa __________ ('aswad).*
5. *al-fuuTa __________ ('akhDar).*
6. *as-sayyaara __________ ('azraq).*
7. *al-jubna __________ ('aSfar).*
8. *az-zaHra __________ ('abyaD) __________ (jamiil).*

Exercise 2 Rewrite each of the following sentences with the appropriate pronoun in place of the subject noun.

1. *Layla Taaliba fii miSr.*
2. *al-'aqlaam xalaa T-Taawila.*
3. *Hasan muhandis.*
4. *al-walad tilmiidh.*
5. *al-kumbyuutaraat baahiDHa.*
6. *al-'awlaad fii ghurfati n-nawm.*
7. *al-kutub fii l-maktab.*
8. *ar-rijaal 'asaatidha.*

Exercise 3 Translate each of the following sentences.

1. *'akaltu khubz.*
2. *sharibat maa'.*
3. *'ishtaraynaa l-kitaab.*
4. *'akala l-'aruzz.*
5. *'akalnaa l-jubna.*
6. *katabuu l-kutub.*
7. *sharibuu l-Haliib.*
8. *'ishtaraytu s-samak.*

Exercise 4 Now rewrite each of the sentences in exercise 3, substituting a direct object pronoun for the direct object nouns.

9G Pronunciation Practice *hamza*

In this lesson we'll take a closer look at the sound which is called *hamza* in Arabic, and which is transcribed in this course as an apostrophe ('). There are three important things to keep in mind about *hamza*. First, it's a sound that you know how to make already and make very often in English. It's technically called a "glottal stop," but if that terminology doesn't help you, just imagine the Cockney pronunciation of "bottle" (boh'le) or the little catch in your voice when you say "uh-oh!" In fact, every time you pronounce a word that begins with a vowel (eat, are, ice, up, over, inquire . . .), you're saying a *hamza* at the very beginning. Second, this sound is a regular consonant in Arabic, so it can appear not just at the beginning of a word, but also in the middle or at the end. Finally, all Arabic words that sound like they begin with a vowel actually begin with a *hamza*, which is why you've learned a lot of words that begin with a *hamza* followed by a vowel (*'akala, 'anaa, 'amriikiyya, 'ustaadh*, etc.). And since this is really the same as English words that begin with vowels (eat, are, ice, up, over, inquire . . .) you don't have to do anything special in these cases. Practice with these words, where *hamza* appears in different positions in a word.

'ustaadh, 'akala, 'injiltra, 'aakhudhu, 'anaa, 'antum, 'isbaaniyaa

shay'in, ka's, 'ulaa'ika, haa'ulaa'i, Taa'ira, su'aal, saa'iq, qaa'ima, 'imra'a

binaa', khaTa', baa', taa', DHaa', bayDaa', zarqaa', nisaa'

9H Arabic Script The letters *Taa'* and *DHaa'*

Now let's focus on the second two emphatic consonants *Taa'* and *DHaa'* in Arabic script. This pair also has similar shapes—a flattened oval loop with a bar instead of a hook—but *DHaa'* has a dot.

	isolated	initial	medial	final
T	ط	طـ	ـطـ	ـط
DH	ظ	ظـ	ـظـ	ـظ

طائِرَة	*Taa'ira* (airplane)	طَوِيل	*Tawiil* (tall, long)
ظَهْر	*DHahr* (back)	ظَلَام	*DHalaam* (darkness)

For more practice, continue *Group 7:* ص *S,* ض *D,* ط *T, and* ظ *DH* and reading practice 8 of *Part 2: Arabic Script* in the *Complete Guide to Arabic Script*. You can also practice writing with Group 7 and writing practices 17–19 of *Part 3: Writing Arabic*.

91 **Cultural Note** Traditional Clothing in the Middle East

Long, flowing robes and garments play a central role in traditional clothing in the Middle East. One of the most popular is the *jallaabiyya*, a full-length, loose outer garment with long sleeves and a hood. It's very popular for both men and women, although women find it especially useful. Because of religious law, some Muslim societies such as Saudi Arabia require women to conceal themselves rather heavily. This includes hair, hands, and face. The *jallaabiyya* and variations of it permit a woman to follow Islamic guidelines without being overly restricted, as the garment is loose-fitting and allows for a wide range of movement.

Other traditional women's garments include the *xabaaya*, which is a robe-like dress without a hood, and the *niqab* or *burqux*, a veil which covers the entire head and face but has a slit in front of the eyes. *Hijaab* is a religious dress code requiring a shawl or scarf which covers the head but leaves the face uncovered. For men there is the *bisht* or *xabaa'*, which is a loose outer robe, usually in black, and the *thawb* or *dishdaasha*, which is a long white shirt worn underneath the *bisht* or *xabaa'*. The traditional headdress that men wear is called the *ghutra*, and it is held in place on the head with the *xiqaal*, a ring or headband that fits over the *ghutra*.

But keep in mind that not all Arabs adhere to strict religious rules or traditional customs regarding clothing, and by no means do all Arab countries impose these rules as a matter of law. In many places throughout the Middle East you're as likely to see people in jeans, suits, dresses, skirts, or tee shirts as you are anywhere else.

Lesson 9 Answer Key

Vocabulary Practice: 1. *qamiiS wa Hizaam*; 2. *sirwaal wa djiinz*; 3. *al-fustaan wa l-Hidhaa'*; 4. *'aqmiSa ghaaliya*; 5. *laaxib as-siidii rakhiiS*; 6. *Haasuub/kumbyuutar jadiid*; 7. *al-muSawwiraat al-qadiima*; 8. *as-saaxa kabiira wa l-khaatim Saghiir*; 9. *'ishtaraa qamiiS jadiid*. 10. *'ishtarat fustaan jadiid* 11. *aT-Taalib 'ishtaraa Haasuub/kumbyuutar jadiid* 12. *bikam haadhihi l-muSawwira*? **Exercise 1:** *al-kitaab al-'azraq xalaa T-Taawila.* / The blue book is on the table. 2. *aT-Taa'ira kabiira wa bayDaa'.* / The airplane is big and white. 3. *al-warda Hamraa' wa jamiila.* / The rose is red and beautiful. 4. *al-funduq 'abyaD wa 'aswad.* / The hotel is white and black. 5. *al-fuuTa khaDraa'.* / The towel is green. 6. *as-sayyaara zarqaa'.* / The car is blue. 7. *al-jubna Safraa'.* / The cheese is yellow. 8. *az-zaHra al-bayDaa' jamiila.* / The white flower is beautiful. **Exercise 2:** 1. *hiya Taaliba fii miSr*. 2. *hiya xalaa T-Taawila*. 3. *huwa muhandis*. 4. *huwa tilmiidh*. 5. *hiya baahiDHa*. 6. *hum fii ghurfati an-nawm*. 7. *hiya fii l-maktab*. 8. hum 'asaatidha. **Exercise 3:** 1. I ate bread. 2. She drank water. 3. We bought the book. 4. He ate the rice. 5. We ate the cheese. 6. They wrote the books. 7. They drank the milk. 8. I bought the fish. **Exercise 4:** 1. *'akaltuhu*. 2. *sharibat-hu*. 3. *'ishtaraynaahu*. 4. *'akalahu*. 5. *'akalnaahaa*. 6. *katabuuhaa*. 7. *sharibuuhu*. 8. *'ishtaraytuhu*.

LESSON 10

I'LL SEE YOU ON WEDNESDAY *sa-'araaki l-'arbixaa'*

In lesson 10 you'll learn important vocabulary for making appointments, including the names of the days of the week and months, and also how to express dates. You'll also build on your knowledge of verbs by learning the present tense.

10A Dialogue

Listen in as Sara walks into a "phone boutique" in Amman, Jordan to make a call to the doctor's office to schedule an appointment.

sara ***hal yumkin 'an 'astaxmila l-haatif?***

al-baa'ix ***Tabxan.***

sara ***'axTiinii biTaaqa li l-haatif min faDlika.***

al-baa'ix ***hal turiidiina biTaaqa li khamsat danaaniir aw xashrat danaaniir?***

sara ***xashrat danaaniir min faDlika. hal xindaka daliil al-haatif?***

al-baa'ix ***tafaDDalii.***

sara ***shukran.***

xalaa l-haatif

sara ***'allo. 'uriidu 'an 'atakallama maxa T-Tabiib.***

al-mumarriDa ***'aasifa, huwa laysa hunaa l-'aan. hal turiidiina 'an tatrukii khabaran?***

sara ***naxam. 'uriidu mawxidan maxa T-Tabiib yawma l-khamiis. hal haadhaa mumkin?***

al-mumarriDa ***'ibqay xalaa l-haatif min faDliki. huwa laysa hunaa l-khamiis. yadh-habu 'ilaa 'irbid kulla khamiis. yaxmalu fii l-mustashfaa hunaaka. hal ath-thulathaa' yuwaafiquki?***

sara ***'anaa fii l-maktab ath-thulathaa' wa 'antahii min al-xamal fii l-layl.***

al-mumarriDa ***hal 'anti fii l-maktab al-'arbixaa'?***

sara ***al-'arbixaa' jayyid. 'ay waqt min faDlik?***

al-mumarriDa ***sa-yakuunu hunaaka fii s-saaxa l-waaHida.***

sara ***haadhaa jayyid. shukran jaziilan.***

al-mumarriDa	***'ilaa l-'arbixaa' fii s-saaxa l-waaHida.***
sara	***shukran. maxa s-salaama***
al-mumarriDa	***maxa s-salaama.***
Sara	Is it possible for me to use the phone?
Clerk	Of course.
Sara	Please give me a phone card.
Clerk	Would you like a card for five dinars or ten dinars?
Sara	Ten dinars, please. Do you have a phone book?
Clerk	Here you go.
Sara	Thank you.

On the phone . . .

Sara	Hello. I'd like to speak with the doctor.
Nurse	I'm sorry, but he's not in now. Would you like to leave a message?
Sara	Yes. I'd like an appointment with the doctor on Thursday. Is that possible?
Nurse	Please hold the line. He's not here on Thursday. He goes to Irbid on Thursdays. He works in the clinic there. Is Tuesday good for you?
Sara	I'm in the office on Tuesday, and I finish at night.
Nurse	Are you in the office on Wednesday?
Sara	Wednesday is good. What time, please?
Nurse	He's going to be here at one o'clock.
Sara	That's good. Thank you very much.
Nurse	See you Wednesday at one o'clock.
Sara	Thank you. Good bye.
Nurse	Good bye.

10B Language Notes

For various reasons ranging from government bureaucracy to lack of adequate infrastructure, the number of fixed lines in most Middle Eastern countries, especially in North Africa, is limited. Over the last few years, cell phones have become ubiquitous because of low cost and accessibility. Also, phone boutiques, small stores that specialize in phone communications, have multiplied. Local residents, tourists, and others wanting to make phone calls simply go to a phone boutique, purchase a card with a certain number of units, and then place calls to any country in the world.

Remember that the phrase *hal yumkin 'an 'astaxmila* literally means "is it possible for me to use . . ." but can also be translated as "Can I use . . . " or "May I use . . . " The word *'an* is called a particle, and it can be translated as "to" or "for [me, you, him, her . . .] to." As you saw earlier in the course, it's followed by a special form of the verb called the subjunctive. We'll come back to this particle and verb form later.

Another useful command is *'axTinii*, or "give me." You should recognize the ending, *-nii*, as an attached pronoun meaning "me."

Notice the use of the preposition *li*, or "for," in the expressions *biTaaqa li l-haatif* (phone card, card for the phone) and *biTaaqa li khamsat daraahim* (a card for five dirhams).

The word *xindaka* in the expression *xindaka daliil al-haatif* is a construction meaning "you have." We'll cover this construction in lesson 11.

Notice that a common way of answering a phone is *'allo*. Other common expressions are *as-salaamu xalaykum*, and *'ahlan wa sahlan*.

You learned the word *laysa* in lesson 5. Remember that it's one of the negative forms of "to be."

To express "Until Wednesday" or "See you on Wednesday," the receptionist uses the preposition *'ilaa*, which can also mean "to" or "toward." The title of the lesson, *sa-'araaki l-'arbixaa'*, literally means "I'll see you on Wednesday," with the suffix *-ki* (you) on the verb *sa-'araa* (I will see).

10C Vocabulary

In this list you'll begin to see two forms of new verbs. For example, for "speak, talk" you'll see *takallama / yatakallamu*. The first form is the *huwa* past tense, and the second form is the *huwa* present tense. Both of these forms give you the information you need to use the verb in the past and present tense. You'll learn more about this in the Grammar and Usage section.

haatif / hawaatif	telephone
haatif xumuumiyy	public phone, payphone
mukaalama haatifiyya	phone call
mukaalamaat haatifiyya	phone calls
mukaalama xalaa Hisaab al-mutalaqqii	collect call
mukaalama duwaliyya	international call
mukaalama maHaliyya	domestic call
haatif mutajawwil	cell phone
raqm / 'arqaam	number
xadad / 'axdaad	number
raqm al-haatif	telephone number
xaamil haatifiyy / xummaal haatifiyyuun	operator
muwaDHDHafat al-'istiqbaal	receptionist
rasm / rusuum	fee
maxluuma / maxluumaat	information
daliil al-haatif / 'adillat al-haatif	telephone book
ghurfat al-haatif	phone booth
mawxid / mawaaxiid	appointment
jadwal al-'awqaat / jadaawil al-'awqaat	schedule
rakkaba r-raqm / yurakkibu r-raqm	dial (the number)
kallama / yukallimu	call
'ajaaba / yujiibu	answer
xamila / yaxmalu	work
takallama / yatakallamu	speak, talk
faaDii	free, available
mashghuul / –uun	busy, booked
kasuul / –uun	lazy
muthaabir / –uun	hard-working
yawm / 'ayyaam	day
'usbuux / 'asaabiix	week
sana / sanawaat	year
shahr / 'ash-hur	month
daa'iman	always
'abadan	never
ixtiyaadiyan	usually
al-'aan	now
aHyaanan	sometimes

10D Vocabulary Practice

Translate each of the following words and expressions.

1. phonebook
2. dial the number (he dialed the number)
3. telephone number
4. international call
5. domestic call
6. phone call
7. Where is the payphone?
8. This is the telephone.
9. collect call
10. The receptionist is busy.
11. The operator is here.
12. International calls are expensive.

10E Grammar and Usage

1 Days of the Week

The days of the week in Arabic are mostly derived from numbers, which we covered in lesson 5.

Sunday	*al-'aHad*
Monday	*al-'ithnayn*
Tuesday	*ath-thulaathaa'*
Wednesday	*al-'arbixaa'*
Thursday	*al-khamiis*
Friday	*al-jumuxa*
Saturday	*as-sabt*

The names of Sunday through Thursday are of course based on the numbers one through five: *waaHid, 'ithnayn, thalaatha, 'arbaxa,* and *khamsa.* But notice that there are some alterations. The word for Friday is derived from the word *jamaxa,* meaning "gathering," and the word for Saturday is derived from *sabt,* meaning "rest."

In the original Islamic calendar, Sunday was the first day, Monday was the second day, Tuesday was the third day,

Wednesday was the fourth day, Thursday was the fifth day, Friday was the day of gathering, and Saturday was the day of rest. You can see the similarity between *as-sabt* and the words Sabbath or Shabbat, which also refer to a day of rest.

To say that you do something on a particular day, or on a day in general, just use the name of the day. Notice that the word *yawm* (day) can be added to clear up any possible confusion in meaning, specifiying that *al-khamiis, al-'ithnayn, al-'arbixaa'*, etc. refer to days and not numbers.

aT-Tabiib laysa hunaa yawm al-khamiis.
The doctor is not here on Thursday.

dhahabtu 'ilaa l-maktaba yawm al-'ithnayn.
I went to the library on Monday.

yaxmaluuna daa'iman yawm al-'arbixaa'.
They always work on Wednesday.

2 Months, Seasons, and Dates

There are three types of calendars used in Arabic—the Gregorian, the Islamic, and the Lunar. The Gregorian is the calendar used in the West. The Lunar calendar is widely used in religious circles and in religious contexts in the Middle East. The Islamic calendar is used in both religious and secular parts of the Middle East. Many newscasts will include the date in both the Gregorian and the Islamic calendar. You'll be able to get by in most places with the Arabic translation of the Gregorian calendar, so we'll start with that.

January	*yanaayir*	July	*yuulyuu*
February	*fabraayir*	August	*aghusTus*
March	*maaris*	September	*sibtambir*
April	*abriil*	October	*uktuubir*
May	*maayuu*	November	*nufambir*
June	*yuunyuu*	December	*disambir*

It is also important to gain exposure to the Islamic and lunar calendars, as some countries, such as Saudi Arabia, use them exclusively. The months of the Islamic calendar start when the moon is first visible, so the months do not of course correlate directly to months on the Gregorian calendar. The Islamic months, in order, are: *muHarram, Safar, rabiix al-'awwal, rabiix ath-thaanii, jumaadaa l-'uulaa, jumaada th-thaania, rajab, shaxbaan, ramaDaan, shawwaal, dhuu l-qaxda, dhuu l-Hijja*. You probably recognize the name of the ninth month, Ramadan, which is fairly well known in the West. On the Islamic calendar, the years are shorter than on the Gregorian calendar, and they are counted from the beginning of the Hijra, the start of the prophet Muḥammad's pilgrimage to Medina in 622 AD. Therefore the year 2000, for example, on the Gregorian calendar corresponded to the year 1421 on the Islamic calendar. This is written 1421 AH, AH meaning *Anno Hegirae*, year of the Hijra.

The months of the lunar calendar, in the order of their correspondence to Gregorian months, are *kaanuun ath-thaaniyy, shubbaat, 'aadhaar, niisaan, 'ayyaar, Huzayran, tammuuz, 'aab, 'ayluul, tishriin al-'awwal, tishriin ath-thaanii,* and *kaanuun al-'awwal.*

The lunar calendar is based on the lunar cycle, and therefore does not overlap with the Gregorian calendar. It does contain twelve months, but it is consistently shorter than the Gregorian calendar because one lunar month comprises roughly 29 days. Hence the lunar calendar, like the Islamic calendar, is shorter than the Gregorian. It is used primarily by Islamic scholars to determine holy months and holy days, such as the start and end of the fasting period during the month of Ramadan.

To give a date in Arabic, you need to know that *'alf* means one thousand and *'alfayn* means two thousand. You also need to know that when you are saying a double-digit number you have to start by saying the number in the ones place followed by the number in the tens place. For example, 24 is *'arbaxa wa xishruun*, "four and twenty." Notice that *'arbaxa* (four) comes before *xishruun* (twenty). 96 is *sitta wa tisxuun. sitta* is six and *tisxuun* is ninety. The word *wa* (and) must always separate all the numbers.

If you want to say 124 you begin with the number in the hundreds and then apply the rule above, where you say the number in the ones place followed by the number in the tens place. For example, 124 is *mi'a* (one hundred) *wa 'arbaxa* (and four) *wa xishruun* (and twenty). The same rule applies if you want to say 1124. You begin with the thousands, then the hundreds, then the ones, and the tens. So 1124 is *'alf* (one thousand) *wa mi'a* (and one hundred) *wa 'arbaxa* (and four) *wa xishruun* (and twenty). The word for two thousand is *'alfayni.*

Here are some examples of dates. Notice that the number of the day comes first, as is common in many European languages.

'arbaxa wa xishruun nufambar	November 24
yawm ath-thulaathaa', ath-thaalith min yunyu	Tuesday, June 3
'alfayni wa sabxa	2007
sabxa wa xishruun yanaayir, 'alfayni wa sitta	January 27, 2006
kataba kitaabahu fii 'alf wa tisxi mi'a wa khamsa wa tisxiin.	He wrote his book in 1995.
dhahabuu 'ilaa qaTar yawm tisxa siptambar.	They went to Qatar on September 9.

Finally, let's take a look at the names of the seasons in Arabic. Thankfully, there are only four of them, and only one system to name them!

spring	*ar-rabiix*
summer	*aS-Sayf*
autumn	*al-khariif*
winter	*ash-shitaa'*

Use the preposition *fii* (in) to say that you do something in a particular season.

nadh-habu 'ilaa sh-shaaTi' fii S-Sayf.
We go to the beach in the summer.

3 The Present Tense of Verbs

The present is the second of the two major tenses in Arabic. It describes both a habitual action (I work, she speaks, we do) and an ongoing action (I am working, she is speaking, we are doing). The formation of the present tense is slightly more complicated than the past tense, because both a suffix and a prefix are added to the consonant root, and a vowel (either *a*, *i*, or *u*) is added after the second root consonant.

For example, while *katabti* means "you (f.) wrote," *taktubiina* means "you write" or "you are writing." As you can see, to the basic root *k-t-b*, the prefix *ta-* and the suffix *-iina* are added, and the vowel *-u-* is inserted between the second and third root consonant. One important point to keep in mind is that while the suffixes and prefixes follow a predictable pattern, you'll have to memorize which vowel is inserted after the second root consonant. For each new verb you learn in this course, you'll see the *huwa* form in both the past and present tense, and that present tense form will contain the vowel you'll insert. For example, for "write," you'll see *kataba / yaktubu*, telling you that *-u-* is the vowel to insert in the present tense.

Now let's take a look at the full present tense conjugation of *faxala / yafxalu* (do) and *darasa /yadrusu* (study) to illustrate this. The prefixes and suffixes have been underlined.

***faxala / yafxalu*—do**		***darasa / yadrusu*—study**	
'anaa 'afxalu	*naHnu nafxalu*	*'anaa 'adrusu*	*naHnu nadrusu*
'anta tafxalu	*'antum tafxaluuna*	*'anta tadrusu*	*'antum tadrusuuna*
'anti tafxaliina	*'antunna tafxalna*	*'anti tadrusiina*	*'antunna tadrusna*
huwa yafxalu	*hum yafxaluuna*	*huwa yadrusu*	*hum yadrusuuna*
hiya tafxalu	*hunna yafxalna*	*hiya tadrusu*	*hunna yadrusna*
	humaa (m.) yafxalaani		*humaa (m.) yadrusaani*
'antumaa tafxalaani	*humaa (f.) tafxalaani*	*'antumaa tadrusaani*	*humaa (f.) tadrusaani*

Notice that the forms for *'anaa*, *'anta*, *huwa*, *hiya*, and *naHnu* have a *-u* suffix. This ending is very often dropped in spoken Arabic, but you'll see it used throughout this course because it will help distinguish the present tense from other important verb forms you'll learn later. Just remember that both *'anaa 'afxal* and *'anaa 'afxalu,* and so on for the other forms listed above, are possible. It's better to learn the more grammatically "rigid" forms in a new language first, and then as you become more confident, you can begin to relax these rules as your speaking becomes more natural.

To summarize the formation of the present tense, the first step is to take the basic consonant root, such as *k-t-b*. Then, insert either *a*, *i*, or *u*, depending on the verb, after the second consonant in the root, giving you *ktub* in the case of *k-t-b*. Finally, add the correct prefix and suffix, for example *ya–* and *–na* for the *hunna* form, giving you *yaktubna*. Here is a table summarizing the prefixes and suffixes. Remember that the *–u* suffix is usually not pronounced in the spoken language, but it will be helpful for you to get used to it in the beginning.

'anaa	*'a–u*	*naHnu*	*na–u*
'anta	*ta–u*	*'antum*	*ta–uuna*
'anti	*ta–iina*	*'antunna*	*ta–na*
huwa	*ya–u*	*hum*	*ya–uuna*
hiya	*ta–u*	*hunna*	*ya–na*
		humaa (m.)	*ya–aani*
'antumaa	*ta–aani*	*humaa (f.)*	*ta–aani*

Here are a few examples of verbs that you've already seen, used here in the present tense.

Hasan yadrusu al-lugha al-faransiyya fii l-jaamixa.
Hassan studies the French language at the university.

'anaa 'axmalu fii maktaba kabiira fii l-madiina.
I work in a big bookstore in the city.

laylaa tadh-habu daa'iman 'ilaa s-sinimaa maxa Sadiiqa.
Layla always goes to the movies with a friend.

ar-rijaal yaqra'uuna daa'iman al-jariida fii l-muntazah.
The men always read the newspaper in the park.

Here is a summary of basic verbs and their past and present *huwa* forms.

kataba / yaktubu write
faxala / yafxalu do
darasa / yadrusu study
qara'a / yaqra'u read
dhahaba / yadh-habu go

takallama / yatakallamu	speak
rajaxa / yarjixu	go back
xaTafa / yaxTufu	turn
'akala / ya'kulu	eat
shariba / yashrabu	drink (Note the *–i* in the past tense)
sa'ala / yas'alu	ask
'akhadha / ya'khudhu	take
xamila / yaxmalu	work (Note the *–i* in the past tense)
fataHa / yaftaHu	open
dakhala / yadkhulu	enter, go in
Tabakha / yaTbukhu	cook
fahima / yafhamu	understand (Note the *–i* in the past tense)
tadhakkara / yatadhakkaru	remember
xarafa / yaxrifu	know
sakana / yaskunu	live, reside
'istamaxa / yastamixu	listen

There's one important minor variation on the regular present tense conjugation, but it only involves a simple vowel change in the fixed prefixes. Certain verbs take a *–u–* in all of their prefixes instead of an *–a*. But these verbs also always take an *–i–* as the vowel that's inserted in the present tense, so they're more predictable in that sense. If you look at the list below, you'll see that all of these verbs have either double second root consonants (***ka<u>ll</u>ama, da<u>rr</u>asa, kha<u>ll</u>aSa***) or they have long *–aa–* after their first root consonant (***s<u>aa</u>fara / yus<u>aa</u>firu, sh<u>aa</u>hada / yush<u>aa</u>hidu***). Also note that in the present tense *huwa* form, the first and second root consonants are separated by a vowel instead of written together (***yud<u>a</u>rrisu*** instead of ***yadrusu***).

khallaSa / yukhalliSu	pay
kallama / yukallimu	call
'ajaaba / yujiibu	answer
darrasa / yudarrisu	teach
shaahada / yushaahidu	watch
saafara / yusaafiru	travel

Whenever you see a present tense *huwa* form that begins with a *yu–* instead of a *ya–*, you'll know that the verb takes *–u–* in all the prefixes instead of *–a*, and that its present tense inserted vowel will always be *–i–*. So, it will follow this slightly modified pattern:

'anaa	*'u –i– u*	*naHnu*	*nu –i– u*
'anta	*tu –i– u*	*'antum*	*tu –i– uuna*
'anti	*tu –i– iina*	*'antunna*	*tu –i– na*
huwa	*yu –i– u*	*hum*	*yu –i– uuna*
hiya	*tu –i– u*	*hunna*	*yu –i– na*
		humaa (m.)	*yu –i– aani*
'antumaa	*tu –i– aani*	*humaa* (f.)	*tu –i– aani*

4 The Negative Present Tense

In English, you can make a verb negative simply by adding "not" to the sentence. "He has left" becomes "he has not left." But sometimes you also have to add a helping verb, such as "does" or "did." "She came to the party" becomes "she did not come to the party." It's much simpler to negate a present tense verb in Arabic. Just add *laa* (no, not) before the verb.

haadhihi l-'ustaadha tudarrisu Saff kabiir.
This professor teaches a big class.

haadhihi l-'ustaadha laa tudarrisu Saff kabiir.
This professor doesn't teach a big class.

'aktubu l-kutub daa'iman.
I always write books.

laa 'aktubu l-kutub daa'iman.
I do not always write books.

5 "To Be" in the Past Tense

In lesson 5 you learned that even though there is no present tense form of the verb "to be" in Arabic—no "am," "are," or "is"—there is a negative form—*'anaa lastu*, *'anta lasta*, *'anti lasti*, etc. There are also past tense forms of the verb "to be," the equivalent of "was" and "were." Notice that while the vowel in the stem changes from *u* to *aa*, the endings are the same endings used for other verbs in the past tense.

'anaa kuntu	*I was*	*naHnu kunnaa*	*we were*
'anta kunta	*you (m.) were*	*'antum kuntum*	*you (m. pl.) were*
'anti kunti	*you (f.) were*	*'antunna kuntunna*	*you (f. pl.) were*
huwa kaana	*he, it, was*	*hum kaanuu*	*they (m.) were*
hiya kaanat	*she, it, was, they were**	*hunna kunna*	*they (f.) were*
		humaa (m.) kaanaa	*the two of them were*
'antumaa kuntumaa	*you two were*	*humaa (f.) kaanataa*	*the two of them were*

'anaa kuntu fii l'maktaba al-baariHa.
I was at the library yesterday.

man kaana maxa dhaalika r-rajul?
Who was with that man?

at-tilifizyuunaat kaanat hunaaka xalaa T-Taawila.
The televisions were there on the table.

10F Grammar and Usage Exercises

Exercise 1 Connect the names of the days of the week.

al-'ithnayn	Tuesday
ath-thulaathaa'	Thursday
al-'arbixaa'	Saturday
al-khamiis	Monday
al-jumuxa	Sunday
as-sabt	Friday
al-'aHad	Wednesday

Exercise 2 Write the months of the year in the Gregorian calendar.

Exercise 3 Translate the following phrases and sentences.

1. January 5
2. October 19
3. Monday, August 17

*As usual, don't forget that non-human plurals are treated as feminine singulars. So, *hiya kaanat* can sometimes mean "they were" when referring to televisions, computers, dogs, mountains, etc. Another point to remember is that *hum* is only used with human beings, either for masculine or mixed groups. So, *hunna* is used only for groups of female humans.

4. Wednesday, March 29
5. They came back on Sunday.
6. I paid on Saturday, June 6.
7. Hassan went to Amman (*xammaan*) on Friday, November 12.
8. 2006

Exercise 4 Give the complete present tense conjugations of the verbs *kataba / yaktubu* (write), *shariba / yashrabu* (drink), and *darrasa / yudarrisu* (teach).

Exercise 5 Fill in the blanks in the following sentences with the correct present tense form of the verb given in parentheses.

1. *al 'awlaad __________ fii l-madrasa. (darasa / yadrusu)*
2. *'anti __________ xalaa s-saaxa l-waaHida. ('akala / ya'kulu)*
3. *al-bint __________ al-Haliib. (shariba / yashrabu)*
4. *'anta __________ 'ilaa l-maktab. (dhahaba / yadh-habu)*
5. *aT-Tabiib __________ fii l-mustashfaa. (xamila / yaxmalu)*
6. *naHnu __________ 'ilaa l-masjid. (dhahaba / yadh-habu)*
7. *an-nisaa' __________ al-lugha al-injiliiziyya. (darrasa / yudarrisu)*
8. *ar-rijaal __________ daa'iman. (xamila / yaxmalu)*

Exercise 6 Now rewrite each of the answers from exercise 5 in the negative.

10G Pronunciation Practice *th* vs. *dh*, *k* vs. *q*

In this lesson we're going to contrast two pairs of sounds which may be giving you trouble. The first pair, *th* and *dh*, exists in English, and can be heard in the contrasting pairs "ether" and "either" (depending on how you prononce that) or "wry thing" and "writhing." Listen to these Arabic pairs.

thabata, dhabba, thubuut, dhubuul, tharr, dharr, thalama, dhahaba

The second constrasting pair is not heard in English, as *q* is not an English sound. It's important to distinguish between these two sounds in Arabic, though. Remember that *k* is just like the English sound in "kite" or "cat," but *q* is produced much further back in the mouth, and it deepens the vowels around it.

kaada, qaada, kasuul, qaSiir, bakara, baqara, kaaf, qaaf

10H Arabic Script The letters *xayn* and *ghayn*

Now let's take a look at the consonants *xayn* and *ghayn* in Arabic script. The shapes for this pair of letters differ more greatly than most other Arabic letters depending on their position in a word. Notice also that the shape of *ghayn* is the same as *xayn*, except that it has a dot.

	isolated	initial	medial	final
x	ع	عـ	ـعـ	ـع
gh	غ	غـ	ـغـ	ـغ

عَيْن	*xayn* (eye)	بـعِيد	*baxiid* (far)
غَبِيّ	*ghabiyy* (stupid)	تَبَغ	*tabagh* (tobacco)

For more practice, read *Group 8: ع x and غ gh* and reading practice 9 of *Part 2: Reading Arabic* in the *Complete Guide to Arabic Script.* You can also practice writing with Group 8 and writing practices 20–21 of *Part 3: Writing Arabic.*

10I Cultural Note The Concept of Time in the Arab World

As a generalization, time is a "loose" concept in the Middle East, especially when it comes to social engagements. For example, if an informal appointment is made for 3:00, the actual time an Arab friend might arrive may be closer to 3:30 or 3:45. This is typical of many personal meetings, especially among friends. Don't be surprised if it seems that punctuality and watch-checking don't carry the same weight as they do in more time-conscious cultures, where 3:00 means 3:00 or 3:05. You'll have to adjust your own expectations and relationship with the clock if you want to avoid frustration!

However, this is not true of more formal events or appointments, which do indeed start on time. It is expected that everyone be on time for important business meetings, seminars, lectures, etc. Another event that is subject to strict punctuality is the calculation of prayer times. Less important activities will be set aside for prayers by the observant, and meetings and other daily routines will be scheduled around prayers.

Lesson 10 Answer Key

Vocabulary Practice: 1. *daliil al-haatif*; 2. *rakkaba r-raqm*; 3. *raqm al-haatif*; 4. *mukaalama duwaliyya*; 5. *mukaalama maHaliyya*; 6. *mukaalama haatifiyya*; 7. *'ayna l-haatif al-xumuumiyy?*; 8. *haadhaa huwa l-haatif.*; 9. *mukaalama xalaa Hisaabi l-mutalaqqii*; 10. *muwaDHDHafat al-'istiqbaal mashghuula* 11. *al-xaamil al-haatifiyy hunaa*. 12. *al-mukaalamaat ad-duwaliyya ghaaliya*. **Exercise 1:** *al-'ithnayn*–Monday; *ath-thulaathaa'*–Tuesday; *al-'arbixaa'*–Wednesday; *al-khamiis*–Thursday; *al-jumuxa*–Friday; *as-sabt*–Saturday; *al-'aHad*–Sunday **Exercise 2:** *yanaayir, fibraayir, maaris, 'abriil, maayuu, yunyu, yulyu, 'awghustus, siptambar, 'uktuubar, nufambar, disambar* **Exercise 3:** 1. *khamsa yanaayir* 2. *tisxa wa xashar 'uktuubar* 3. yawm *al-'ithnayn, sabxata xashar 'aghusTus / 'uut* 4. *yawm al-'arbixaa', tisxa wa xishruun maaris* 5. *rajaxuu yawm al-'aHad* 6. *khallaStu s-sabt, sitta yunyu / jwaan* 7. *Hasan dhahaba 'ilaa xammaan yawm al-jumuxa, 'ithnayn wa xashar nufambar*. 9. *'alfayn wa sitta* **Exercise 4:** 'anaa *'aktubu; 'anta taktubu; 'anti taktubiina; huwa yaktubu; hiya taktubu; 'antumaa taktubaani; naHnu naktubu, 'antum taktubuuna; 'antunna taktubna; hum yaktubuuna; hunna yaktubna; humaa (m.) yaktubaani; humaa (f.) taktubaani. 'anaa 'ashrabu; 'anta tashrabu; 'anti tashrabiina; huwa yashrabu; hiya tashrabu; 'antumaa tashrabaani; naHnu nashrabu; 'antum tashrabuuna; 'antunna tashrabna; hum yashrabuuna; hunna yashrabna; humaa (m.) yashrabaani; humaa (f.) tashrabaani. 'anaa 'udarrisu; 'anta tudarrisu; 'anti tudarrisiina; huwa yudarrisu; hiya tudarrisu; 'antumaa tudarrisaani; naHnu nudarrisu; 'antum tudarrisuuna; 'antunna tudarrisna; hum yudarrisuuna; hunna yudarrisna; humaa (m.) yudarrisaani; humaa (f.) tudarrisaani*. **Exercise 5:** 1. *yadrusuuna*; 2. *ta'kuliina*; 3. *tashrabu*; 4. *tadh-habu*; 5. *yaxmalu*; 6. *nadh-habu*; 7. *yudarrisna*; 8. *yaxmaluuna* **Exercise 6:** 1. *al-'awlaad laa yadrusuuna fii l-madrasa*. 2. *'anti laa ta'kuliina xalaa s-saaxa l-waaHida*. 3. *al-bint laa tashrabu al-Haliib*. 4. *'anta laa tadh-habu 'ilaa l-maktab*. 5. *aT-Tabiib laa yaxmalu fii l-mustashfaa*. 6. *naHnu laa nadh-habu 'ilaa l-masjid*. 7. *an-nisaa' laa yudarrisna al-lugha l-injiliiziyaa*. 8. *ar-rijaal laa yaxmaluuna daa'iman*.

LESSON 11

THE FAMILY *al-xaa'ila*

In Lesson 11 you'll learn important vocabulary for talking about your own family and asking about others. You'll also learn how to express possession.

11A Dialogue

Mary is invited to her co-worker Ahmed's house to meet his wife Latifa and their son Murad.

'aHmad	***'ahlan wa sahlan. TafaDDalii.***
marii	***shukran jaziilan.***
'aHmad	***haadhihi zawjatii laTiifa. laTiifa, haadhihi marii, zamiila min al-maktab.***
marii	***as-salaamu xalayki yaa laTiifa. kayfa Haaluki?***
laTiifa	***as-salaamu xalayki yaa marii. al-Hamdu lillaah, shukran.***
'aHmad	***wa haadhaa 'ibnii muraad. xumruhu tisxat sanawaat.***
marii	***'ahlan wa sahlan yaa muraad. kayfa l-Haal?***
laTiifa	***'ibnii khajuul. wa taxbaan 'ayDan!***
marii	***'anaa 'afhamu.***
laTiifa	***hal xindaki 'aTfaal, yaa marii?***
marii	***naxam. 'anaa wa zawjii xindanaa bintaani. saara, xumruhaa thamaania sanawaat, wa danyaal xumruhaa khams sanawaat. 'innahaa khajuula 'ayDan!***
Ahmed	Hello. Please come in.
Mary	Thank you very much.
Ahmed	This is my wife Latifa. Latifa, this is Mary, a colleague from the office.
Mary	Hello Latifa. How are you?
Latifa	Hello Mary. I'm doing very well, thank you.
Ahmed	And this is my son Murad. He's nine years old.
Mary	Hi, Murad. How are you?
Latifa	My son is shy. And tired, too!
Mary	I understand.
Latifa.	Do you have children, Mary?
Mary	Yes. My husband and I have two daughters. Sarah is eight years old, and Danielle is five. She's shy, too!

11B Language Notes

In lesson 2 you learned that *kayfa l-Haal* means "how are you?" This is one way of asking that question, and literally it means "how's the health/condition?" In this dialogue you heard Mary ask Latifa *kayfa Haaluki*? This means the same thing, but it's more specific, meaning "how's your health/condition." In Arabic, possessive adjectives (my, your, his) are added onto the end of nouns, just like object pronouns are. You'll learn more about that in this lesson.

Another example of the possessive endings used in an expression you've come across already is *as-salaamu xalayki*. You already know this expression as *as-salaamu xalaykum*, which is a general greeting said to a group of people. The *-ki* ending on *xalayki* specifies that the speaker is addressing one woman. It's related to the ending for the pronoun *'anti*, which you know is the feminine singular.

In the dialogue Ahmed says that Murad is nine years old. He uses the expression *xumruhu tisxa sanawaat.* You already know that *tisxa* is nine, and *sanawaat* is years. The word *xumr* means "age," and *xumruhu* literally means "his age," which is the same construction as *Haaluki*, or "your health." To say your own age, you'd say *xumrii* . . ., or "my age is . . ."

Notice that Ahmed says *haadhihi zawjatii* for "this is my wife" but *haadhaa 'ibnii* for "this is my son." Don't forget that *haadhaa* is a masculine form, while *haadhihi* is a feminine form.

Did you notice the use of the dual form, *bintaani*, in Mary's answer to the question *hal xindaki 'aTfaal*? Remember that *bint* means "one girl" or "one daughter", *banaat* means "daughters" and *bintaani* means "two daughters" or "a pair of daughters." Notice that the *-ayni* ending of the dual is often shortened to *-ayn* in spoken Arabic. In fact, as you hear more and more spoken Arabic, you'll notice that a lot of final vowels of endings may be dropped—for example, *'anaa 'adrus* instead of *'anaa 'adrusu* (I study), *'anti taskuniin* instead of *'anti taskuniina* (you live) or *hum yaxfaluun* instead of *hum yaxfaluuna* (they work).

Back in lesson 5 you saw the sentence *'innahu qariib min maHattati l-qitaar*, "it is close to the train station." You saw in the language notes that *'inna* is often used in "to be" sentences in Arabic, and that it takes certain endings to show the subject. In the dialogue above you saw another example of this, *'innahaa khajuula 'ayDan,* meaning "she's shy, too." Note that the ending *–haa* on *'inna* means "she." This is the same set of endings that can mean object pronouns or possessives. You'll learn more about them in this lesson.

11C Vocabulary

xaa'ila / xaa'ilaat	family
shakhS / 'ashkhaaS	person
rajul / rijaal	man
imra'a / nisaa'	woman (irregular singular/plural)
zawj / 'azwaaj	husband
zawja / zawjaat	wife
'ibn / 'abnaa'	son
walad / 'awlaad	son, boy
bint / banaat	daughter, girl
'akh / 'ikhwa	brother
'ukht / 'akhawaat	sister
'umm / 'ummahaat	mother
'ab / 'aabaa'	father
khaala / khaalaat	aunt (maternal side)
xamma / xammaat	aunt (paternal side)
khaal / 'akhwaal	uncle (maternal side)
xamm / 'axmaam	uncle (paternal side)
ibn xamm*	cousin, paternal side, male
ibn khaal	cousin, maternal side, male
bint xamm	cousin, paternal side, female
bint khaal	cousin, maternal side, female
jadd / juduud	grandfather
jadda / jaddaat	grandmother
Sadiiq / 'aSdiqaa'	friend (m.)
Sadiiqa / Sadiiqaat	friend (f.)
zamiil / zumalaa'	colleague (m.)
zamiila / zamiilaat	colleague (f.)

The word for cousin in Arabic is simply "son" ('ibn*) or "daughter" (*bint*) of one of the four words meaning "aunt" or "uncle"–*khaala, xamma, khaal, xamm*. So, *'ibn xamm* is a cousin who is specifically the son of a paternal uncle, and *bint khaal* is a cousin who specifically is the daughter of a maternal uncle.

ghariib / ghurabaa'	strangers
mumaththil / mumaththiluun	actor
muhandis / muhandisuun	architect
fannaan / fannaanuun	artist
Hallaaq /Hallaaquun	barber
simsaar	broker
muHaasib	accountant
rajul 'axmaal	businessman
'imra'at 'axmaal	businesswoman
taajir	merchant, trader
Tabbaakh	cook/chef
Tabiib / 'aTibbaa'	doctor
muHarrir / muHarriruun	editor
muHaamii	lawyer
mumarriDa / mumarriDaat	nurse
mutarjim	translator
muxallim	teacher
kaatib	writer
khajuul / –uun	shy
taxbaan / –uun	tired, sleepy
farHaan / –uun	happy
Haziin / Huzanaa'	sad
dhakiyy / 'adhkiyaa'	smart, intelligent
jaahil / juhalaa'	foolish, ignorant
mariiD / marDaa	sick, ill
'ayDan	also
marratan 'ukhra	again, another time
jiddan	very

11D Vocabulary Practice

Translate the following words, phrases, and sentences.

1. lawyer
2. the nurse (f.)
3. son
4. wife
5. the student (m.)
6. barber
7. daughters

8. husband
9. doctor
10. families
11. The boy is tired.
12. The little girl is very intelligent.
13. The man travels a lot.
14. The children do not understand.

11E Grammar and Usage

❸ "To Have" in Arabic

There is no verb "to have" in Arabic. Instead there are certain prepositional constructions that can be used to show ownership or possession. The most common prepositions used to show possession are *li* (to, for) and *xinda* (with).

li-musTafaa sayyaara Hamraa'.	Mustafa has a red car.
li-maryam luxba jadiida.	Myriam has a new toy.
xindii daftar wa qalam.	I have a notebook and a pen.
xindanaa bayt Saghiir fii l-madiina.	We have a small house in the city.

Notice the suffixes *–ii* and *–naa* on the preposition *xinda*; these are same suffixes as the attached direct object pronouns that you learned in lesson 9. Here are all of these suffixes attached to *xinda*, which is the most common way to express "I have," "you have," "he has," etc.

xindii	"I have"	*xindanaa*	"we have"
xindaka	"you have"	*xindakum*	"you have"
xindaki	"you have"	*xindakunna*	"you have"
xindahu	"he, it has"	*xindahum*	"they have"
xindahaa	"she, it has"		
	"they have" (non-human)	*xindahunna*	"they have"
xindakumaa	"you two have"	*xindahumaa*	"the two of them have" (m. or f.)

This construction is not a verb, but instead a prepositional phrase that literally means something along the lines of "by/with/to me there is a car." So, to negate it, you can't use *laa* as you would with verbs. Instead, use either *laysa* ("it isn't," see lesson 5) or *maa* in more informal speech.

laysa xindii daftar wa 'aqlaam.	I don't have a notebook and pens.
maa xindahu kitaabii.	He doesn't have my book.

❷ Possessive Suffixes

In lesson 9 you learned that direct object pronouns are attached as suffixes to verbs. Those endings are the same as what you just learned can be attached to *xinda*: *–ii* (me), *–ka* (you, m.), *–ki* (you, f.), *–hu* (him, it), *–haa* (her, it, non-human them), *–naa* (us), *–kum* (you, pl. m.), *–kunna* (you, pl. f.), *–hum* (them, m. and mixed),*–hunna* (them, f.) *–kumaa* (you two), and *–humaa* (the two of them, m. or f.).

As you saw in the dialogue, these endings express possession when attached to nouns instead of verbs. In these cases they are translated as the possessive adjectives "my," "your," "his," "her," etc.

kayfa Haaluki?	How are you? / How's your health? (to a woman)
haadhaa 'ibnii.	This is my son.
baytunaa kabiir wa 'abyaD.	Our house is big and white.
maktabuhaa laysa baxiid.	Her office is not far.

The possessive endings are the same as the direct object endings, except *–nii* (me) becomes *–ii* (my). Let's see how they attach to the noun *Sadiiq* (friend).

Sadiiqii	my friend	*Sadiiqunaa*	our friend
Sadiiquka	your (m.) friend	*Sadiiqukum*	your (m. pl.) friend
Sadiiquki	your (f.) friend	*Sadiiqukunna*	your (f. pl.) friend
Sadiiquhu	his friend	*Sadiiquhum*	their (m.) friend
Sadiiquhaa	her friend	*Sadiiquhunna*	their (f.) friend
Sadiiqukumaa	the friend of the two of you	*Sadiiquhumaa*	the friend of the two of them (m. or f.)

If you attach a possessive suffix to a feminine noun ending in *–a*, then the "hidden t" is pronounced. Take the example of *Sadiiqa*:

Sadiiqatii	my friend	*Sadiiqatunaa*	our friend
Sadiiqatuka	your (m.) friend	*Sadiiqatukum*	your (m. pl.) friend
Sadiiqatuki	your (f.) friend	*Sadiiqatukunna*	your (f. pl.) friend
Sadiiqatuhu	his friend	*Sadiiqatuhum*	their (m.) friend
Sadiiqatuhaa	her friend	*Sadiiqatuhunna*	their (f.) friend
Sadiiqatukumaa	the friend of the two of you	*Sadiiqatuhumaa*	the friend of the two of them (m. or f.)

Notice that *–u–* is inserted before all of the endings but *–ii* after nouns that end in consonants, such as *Sadiiq,* or after the "hidden t" of feminine nouns, such as *Sadiiqa(t).* But this *–u* changes to *–i* after prepositions or in possessive constructions, which you'll learn about in the next section. It can also change to *–a* in certain grammatical instances. This is all a question of something called a "noun case," which is a point of Arabic grammar that you usually don't have to worry about. If you're curious about the big picture of noun cases, take a look at that section in the Grammar Summary at the end of this book. If you're not curious about them, you'll be happy to know that except in very formal Arabic, they only turn up in few circumstances, such as this *–u* or *–i* or *–a* inserted before possessive suffixes.

baytuhaa fii haadhaa n-nahj.	Her house is on this street. (*bayt* is the subject).
naHnu fii baytihaa.	We're in her house. (*bayt* follows a preposition)
'anaa 'araa baytahaa.	I see her house. (*bayt* is the direct object.)
Sadiiquka laTiif jiddan.	Your friend is very nice. (*Sadiiq* is the subject.)
dhahabtu maxa Sadiiqika.	I went with your friend. (*Sadiiq* follows a preposition.)
laa 'axrifu Sadiiqaka.	I don't know your friend. (*Sadiiq* is the direct object.)

In very formal Arabic, such as television interviews or scholarly discussions, these case endings can appear on all nouns, but for everyday speaking, you'll most likely only come across them in very limited situations, such as the examples above that include possessive suffixes. Another common situation that calls for a case ending is after that same "hidden t" of the feminine *–a* ending in possessive noun constructions, which you'll learn about next.

3 Possessive Noun Constructions

A possessive noun construction is a phrase where one noun is the possessor or owner of a second noun. In English, this is most often expressed by adding 's (apostrophe s) after the possessor, as in "the man's house" or "the boy's dog." In Arabic, the word order is reversed—the possessor or owner is second instead of first, similar to the alternate English word order for possession, "the house of the man" or "the dog of the boy." Note that in Arabic, though, there is no preposition "of," and only the second noun is always in the definite form. The first noun, expressing what is possessed or owned, does not take the definite article, but it is still grammatically definite.

daar ar-rajul	the man's house (the house of the man)
kalb al-'imra'a	the woman's dog (the dog of the woman)
'umm al-walad	the boy's mother (the mother of the boy)
baab al-maktab	the door of the office
Sadiiq 'ukhtii	my sister's friend (the friend of my sister)

Notice that in that last example, the second noun does not take *al-*, but it is still definite, because it ends in a possessive suffix.

If the first noun is feminine and ends in *–a*, then the "hidden t" is pronounced, and it is likely to be followed by *–u*, or *–i* after prepositions, or even *–a*. This is the other situation where you're likely to encounter case endings in spoken Arabic.

ghurfatu n-nawm laysat kabiira.	The bedroom is not big.
sayyaaratu r-rajul bijaanibi baytinaa.	The man's car is next to our house.
naHnu fii ghurfati n-nawm.	We are in the bedroom.
dhahabtu maxa Sadiiqati 'ukhtii.	I went with my sister's friend.
'akhadhtu biTaaqata l-'istilaaf.	I took the credit card.

If the second noun ends in a possessive suffix, it will have an *–i* before that suffix. Also, if that second noun is a masculine sound plural, the ending will be *–iin* or *–iina* instead of *–uun*.

baab baytinaa 'azraq.	The door of our house is blue.
'umm Sadiiqatihaa laTiifa jiddan.	The mother of her friend / her friend's mother is very nice.

bayt al-miSriyyiin laysa baxiid.	The house of the Egyptians / the Egyptians' house is not far.
kuumbyuutaraat al-mudiiriina jadiida.	The directors' computers are new.

If you'd like to use an adjective to describe either of the nouns in a possessive noun construction, it must of course agree in gender and number, but it must always be definite and it must be placed after the entire phrase. This can, sometimes, create ambiguity, but context will usually make the meaning clear.

bayt ar-rajul al-kabiir	the old man's house or the man's big house
kitaab al-'ustaadh al-jadiid	the young professor's book or the professor's new book
bint al-'imra'a l-Saghiira	the short woman's daughter or the woman's short daughter.

But of course if one of the nouns is masculine and the other is feminine, or if one is plural and the other singular, it will be clear which noun the adjective is describing.

zawjat ar-rajul al-laTiif	the friendly man's wife
zawjat ar-rajul al-laTiifa	the man's friendly wife
'umm al-walad al-mariiD	the sick boy's mother
'umm al-walad al-mariiDa	the boy's sick mother

And finally, don't forget the difference between a phrase and a sentence. If those last adjectives are indefinite instead of definite, complete sentences are created.

zawjat ar-rajul laTiifa.	The man's wife is friendly.
'umm al-walad mariiDa.	The boy's mother is sick.

11F Grammar and Usage Exercises

Exercise 1 Combine the preposition *xinda* with the suffixes that correspond to the pronouns in brackets in order to form "to have" sentences.

1. *['anaa + xinda] 'ukht.*
2. *[hiya + xinda] 'akh.*
3. *[naHnu + xinda] bint wa 'ibn.*
4. *[naHnu + xinda] bayt Saghiir.*
5. *hal ['anti + xinda] kalb?*
6. *['anaa + xinda] sayyaara zarqaa'*

7. *hal ['anta + xinda] qamiiS jadiid?*
8. *hal [hum + xinda] haadhaa l-kitaab?*

Exercise 2 Now combine the following sentences using possessive suffixes. Follow this example: *xindii haatif. huwa jadiid. = hatiifii jadiid.*

1. *xindii kalb. huwa kabiir wa 'aswad.*
2. *xindanaa kutub. hiya jadiida.*
3. *xindahu qamiiS. huwa 'abyaD.*
4. *xindahu sayyaara. hiya zarqaa'.*
5. *xindahum bayt. huwa kabiir wa jadiid.*
6. *xindanaa 'ukht. hiya laTiifa.*
7. *xindii Sadiiq. huwa miSriyy.*
8. *xindanaa shuqqa. hiya Saghiira.*

Exercise 3 Translate each of the following into Arabic.

1. the girl's friend (m.)
2. the girls' friend (m.)
3. the window of the office
4. the son's bedroom (Remember–only one definite article!)
5. the woman's husband
6. the living room of the apartment
7. the door of the house
8. the tall boy's book
9. the boy's new books
10. The boys' books are new.
11. The door of the apartment is small.
12. The man's shirt is red.

11G Pronunciation Practice *h* vs. *H* vs. *kh*

In this lesson we'll contrast the sounds *h, H* and *kh*. Remember that *h* is the same sound as the first consonant in the English words "house" or "here." *H*, on the other hand, is a deep, "throaty" sound that's similar to the sound you make when you blow on glasses to clean them or when you lower yourself into a hot bath. You should be able to feel the muscles over your adam's apple constrict when you pronounce *H*. The sound *kh* is produced in an area of your mouth between *h* and *H*. It's the sound that you hear in the Scottish pronunciation of "loch" or the German pronunciation of "Bach." Now listen to these words and repeat. Notice that each of these letters can appear anywhere in a word—at the beginning, in the middle, or even at the end.

haadhaa, Hammaam, khayr, hum, Hubb, khubz, nahj, 'uHibbu, 'ukht, zahra, naHnu, wasikha, wajh, jarraaH, maTbakh, 'allaah, miSbaaH, 'akh

11H **Arabic Script** The Letters *faa'* and *qaaf*

In this lesson we'll focus on the consonants *faa'* and *qaaf* in Arabic script. Both of these letters are essentially circles, but *faa'* has one dot over it while *qaaf* has two. Also notice that the tail of *qaaf* in its isolated or final form dips below the line.

	Isolated	Initial	medial	final
f	ف	فـ	ـفـ	ـف
q	ق	قـ	ـقـ	ـق

فِكْرَة	*fikra* (idea)	خَفِيف	*khafiif* (light, nimble)
قَصِير	*qaSiir* (short)	العِرَاق	*al-xiraaq* (Iraq)

For more practice, read *Group 9:* ف *f and* ق *q* and reading practice 10 of *Part 2: Reading Arabic* in the *Complete Guide to Arabic Script*. You can also practice writing with Group 9 and writing practices 22–23 of *Part 3: Writing Arabic*.

11I **Cultural Note** The Family in the Middle East

The family is the cornerstone of Middle Eastern society. Families are very close-knit units, and the typical Middle Eastern family is different from the typical nuclear family prevalent in the West. A typical family in the Middle East is extended, meaning that the concept of family includes aunts, uncles, cousins, grandparents, in-laws, and other relatives to a far greater extent than in many Western families. As in most societies, parents and children tend to live together. An affluent Middle Eastern family may have a very large house with close relatives living in different quarters within the same house. But familial ties are expressed even in modest homes. For example, grandparents typically live with their adult children upon reaching retirement. It is important to most Arabs to keep grandparents close to the extended family unit, so generally speaking, people in the Middle East look unfavorably on the concept of retirement homes.

The close-knit extended family unit of the Middle East is one expression of the importance of kinship ties. This importance can also be seen in some marriages, which may be arranged as a means of strengthening strategic alliances between two extended families. This system has its roots in a clan-based society, where kinship and tribal relations have evolved as a crucial layer of social and political organization. Of course, it is true that some Arab societies are moving away from this traditional structure under the influence of a variety of social and economic factors. Still, the extended family and heavy kinship ties remain the norm in most Middle Eastern countries.

Lesson 11 Answer Key

Vocabulary Practice: 1. *muHaamii*; 2. *al-mumarriDa*; 3. *'ibn*; 4. *zawja*; 5. *aT-Taalib*; 6. *Hallaaq*; 7. *banaat*; 8. *zawj*; 9. *Tabiib*; 10. *xaa'ilaat* 11. *al-walad taxbaan.* 12. *al-bint aS-Saghiira dhakiyya jiddan.* 13. *ar-rajul yusaafiru kathiiran.* 14. *al-'aTfaal laa yafhamuuna.* **Exercise 1:** 1. *xindii 'ukht.* 2. *xindahaa 'akh.* 3. *xindanaa bint wa 'ibn.* 4. *xindanaa bayt Saghiir.* 5. *hal xindaki* kalb? 6. *xindii sayyaara zarqaa'.* 7. *hal xindaka qamiiS jadiid?* 8. *hal xindahum haadhaa l-kitaab?* **Exercise 2:** 1. *kalbii kabiir wa 'aswad.* 2. *kutubunaa jadiida.* 3. *qamiiSuhu 'abyaD.* 4. *sayyaaratuhu zarqaa'.* 5. *baytuhum kabiir wa jadiid.* 6. *'ukhtunaa laTiifa.* 7. *Sadiiqii miSriyy.* 8. *shuqqatunaa Saghiira.* **Exercise 3:** 1. *Sadiiq al-bint*; 2. *Sadiiq al-banaat*; 3. *shubbaak al-maktab*; 4. *ghurfat nawm al-'ibn*; 5. *zawj al-imra'a*; 6. *ghurfat juluus ash-shuqqa*; 7. *baab ad-daar/al-bayt*; 8. *kitaab al-walad aT-Tawiil*; 9. *kutub al-walad al-jadiida*; 10. *kutub al-'awlaad jadiida.* 11. *baab ash-shuqqa Saghiir.* 12. *qamiiS ar-rajul 'aHmar.*

LESSON 12

MY HEAD HURTS! *ra'sii yu'limunii!*

In lesson 12 you'll learn important vocabulary for talking about health and the body. You'll also learn how to talk about future actions and give and understand a few essential commands, and you'll take a look at some common irregular verbs.

12A Dialogue

Bill Stephens is visiting friends in Bahrain, but he hasn't been feeling well. Let's listen in as he visits the doctor.

aT-Tabiib	***maadhaa yu'limuka, yaa sayyid stiifins?***
bil	***laa 'axrifu, yaa duktuur Hasan. 'aDHunnu 'anna xindii l-'unfluwanza.***
aT-Tabiib	***hal tasxulu kathiiran?***
bil	***naxam, kathiiran. wa 'anfii masduud.***
aT-Tabiib	***hal ra'suka yu'limuka?***
bil	***naxam. ra'sii yu'limunii kathiiran. lam 'astaTix 'an 'anaama l-baariHa.***
aT-Tabiib	***hal tuHissu bi l-ghathayaan? hal xindaka 'is-haal?***
bil	***laa, 'abadan. ra'sii wa ri'ataaya yu'limaananii kathiiran.***
aT-Tabiib	***sa-naraa 'idhaa xindaka Hummaa. 'iftaH famaka min faDlik wa sa-'aakhudhu Haraarataka.***

baxda laHaDHaat . . .

aT-Tabiib	***naxam, xindaka Hummaa. sa-nastamixu 'ilaa ri'atayka. 'ikhlax thiyaabaka min faDlik. tanaffas xamiiqan. ri'ataaka masduudataani.***
bil	***maadhaa yajibu 'an 'afxala ya duktuur?***
aT-Tabiib	***al-yawm sa-tadh-habu 'ilaa l-manzil, wa tastariiH fii s-sariir. Wa sa-tanaamu. haadhaa 'aHsan xilaaj.***
bil	***hal 'aHtaaju 'ilaa 'adwiya?***
aT-Tabiib	***yumkin 'an ta'khudha 'asbiriin li ra'sika wa li l-Hummaa. 'ishrab maa'an kathiiran wa naam kathiiran! sa-tashxuru 'annaka jayiddun ghadan.***

Doctor	What's the problem, Mr. Stevens?
Bill	I don't know, Dr. Hassan. I think I have the flu.
Doctor	Are you coughing a lot?
Bill	Yes, very much. And my nose is congested.
Doctor	Do you have a headache?
Bill	Yes, my head hurts a lot. And I couldn't sleep last night.
Doctor	Are you nauseous? Do you have diarrhea?
Bill	No, not at all. My head and my lungs hurt a lot.
Doctor	Let's see if you have a fever. Open your mouth and I will take your temperature.

A few minutes later . . .

Doctor	Yes, you have a fever. Let's listen to your lungs. Please take your shirt off. Now breathe deeply. Your lungs are congested.
Bill	What do I have to do, Dr.?
Doctor	Tonight you'll go home and get into bed. Then you'll sleep. That's the best remedy.
Bill	Do I need medication?
Doctor	You can take aspirin for your head and fever. Drink a lot of water and sleep a lot! You'll feel better tomorrow.

12B Language Notes

Notice the many examples in this dialogue of possessive or object suffixes: *maadhaa yu'limuka* (what hurts you?), *'anfii* (my nose), *ra'suka* (your head), *ra'sii* (my head), *yu'limunii* (hurts me), and so on. Also notice the many examples of *xinda* with these same endings which mean "have."

Notice the expression *'aDHunnu 'anna* . . . (I think that . . .) The word *'anna* functions as the English conjunction "that." It can introduce an entire thought after verbs like *DHanna / yaD-Hunnu* (think).

Some of the verbs in the dialogue have an *–a* ending instead of the *–u* of the present tense: *lam 'astaTix 'an 'anaama l-baariHa.* (I couldn't sleep last night.) *maadhaa yajibu 'an 'afxala?* (What do I have to do?) These forms are what is called the subjunctive, which you've already seen after the words *mumkin / yumkin* (possible), and which you'll learn in lesson 13. As you can see from these examples, this form is used after verbs such as "can" or "must" and is often introduced by the particle *'an*.

12C Vocabulary

There are several nouns in this list that do not end in the feminine *–a*, but that are still feminine. Notice that these all denote parts of the body that come in pairs, such as eyes, ears, arms, etc, so the most logical plural forms are actually dual forms.

jasad / 'ajsaad body
jild skin
ra's / ru'uus head
fam mouth
lisaan tongue
sinn / 'asnaan tooth
wajh / wujuuh face
xayn / xuyuun eye (feminine)
'anf nose
'udhun / 'udhunaani ear (feminine)
shaxr hair
katif / katifaani shoulder (feminine)
Sadr chest
maxida belly, abdomen
dhiraax / dhiraaxaani arm (feminine)
yad / yadaani hand (feminine)
'iSbax / 'aSaabix finger
rijl / rijlaani leg (feminine)
qadam / qadamaani foot (feminine)
'iSbax al-qadam / 'aSaabix al-qadam toe
rukba / rukbataan knee
dimaagh brain
qalb / quluub heart
nafas breath
ri'a / ri'ataani lung

xaDHm / xiDHaam	bone
damm	blood
Tabiib	doctor
maraD	sickness
maraD al-Hasaasiyya	allergy
wajax aDH-DHahr	backache
suxaal	cough
Harq	burn
raDDa	bruise
bard	cold
xindii Sudaax.	I have a headache.
xindii bard.	I have a cold.
xindii l-'unfluwanza.	I have the flu.
xindii Haraara.	I have a temperature.
'adwiya	medication, drugs
'asbiriin	aspirin
sharaab as-suxaal	cough syrup
xilaaj	remedy
xiyaada	clinic
mustashfaa	hospital
jarraaH	surgeon
Suurat ashixxa	x-ray
jalasa / yajlisu	sit
waqafa / yaqifu	stand
mashaa / yamshii	walk
rafaxa / yarfaxu	lift, raise
fataHa / yaftaHu	open
saxala / yasxulu	cough
khalaxa / yakhlaxu	take off (clothes)
labisa / yalbasu	put on (clothes)
naama / yanaamu	sleep
DHanna / yaDHunnu	think
'anna . . .	that . . .
'aHsan . . .	the best . . .
mariiD	sick
qawiyy	strong
saliim	healthy
kathiir(an)	a lot
qaliil(an)	a little

12D Vocabulary Practice

Translate the following words, phrases, and sentences.

1. knee
2. the heart
3. my nose
4. a good surgeon
5. the red blood
6. his brain
7. my doctor (both m. and f.)
8. your (m.) eye
9. I have a headache.
10. Do I have a temperature?
11. Her arm is small.
12. The girl's face is pretty.
13. Where is the hospital?
14. I don't know.
15. We are sitting.
16. I'm not opening the window. / I don't open the window.

12E Grammar and Usage

❶ Expressing the Future

As you know, there are only two basic tenses in Arabic—the past and the present. There is no future tense, but there is a very easy way to express future actions. Simply add the prefix *sa–* onto the present tense form of the verb, or place the word *sawfa* before the present tense form of the verb. These are interchangeable.

sa-'aqra'u l-kitaab fii l-ghad.	I will read the book tomorrow.
sa-na'kulu xalaa s-saaxa th-thaalitha.	We will eat at three o'clock.
sawfa tashrabiina ka's min al-khamr.	You will drink a glass of wine.
mataa sa-yakuunu fii l-bayt?	When will he be home?

❷ Common Irregular Verbs

You've learned how to form the past and present tenses in Arabic, and you've also learned that you can use *sa–* or *sawfa* with the present tense to express future events or actions. But as you might guess, Arabic, like most languages, has several common irregular verbs, or verbs that don't quite follow the normal pattern. The prefixes and suffixes are the same as what you've already learned, but the stems themselves undergo changes you might not expect. The best way to learn irregular verbs is to memorize them, but keep it in the back of your mind that even irregular verbs tend to follow patterns, and overall, verb irregularities in Arabic are not as complicated or random as in many languages you may have studied. First let's take a look at the most important patterns irregular verbs in Arabic follow. Then we'll look at some important individual irregular verbs, some of which you've already seen.

Verbs with *w* or *y*—"Weak Verbs"

Verbs that have a *–w–* or *–y–* as one of the root consonants are considered irregular because these consonants are "weak" and can drop out of the root in conjugation or become vowels. Keep in mind that the same Arabic letters are used for *w* and *uu* and for *y* and *ii*, so this back-and-forth from vowel to consonant isn't as crazy as it may seem.

If the first consonant is weak (almost always a *w-*) the verb is regular in the past tense, but it loses the *w–* in the present tense. In traditional Arabic grammars you'll see these referred to as "assimilated verbs." You may have noticed this pattern with *waSala / yaSilu* (arrive).

waSala / yaSilu—arrive

Past: *'anaa waSaltu, 'anta waSalta, 'anti waSalti, huwa waSala, hiya waSalat, 'antumaa waSaltumaa, naHnu waSalnaa, 'antum waSaltum, 'antunna waSaltunna, hum waSaluu, hunna waSalna, humaa (m.) waSalaa, humaa (f.) waSalataa.*

Present: *'anaa 'aSilu, 'anta taSilu, 'anti taSiliina, huwa yaSilu, hiya taSilu, 'antumaa taSilaani, naHnu naSilu, 'antum taSiluuna, 'antunna taSilna, hum yaSiluuna, hunna yaSilna, humaa (m.) yaSilaani, humaa (f.) taSilaani.*

Other common verbs that follow this pattern are *wajada / yajidu* (find), *waDaxa / yaDaxu* (put or lay down) and *waqafa / yaqifu* (stand).

If the *-w-* or *-y-* is the second root letter, it will often be replaced by (or pronounced as) a vowel. Again, if you remember that in Arabic script *w* and *uu* are the same thing, and *y* and *ii* are the same thing, this will make more sense. Traditionally these are called "hollow verbs," because instead of having a *w* or *y* as the second root consonant, there is a "hollow" space that is filled by a vowel, either *uu* or *u*, *ii* or *i*, or even *aa*. Some of the most commonly used verbs in Arabic are hollow verbs, so it's worth taking a closer look at the general patterns.

In the past tense, hollow verbs have a long *aa* instead of a second root consonant in the *huwa*, *hiya*, *hum*, and *humaa* forms. The other forms in the past have a short *i* or *u*. To illustrate this, here are two examples, *zaara / yazuuru* (visit) and *baaxa / yabiixu* (sell).

***zaara / yazuuru*—visit**

Past: *'anaa zurtu, 'anta zurta, 'anti zurti, huwa zaara, hiya zaarat, 'antumaa zurtumaa, naHnu zurnaa, 'antum zurtum, 'antunna zurtunna, hum zaaruu, hunna zurna, humaa (m.) zaaraa, humaa (f.) zaarataa.*

***baaxa / yabiixu*—sell**

Past: *'anaa bixtu, 'anta bixta, 'anti bixti, huwa baaxa, hiya baaxat, 'antumaa bixtumaa, naHnu bixnaa, 'antum bixtum, 'antunna bixtunna, hum baaxuu, hunna bixna, humaa (m.) baaxaa, humaa (f.) baaxataa.*

Again, the important thing to keep in mind about hollow verbs in the past is the unexpected *-aa-* in the *huwa*, *hiya*, *hum*, and *humaa* forms, and also the short *i* or *u* in all the other past forms.

In the present tense, hollow verbs have long *ii* (instead of *y*) or *uu* (instead of *w*) in all the forms except the feminine plural *antunna* and *hunna*, where the short *i* or *u* appears.

***zaara / yazuuru* (visit)**

Present: *'anaa 'azuuru, 'anta tazuuru, 'anti tazuuriina, huwa yazuuru, hiya tazuuru, 'antumaa tazuuraani, naHnu nazuuru, 'antum tazuuruuna, 'antunna tazurna, hum yazuuruuna, hunna yazurna, humaa (m.) yazuuraani, humaa (f.) tazuuraani.*

***baaxa / yabiixu* (sell)**

Present: *'anaa 'abiixu, 'anta tabiixu, anti tabiixiina, huwa yabiixu, hiya tabiixu, 'antumaa tabiixaani, naHnu nabiixu, 'antum tabiixuuna, 'antunna tabixna, hum yabiixuuna, hunna yabixna, humaa (m.) yabiixaani, humaa (f.) tabiixaani.*

Notice that the two places where there is a short *i* or *u* instead of the long *ii* or *uu* are the only positions that are directly followed by two consonants—*tazurna* or *yabixna*, for example. Another common verb that follows this pattern is *Taara / yaTiiru (*fly).

If the *-w-* or *-y-* is the last root letter, the verb will be somewhat regular in the past tense, but that letter will drop out of the *huwa*, *hiya*, *hum*, and *humaa* forms. In the present tense there will be an *-aa-, -ii-, -uu-, -ay-,* or *-aw* in its place. These verbs are called "defective verbs" in traditional grammars. There are rules for determining which long vowel or diphthong will be seen in the present, but the patterns are sometimes difficult to predict. At this point it's sufficient to take a look at two common examples.

***mashaa / yamshii* (walk)**

Past: *'anaa mashaytu, 'anta mashayta, 'anti mashayti, huwa mashaa, hiya mashat, 'antumaa mashaytumaa, naHnu mashaynaa, 'antum mashaytum, 'antunna mashaytunna, hum mashaw, hunna mashayna, humaa (m.) mashayaa, humaa (f.) mashataa.*

Present: *'anaa 'amshii, 'anta tamshii, 'anti tamshiina, huwa yamshii, hiya tamshii, 'antumaa tamshiyaani, naHnu namshii, 'antum tamshuuna, 'antunna tamshiina, hum yamshuuna, hunna yamshiina, humaa (m.) yamshiyaani, humaa (f.) tamshiyaani.*

***'ishtaraa / yashtarii* (buy)**

Past: *'anaa 'ishtaraytu, 'anta 'ishtarayta, 'anti 'ishtarayti, huwa 'ishtaraa, hiya 'ishtarat, 'antumaa 'ishtaraytumaa, naHnu 'ishtaraynaa, 'antum 'ishtaraytum, 'antunna 'ishtaraytunna, hum 'ishtaraw, hunna 'ishtarayna, humaa (m.) 'ishtarayaa, humaa (f.) 'ishtarataa.*

Present: *'anaa 'ashtarii , 'anta tashtarii, 'anti tashtariina, huwa yashtarii, hiya tashtarii, 'antumaa tashtariyaani, naHnu nashtarii, 'antum tashtaruuna, 'antunna tashtariina, hum yashtaruuna, hunna yashtariina, humaa (m.) yashtariyaani, humaa (f.) tashtariyaani.*

Another verb that follows this pattern is *nasiya / yansaa* (forget).

Doubled Verbs

Verbs whose second and third root consonants are the same—so-called "double verbs"—are also irregular. Their irregularity has to do with whether the doubled consonants are right next to each other (*ra<u>dd</u>a*, "he answered") or separated by a vowel (*ra<u>dad</u>tu*, "I answered.") Take a look at an example, and pay attention to where you see the doubled *-dd-* of the root.

radda / yaruddu (answer)

Past: *'anaa radadtu, 'anta radadta, 'anti radadti, huwa radda, hiya raddat, 'antumaa radadtumaa, naHnu radadnaa, 'antum radadtum, 'antunna radadtunna, hum radduu, hunna radadna, humaa (m.) raddaa, humaa (f.) raddataa.*

Present: *'anaa 'aruddu, 'anta taruddu, 'anti taruddiina, huwa yaruddu, hiya taruddu, 'antumaa taruddaani, naHnu naruddu, 'antum tarudduuna, 'antunna tardudna, hum yarudduuna, hunna yardudna, humaa (m.) yaruddaani, humaa (f.) taruddaani.*

If you look at where the double *-dd-* occurs, you can see that it's limited to positions that are directly followed by a vowel. You might also notice that, in the present tense where the consonant is doubled, the second root consonant shifts position, "sticking" to the third instead of the first. In other words, a regular *'anaa* form would be **'ardudu* (like *'anaa 'aktubu*), but the correct form is *'aruddu*.

Verbs with *hamza*

Another category of verbs that can be considered irregular are verbs that have *hamza* (') as one of their root consonants. If *hamza* is the first root letter, there will be a long *'aa-* prefix in the present tense *'anaa* form instead of the *'a'* that you might expect.

'akala / ya'kulu	eat
'anaa 'aakulu	I eat
'akhadha / ya'khudhu	take
'anaa 'aakhudhu	I take

There are a few other common verbs that are irregular and do not fit into one of the categories that we've just outlined. It's best to memorize each of these common verbs individually.

jaa'a / yajii'u (come)

Past: *'anaa ji'tu, 'anta ji'ta, 'anti ji'ti, huwa jaa'a, hiya jaa'at, 'antumaa ji'tumaa, naHnu ji'naa, 'antum ji'tum, 'antunna ji'tunna, hum jaa'uu, hunna ji'na, humaa* (m.) *jaa'aa, humaa* (f.) *jaa'ataa*

Present: *'anaa 'ajii', 'anta tajii', 'anti tajii'iina, huwa yajii', hiya tajii', 'antumaa tajii'aani, naHnu najii', 'antum tajii'uuna, 'antunna taji'na, hum yajii'uuna, hunna yaji'na, humaa* (m.) *yajii'aani, humaa* (f.) *tajii'aani.*

ra'aa / yaraa (see)

Past: *'anaa ra'aytu, 'anta ra'ayta, 'anti ra'ayti, huwa ra'aa, hiya ra'at, 'antumaa ra'aytumaa, naHnu ra'aynaa, 'antum ra'aytum, 'antunna ra'aytunna, hum ra'aw, hunna ra'ayna, humaa* (m.) *ra'ayaa, humaa* (f.) *ra'ataa.*

Present: *'anaa 'araa, 'anta taraa, 'anti tarayna, huwa yaraa, hiya taraa, 'antumaa tarayaani, naHnu naraa, 'antum tarauna, 'antunna tarayna, hum yarauna, hunna yarayna, humaa* (m.) *yarayaani, humaa* (f.) *tarayaani.*

axTaa / yuxTii (give)

Past: *'anaa 'axTaytu, 'anta 'axTayta, 'anti 'axTayti, huwa 'axTaa, hiya 'axTat, 'antumaa 'axTaytumaa, naHnu 'axTaynaa, 'antum 'axTaytum, 'antunna 'axTaytunna, hum 'axTaw, hunna 'axTayna, humaa* (m.) *'axTayaa, humaa* (f.) *'axTayataa*

Present: *'anaa 'uxTii, 'anta tuxTii, 'anti tuxTiina, huwa yuxTii, hiya tuxTii, 'antumaa tuxTiyaani, naHnu nuxTii, 'antum tuxTuuna, 'antunna tuxTiina, hum yuxTuuna, hunna yuxTiina, humaa* (m.) *yuxTiyaani, humaa* (f.) *tuxTiyaani.*

naama / yanaam (sleep)

Past: *'anaa nimtu, 'anta nimta, 'anti nimti, huwa naama, hiya naamat, 'antumaa nimtumaa, naHnu nimnaa, 'antum nimtum, 'antunna nimtunna, hum naamuu, hunna nimna, humaa* (m.) *naamaa, humaa* (f.) *naamataa*

Present: *'anaa 'anaamu, 'anta tanaamu, 'anti tanaamiina, huwa yanaamu, hiya tanaamu, 'antumaa tanaamaani, naHnu nanaamu, 'antum tanaamuuna, 'antunna tanamna, hum yanaamuuna, hunna yanamna, humaa* (m.) *yanaamaani, humaa* (f.) *tanaamaani.*

yakuunu (be)

'anaa 'akuunu; anta takuunu, 'anti takuuniina, hiya takuunu, huwa yakuu-nu, 'antumaa takuunaani, naHnu nakuunu, antum takuunuuna, antunna takunna, hum yakuunuuna, hunna yakunna, humaa (m.) *yakuunaani, humaa* (f.) *takuunaani.*

When used with *sa–* or *sawfa,* the forms of *yakuunu* translate as the future tense of "to be"—"will be." This verb can also be used in negative statements, which you'll learn in lesson 14.

3 Important Command Forms

The command form, also known as the imperative, is the form of the verb that you use when you want to tell someone to do (or not to do) something. Take a look at the following examples, all of which are practical expressions for a student of Arabic or a traveler to know. Note that these are forms you'd use to address a man.

'axid	Repeat.
takallam bi buT'in	Speak slowly.
'uktub	Write.
'axTinii	Give me . . .
qullii	Tell me . . .
khudhnii 'ilaa . . .	Take/Drive me to . . .
qif	Stop.

Of course, there are other forms to use to address a woman, and in general you can and should soften all of these forms by adding "please," *min faDlika/faDliki.* There are rules for forming the imperative in Arabic, but for now, though, all you need to do is memorize a few practical forms. Here they are again, in full sentences, first in the form you'd use to address a man, and then in the form you'd use to address a woman.

Repeat that please.	*'axid min faDlika.*	*'axiidii min faDliki.*
Speak more slowly.	*takallam bi buT'in.*	*takallamii bi buT'in.*
Write the price.	*'uktub ath-thaman.*	*'uktubii ath-thaman.*
Give me the book.	*'axTinii l-kitaab.*	*'axTiinii l-kitaab.*
Tell me the address.	*qullii l-xunwaan.*	*quliilii l-xunwaan.*
Stop at the corner.	*qif fii l-maqtax.*	*qifii fii l-maqtax.*

Notice that the commands used to address a woman end in *–ii.*

4 Courtesy Expressions

Like any language, Arabic has a lot of important courtesy expressions that have to be memorized. You've already learned many of them, in fact, but let's take a moment to review and add to that list.

When addressing a friend, use the term *Sadiiq(a)* (friend), *'akh* (brother), or *'ukht* (sister). When addressing someone of importance you may use several terms, depending of course on the circumstances. Some common polite Arabic titles are *duktuur(a)* (Doctor), *'ustaadh(a)* (professor), *sayyid* (Sir), or *sayyida* (Ma'am). You may even hear or have the chance to use *shaykh* (Sheikh), *mawlay* (your highness, reserved for royalty), *amiir* (prince), or *amiira* (princess).

A person who has been on the pilgrimage to Mecca becomes *Haajj* (m.) or *Haajja* (f.). This is a prestigious title that many Muslims are honored to have; being called a *Haajj* or a *Haajja* is a sign of respect, often used to refer to senior citizens.

Whenever you address a person directly, don't forget to use *yaa* before the polite title. For example, *yaa sayyid* if you're speaking to a man, or *yaa 'ustaadha* if you're speaking to a female professor.

Here is a brief list of other polite expressions, some of which you already know.

xafwan	I'm sorry/Pardon me. / Excuse me.
maxa s-salaama.	Good bye.
'ilaa l-liqaa'.	Until next time.
'ilaa– l-ghad.	Until tomorrow.
maxaa 'aTyab al-'umniyaat.	With best wishes.
waqtan mumtixan.	Have a good time.
safaran saxiidan.	Have a good trip.
balligh taHiyyaatii.	Give my greetings/regards.
'alf mabruuk!	Congratulations!
xiid miilaad saxiid	Happy birthday!
HaDHDHan saxiidan!	Best of luck!

12F Grammar and Usage Exercises

Excercise 1 Transform each of the following sentences into the future. First use *sa–* and then *sawfa*. Then translate your answers.

1. *taqra'iina l-jariida.*
2. *'adrusu l-xarabiyya.*
3. *yashrabu ka's maa'.*
4. *nadh-habu 'ilaa l-maTaar.*
5. *yarjixuuna.*

Excercise 2 Fill in the missing present forms of the irregular verbs.

a) *waSala / yaSilu–'anaa 'aSilu, __________, 'anti taSiliina, __________, __________, 'antumaa taSilaani, naHnu naSilu, __________, 'antunna taSilna, __________, hunna yaSilna, humaa yaSilaani, __________.*

b) *baaxa / yabiixu–__________, 'anta tabiixu, __________, huwa yabiixu, __________, __________, __________, 'antum tabiixuuna, __________, hum yabiixuuna, hunna yabixna, __________, humaa tabiixaani.*

c) *mashaa / yamshii–__________, 'anta tamshii, __________, __________, hiya tamshii,__________, naHnu namshii, __________ 'antunna tamshiina, __________, hunna yamshiina, humaa yamshiyaani, humaa tamshiyaani.*

d) *jaa'a / yajii'u–__________, __________, 'anti tajii'iina, __________, hiya tajii'u, __________, __________, 'antum tajii'uuna, 'antunna taji'na, __________, __________, humaa yajii'aani, __________.*

e) *ra'aa–yaraa–'anaa 'araa, __________, __________, __________, hiya taraa, 'antumaa tarayaani, __________, 'antum tarawna, __________, __________, hunna yarayna, __________, humaa tarayaani.*

Excercise 3 Translate each of the following sentences.

1. Please speak more slowly, sir.
2. Please write the address, ma'am.
3. Bring me the check, sir.

4. Please repeat that, ma'am
5. Pardon me, sir
6. Have a good trip.
7. Happy Birthday!
8. Congratulations, my friend.
9. Please give me the book, professor.

12G Pronunciation Practice *gh, k,* and *q*

In this lesson we'll compare three similar Arabic sounds: *gh, k,* and *q*. Remember that *k* is the same consonant as the one at the beginning of "cat" or "kite." But *gh* is closer to a French *r*, a "gargled" sound produced further back in the mouth. The Arabic *q* is similar to a *k*, but it is produced where the *gh* is produced.

kaaf, qaaf, ghayn, kursiyy, qur'aan, ghurfa, kabiir, qaSiir, ghadan, fikra, 'aqlaam, Saghiir

12H Arabic Script The Letters *kaaf* and *laam*

Let's take a look at the consonants *kaaf* and *laam* in Arabic script. Notice that both the final and isolated forms of *kaaf* have a small *s*-like shape inside the hook of the letter, but the initial and medial forms have a tail above the body of the letter instead. The letter *laam* looks a bit like *'alif*, but it is a connector. Its isolated and final forms have hooks that extend below the line.

	isolated	initial	medial	final
k	ك	كـ	ـكـ	ـك
l	ل	لـ	ـلـ	ـل

فِكْرَة	*fikra* (idea)	مَلِك	*malik* (king)
وَلَد	*walad* (boy)	لَيْل	*layl* (night)

For more practice, begin reading *Group 10: ك k, ل l, م m and ن n* and reading practice 11 of *Part 2: Reading Arabic* in the *Complete Guide to Arabic Script.*

121 **Cultural Note** Visiting the Doctor

A common preconception about going to the doctor in the Middle East is that male doctors are not permitted to see female patients, regardless of the emergency at hand, because of a religious belief that the woman's body is sacred and may only be seen by a close male relative. This is really not the case in most Middle Eastern countries, which do not have such strict rules regarding contact between doctors and their patients. This very strict application of codes of modesty applies mostly to Saudi Arabia, and many in the West have come to associate them, inaccurately and unfairly, with the entire region.

Even in Saudi Arabia, though, most hospitals are staffed by women doctors who deal exclusively with female patients. This allows hospitals to provide proper medical attention to all patients while still respecting religious and cultural beliefs. There is no clear protocol regarding female doctors examining male patients, but the expected norm is that male doctors examine male patients. In an emergency these rules can be bent and a female doctor can attend to a male patient. Rules in the reverse direction—male doctors attending to female patients—are not quite as flexible. It's therefore important to keep in mind the unique strictness of religious interpretation regarding the human body, even in medicine, when living or traveling in Saudi Arabia.

Lesson 12 Answer Key

Vocabulary Practice: 1. *rukba*; 2. *al-qalb*; 3. *'anfii*; 4. *jarraaH jayyid*; 5. *ad-damm al-'aHmar*; 6. *dimaaghuhu*; 7. *Tabiibii, Tabiibatii*; 8. *xaynuka*. 9. *xindii Sudaax*. 10. *hal xindii Haraara*? 11. *dhiraaxuhaa Saghiira*. 12. *wajh al-bint jamiil* 13. *'ayna l-mustashfaa*? 14. *laa 'axrifu*. 15. *(naHnu) najlisu*. 16. *laa 'aftaHu sh-shubbaak*. **Exercise 1:** 1. *sa-taqra'iina l-jariida*. / *sawfa taqra'iina l-jariida*. (You will read the newspaper.) 2. *sa-'adrusu l-xarabiyya*. / *sawfa 'adrusu l-xarabiyya*. (I will study Arabic.) 3. *sa-yashrabu ka's maa'*. / *sawfa yashrabu ka's maa'*. (He will drink a glass of water.) 4. *sa-nadh-habu 'ilaa l-maTaar*. / *sawfa nadh-habu 'ilaa l-maTaar*. (We will go to the airport.) 5. *sa-yarjixuuna*. / *sawfa yarjixuuna*. (They will come back.) **Exercise 2:** a): *'anta taSilu, huwa yaSilu, hiya taSilu, 'antum taSiluuna, hum yaSiluuna, humaa taSilaani*; b): *'anaa 'abiixu, 'anti tabiixiina, hiya tabiixu, 'antumaa tabiixaani naHnu nabiixu, 'antunna tabixna, humaa yabiixaani*; c): *'anaa 'amshii, 'anti tamshiina, huwa yamshii, 'antumaa tamshiyaani*, / *'antum tamshuuna, hum yamshuuna*; d): *'anaa 'ajii'u, 'anta tajii'u, huwa yajii'u, 'antumaa taiii'aani, naHnu najii'u, hum yajii'uuna, hunna yaji'na, humaa tajii'aani*; e): *'anta taraa, 'anti tarayna, huwa yaraa, naHnu naraa, 'antunna tarayna, hum yarawna, humaa yaraani*. **Exercise 3:** 1. *takallam bi buT'in min faDlika, yaa sayyid*. 2. *'uktubii al-xunwaan min faDliki yaa sayyida*. 3. *'axTinii l-faatuura, yaa sayyid*. 4. *'axiidii min faDliki, yaa sayyidati*. 5. *xafwan, yaa sayyidii*. 6. *safaran saxiidan*. 7. *xiid milaad saxiid*! 8. *'alf mabruuk, yaa Sadiiqii / Sadiiqatii*. 9. *'axTinii l-kitaab min faDlika, ya 'ustaadh / 'axtiinii l-kitaab min faDliki, yaa 'ustaadha*.

LESSON 13

WHERE DO YOU WORK? *maa hiya mihnatuka?*

In Lesson 13 you'll learn how to speak about your job, including important vocabulary for the office. You'll also learn the first of two important variations of the present tense that you can use with verbs such as "can" or "want" or "like."

13A Dialogue

bashiir	***amiir?***
amiir	***bashiir, 'ahlan wa sahlan! hal turiidu musaaxadatii?***
bashiir	***'ahlan wa sahlan. hal katabta at-taqriir?***
amiir	***naxam. katabtuhu haadhaa S-SabaaH. wa 'arsaltuhu 'ilaa l-mudiir.***
bashiir	***mumtaaz! hal yumkin 'an tufarriqahu xalaa kull mudiir 'ayDan? yajibu 'an tufarriqahu qabla haadhaa l-masaa'.***
amiir	***tabxan. sawfa 'ursiluhu bi l-faaks 'ilaa l-maktab fii nyuu yuurk 'ayDan.***
bashiir	***jayyid, amiir. hal xindaka waqt faarigh yawm al-jumuxaa'?***
amiir	***'anaa mashghuul baxda l-ghadaa', wa laakin xindii waqt faarigh fii S-SabaaH. hal xindaka 'ijtimaax?***
bashiir	***xindanaa zabuun jadiid fii s-saaxa 'iHda xashar, wa 'uriidu 'an takuuna hunaaka. haadhaa z-zabuun muhimm.***
amiir	***Tabxan. sawfa 'akuunu hunaaka.***
Bashiir	Amiir?
Amiir	Bashiir, hello! Do you want my help?
Bashiir	Hello. Have you written the report?
Amiir	Yes. I wrote it this morning, and I sent it to the director.
Bashiir	Great! Can you distribute it to all the directors, too? You need to distribute it before this evening.
Amiir	Of course. I'll also fax a copy to the New York office.
Bashiir	Good, Amiir. Do you have some free time on Friday?

Amiir	I'm busy after lunch, but I have free time in the morning. Do you have a meeting?
Bashiir	We have a new client at 11:00, and I want you to be there. This client is important.
Amiir	Of course. I'll be there.

13B Language Notes

Notice that the name of this lesson is *maa hiya mihnatuka*, translated as "Where Do You Work?" A more literal translation of the phrase, though, is "What is Your Profession," and word-for-word the phrase is "What [is] She/it, Your Work?" Don't forget that since the word *mihna* (work, profession) is feminine, the pronoun *hiya* (she, it) must step in to replace it. By using both the pronoun *hiya* and the noun *mihna*, the topic of the question receives more focus in Arabic. You'll see many sentences in Arabic that use both nouns and corresponding pronouns, as you learned in lesson 9.

When the possessive suffix *-ka* is added to the noun *mihna*, notice that the "hidden t" is pronounced, giving you *mihnatuka*. In other grammatical circumstances, it could be *mihnatika* or *mihnataka*, as you saw in lesson 11.

Did you notice all of the possessive and direct object prefixes in the dialogue? For example, *musaaxadatii* (my help) or *katabtuhu* (I wrote it).

In this dialogue you saw a lot of verbs such as *'uriidu* (I want) or *yajibu* (must, have to) followed by *'an* and then another verb. This is the equivalent of the English "want to" or "have to" plus another verb, and in Arabic, that second verb will be in a form known as the subjunctive. It's very similar to the regular present tense, and you'll learn all about it in this lesson.

Notice that when Bashir says "I want you to be there" he uses that special form of "be" that you learned in the last lesson—*'uriidu 'an takuuna hunaaka*. Literally, that's "I want that you be there." Since there are no infinitives (to be, to go, to do, etc.) in Arabic, a construction with *'an* plus the subjunctive is used here.

13C Vocabulary

xamal	job
mihna / mihan	profession, work
sharika / sharikaat	company
maxmal	factory
zabuun	client
muwaDHDHaf / −uun	employee
mudiir / −uun	director
ra'iis / ru'asaa'	manager/head
daa'ira	department
daa'irat al-bayx	sales department
kaatiba	secretary
kaatib	secretary, clerk
muHaasib	bookkeeper/accountant
simsaar	broker
baa'ix	salesman
'ijtimaax	meeting
taqriir	report
Suura / Suwar	copy, picture, photograph
al-faaks	fax
jadwal / jadaawil	schedule
Haasuub, kumbyuutar	computer
milaff / milaffaat	file
mashghuul / −uun	busy
waqt faarigh	free time
muhimm / −uun	important
Tawiil	long, lengthy
qaSiir	short, brief
xamila / yaxmalu	work
farraqa / yufarriqu	give out, distribute
Sawwara / yuSawwiru	copy
bada'a / yabda'u	begin, start
kammala / yukammilu	finish, complete

13D Vocabulary Practice

Translate the following sentences.

1. I have a new job.
2. This is the new director.
3. The sales department is not big.

4. This important client will come to the office.
5. They worked a lot.
6. We wrote the important file.
7. The file is at the office.
8. The computer and the report are in the office.
9. She is busy on Thursday.
10. The meeting was long.

13E Grammar and Usage

1 The Subjunctive

You've already learned that there are two basic tenses in Arabic—the past and the present. These are the verb forms that you'll use most of the time. However, there are a few important situations where you'll have to use a special "mood" or variation of the present tense. There are two of these moods or variations in Arabic, technically called the subjunctive and the jussive. Their forms are very similar to the present tense. In this lesson we'll focus on the subjunctive.

The forms of the subjunctive are almost identical to the present tense. The first major difference is that the *-na* / *-ni* endings in the present tense *'anti*, *'antum*, *hum*, and dual forms are dropped in the subjunctive. The other difference is that the *-u* of the *'anaa*, *'anta*, *huwa*, *hiya*, and *naHnu* becomes an *-a*. But remember that the *-u* of the present tense is often dropped in informal spoken Arabic, and so is the *-a* of the subjunctive. So, in many cases, the *'anaa, 'anta, huwa, hiya*, and *naHnu* forms will sound alike in the present tense and subjunctive. Let's compare the present tense and subjunctive forms of *faxala* / *yafxalu-* (do) and *darasa* / *yadrusu-* (study). Again, you'll see the *-u* and *-a* endings to help you distinguish between the forms.

	***faxala*– pres.**	***faxala*– subj.**	***darasa*– pres.**	***darasa*– subj.**
'anaa	*'afxalu*	*'afxala*	*'adrusu*	*'adrusa*
'anta	*tafxalu*	*tafxala*	*tadrusu*	*tadrusa*
'anti	*tafxaliina*	*tafxalii*	*tadrusiina*	*tadrusii*
huwa	*yafxalu*	*yafxala*	*yadrusu*	*yadrusa*
hiya	*tafxalu*	*tafxala*	*tadrusu*	*tadrusa*
'antumaa	*tafxalaani*	*tafxalaa*	*tadrusaani*	*tadrusaa*
naHnu	*nafxalu*	*nafxala*	*nadrusu*	*nadrusa*
'antum	*tafxaluuna*	*tafxaluu*	*tadrusuuna*	*tadrusuu*
'antunna	*tafxalna*	*tafxalna*	*tadrusna*	*tadrusna*
hum	*yafxaluuna*	*yafxaluu*	*yadrusuuna*	*yadrusuu*
hunna	*yafxalna*	*yafxalna*	*yadrusna*	*yadrusna*
humaa (m.)	*yafxalaani*	*yafxalaa*	*yadrusaani*	*yadrusaa*
humaa (f.)	*tafxalaani*	*tafxalaa*	*tadrusaani*	*tadrusaa*

There is a subjunctive in English, and its uses are rather limited. For example, the subjunctive is used after "that" with such verbs as "require" or "request"—"I requested that he give me the report" or "It is required that each employee have ID." The situation is similar in Arabic, where the subjunctive is used after certain words such as: *'an* (to), *lan* (will not), *'allaa* (not to), *Hattaa* (so that), and *likay* (in order to). All in all, the subjunctive is used more frequently in Arabic than in English.

yajibu 'an tufarriqahu.
You need to distribute it. (It is required that you . . .)

yajibu 'an yaktuba at-taqriir.
He must write the report. (It is required that he . . .)

ji'tu baakiran likay 'adh-haba 'ilaa l-'ijtimaax.
I arrived early in order to go to the meeting. (. . . in order that I go . . .)

2 Can, Want to, Like to, Have to, and Must

One of the most important uses of the subjunctive is with the verbs *yuriidu* (want), *yuHibbu* (like, love), and *yastaTiixu* (can, be able). These verbs are conjugated and followed by *'an* and then the conjugated form of the second verb in the subjunctive. Here is the full present tense conjugation of each of these important verbs.

(want): *'anaa 'uriidu; 'anta turiidu; 'anti turiidiina; huwa yuriidu; hiya turiidu; 'antumaa turiidaani; naHnu nuriidu; 'antum turiiduuna; antunna turidna; hum yuriiduuna; hunna yuridna; humaa* (m.) *yuriidaani; humaa* (f.) *turiidaani*

(like, love): *'anaa 'uHibbu; 'anta tuHibbu; 'anti tuHibbiina; huwa yuHibbu; hiya tuHibbu; 'antumaa tuHibbaani; naHnu nuHibbu; 'antum tuHibbuuna; antunna tuHbibna; hum yuHibbuuna; hunna yuHbibna; humaa* (m.) *yuHibbaani; humaa* (f.) *tuHibbaani.*

(can, be able): *'anaa 'astaTiixu; 'anta tastaTiixu; 'anti tastaTiixiina; huwa yastaTiixu; hiya tastaTiixu; 'antumaa tastaTiixaani; naHnu nastaTiixu; 'antum tastaTiixuuna; 'antunna tastaTixna; hum yastaTiixuuna; hunna yastaTixna; humaa* (m.) *yastaTiixaani; humaa* (f.) *tastaTiixaani*

al-mudiir yuriidu 'an yadh-haba 'ilaa l-'ijtimaax.
The director wants to go to the meeting.

nuHibbu 'an natakallama al-xarabiyya.
We like to speak Arabic.

tuHibbu 'an tadh-haba 'ilaa l-bustaan yawm as-sabt.
You like to go the garden on Saturday.

'uriidu 'an 'adrusa l-xarabiyya.
I want to study Arabic.

Notice that there can be different subjects in the present tense and subjunctive forms. In the English translation, there will be a pronoun followed by an infinitive, such as "you to go" or "me to do."

'ustaadhatunaa turiidu 'an nadrusa l-xarabiyya kathiiran.
Our professor wants us to study Arabic a lot.

al-mudiir yuriidu 'an 'adh-haba 'ilaa l-'ijtimaax 'ayDan.
The director wants me to go to the meeting also.

The subjunctive is also used after *mumkin/yumkin* (possible) and *yajibu* (necessary, must). Remember that *mumkin* and *yumkin* are interchangeable, and they are translated as "can" in the sense of "possible" (as opposed to "able or capable of") The word *yajibu* translates as "have to," "need to" or "must" in the sense of "necessary to" None of these forms changes to agree with the subject. The subject is shown by the conjugation of the verb that follows them, and that verb is in the subjunctive.

yajibu 'an 'adh-haba 'ilaa l-xamal ghadan.
I have to go to work tomorrow.

yajibu 'an yadh-haba 'ilaa l-xamal ghadan.
He has to go to work tomorrow.

Finally, the subjunctive is used to make negative statements in the future. We'll come back to that in lesson 14.

❸ Review of Possessive and Object Suffixes

Remember that both object pronouns (me, you, us) and possessive adjectives (my, your, our) are suffixes in Arabic, which are attached to either a verb or a noun. You saw many examples of them in the dialogue. Let's review them all now.

-ii / –nii	my, me	*-naa*	us, our
-ka	you, your (m.)	-kum	you, your (m. pl.)
-ki	you, your (f.)	-kunna	you, your (f. pl.)
-hu	him, his, it, its	-hum	them, their (m. or mixed)
-haa	her, it, its, them, their	-hunna	them, their (f.)
-kumaa	the two of you, belonging to the two of you	-humaa	the two of them, belonging to the two of them

Don't forget that the ending *–ii* is used with nouns to mean "my," and the ending *–nii* is used with verbs to mean "me." Also remember that in Arabic, non-human plurals are considered feminine singulars, so the ending *–haa* with nouns can mean "her" or "its" (with non-human feminine singular nouns) or even "their" (with non-human plurals). When *-haa* is attached to verbs, then, it can mean "her," "it" or "them."

al-kitaab? 'anaa waDaxtuhu xalaa T-Taawila.	The book? I put it on the table.
al-kutub? 'anaa waDaxtuhaa xalaa T-Taawila.	The books? I put them on the table.
hal taraanii?	Do you see me?
hal taraahum?	Do you see them?

maktabuhu laysa kabiir.	His office is not big.
maktabuki laysa kabiir.	Your office is not big.
hal kalbuka laTiif?	Is your dog friendly?
hal kilaabukum laTiifa?	Are your dogs friendly?

This is a case where you may encounter those "noun case" changes in the form of an *–i* or *–a* instead of *–u* between the noun and the possessive suffix. Even the *–u* of the ending may change to an *–i*, such as in *–hu* or *–hum*.

naHnu fii ghurfatihim maxa Sadiiqihim.	We are in their room with their friend.
turiidu 'an 'adh-haba 'ilaa maktabika.	You want me to go to your office.

And don't forget that the "hidden t" of feminine nouns is pronounced before these suffixes, and it can be followed by a *–u*, *–i*, or *–a* depending on how that noun is used in the sentence.

sayyaaratuki mumtaaza!	You car is great!
hal hunaaka jaamixa fii madiinatika?	Is there a university in your city?

4 Review of Verb Tenses

You've now learned both important tenses, as well as one variation of the present tense. Let's review the system of verb tenses by comparing the forms of two verbs, *kataba / yaktubu*—write, and *fataHa / yaftaHu*—open.

kataba / yaktubu	**Past**	**Present**	**Subjunctive**
'anaa	*katabtu*	*'aktubu*	*'aktuba*
'anta	*katabta*	*taktubu*	*taktuba*
'anti	*katabti*	*taktubiina*	*taktubii*
huwa	*kataba*	*yaktubu*	*yaktuba*
hiya	*katabat*	*taktubu*	*taktuba*
'antumaa	*katabtumaa*	*taktubaani*	*taktubaa*
naHnu	*katabnaa*	*naktubu*	*naktuba*
'antum	*katabtum*	*taktubuuna*	*taktubuu*
'antunna	*katabtunna*	*taktubna*	*taktubna*
hum	*katabuu*	*yaktubuuna*	*yaktubuu*
hunna	*katabna*	*yaktubna*	*yaktubna*
humaa (m.)	*katabaa*	*yaktubaani*	*yaktubaa*
humaa (f.)	*katabataa*	*taktubaani*	*taktubaa*

fataHa / yaftaHu	Past	Present	Subjunctive
'anaa	*fataHtu*	*'aftaHu*	*'aftaHa*
'anta	*fataHta*	*taftaHu*	*taftaHa*
'anti	*fataHti*	*taftaHiina*	*taftaHii*
huwa	*fataHa*	*yaftaHu*	*yaftaHa*
hiya	*fataHat*	*taftaHu*	*taftaHa*
'antumaa	*fataHtumaa*	*taftaHaani*	*taftaHaa*
naHnu	*fataHnaa*	*naftaHu*	*naftaHa*
'antum	*fataHtum*	*taftaHuuna*	*taftaHuu*
'antunna	*fataHtunna*	*taftaHna*	*taftaHna*
hum	*fataHuu*	*yaftaHuuna*	*yaftaHuu*
hunna	*fataHna*	*yaftaHna*	*yaftaHna*
humaa (m.)	*fataHaa*	*yaftaHaani*	*yaftaHaa*
humaa (f.)	*fataHataa*	*taftaHaani*	*taftaHaa*

13F Grammar and Usage Exercises

Exercise 1 Fill in the blanks in the following table, giving the missing subjunctive forms of *Tabakha / yaTbukhu*, cook, and *rajaxa / yarjixu* come back, return.

	Tabakha– pres.	*Tabakha–* subj.	*rajaxa–* pres.	*rajaxa–* subj.
'anaa	*'aTbukhu*		*'arjixu*	
'anta	*taTbukhu*		*tarjixu*	
'anti	*taTbukhiina*		*tarjixiina*	
huwa	*yaTbukhu*		*yarjixu*	
hiya	*taTbukhu*		*tarjixu*	
'antumaa	*taTbukhaani*		*tarjixaani*	
naHnu	*naTbukhu*		*narjixu*	
'antum	*taTbukhuuna*		*tarjixuuna*	
'antunna	*taTbukhna*		*tarjixna*	
hum	*yaTbukhuuna*		*yarjixuuna*	
hunna	*yaTbukhna*		*yarjixna*	
humaa (m.)	*yaTbukhaani*		*yarjixaani*	
humaa (f.)	*taTbukhaani*		*tarjixaani*	

Exercise 2 Fill in the blanks in the following sentences with the proper present tense form of the verb given in parentheses.

1. *maadhaa hiya ___________? (faxala / yafxalu)*
2. *'anaa ___________ 'ilaa l-masjid. (dhahaba / yadh-habu)*

3. *naHnu __________ l-baab. (fataHa / yaftaHu)*
4. *'anta __________ fii l-kulliyya. (darasa / yadrusu)*
5. *ar-rajul __________ l-xashaa'. (Tabakha / yaTbukhu)*
6. *'anaa laa __________ kutub. (qara'a / yaqra'u)*
7. *hum __________ fii l-maktab. (kataba / yaktubu)*
8. *maadhaa 'antum __________? ('akala ya'kulu)*
9. *al-banaat __________ 'ilaa l-maktaba. (dhahaba / yadh-habu)*
10. *al-kalb __________ l-maa'. (shariba / yashrabu)*

Exercise 3 Write the correct form of the verb given in parentheses.

1. *Hasan yuriidu 'an __________ 'ilaa l-maktaba. (dhahaba / yadh-habu)*
2. *laylaa yajibu 'an __________ al-yawm. (darasa / yadrusu)*
3. *'anti turiidiina 'an __________ kitaaban jadiidan. (kataba / yaktubu)*
4. *maadhaa 'antum turiiduuna 'an __________? ('akala / ya'kulu)*
5. *naHnu yajibu 'an __________ al-ghad. (rajaxa / yarjixu)*
6. *maadhaa hum yastaTiixuuna 'an __________? (faxala / yafxalu)*

Exercise 4 Translate each of the following sentences into Arabic.

1. My sister went to the market with my mother.
2. My book is old.
3. This book? I read it yesterday.
4. We have to write the report.
5. His computer is new.
6. Bashiir, your office is close to my office.

13G Pronunciation Practice *s, d, t,* and *dh* vs. *S, D, T,* and *DH*

Let's review the differences in pronunciation between the so-called "emphatic" consonants *S, D, T,* and *DH* and their non-emphatic counterparts *s, d, t,* and *dh*. Remember that the emphatic consonants are pronounced with the tongue low in the mouth, cradled between the lower teeth. This gives the vowels near emphatic consonants a very deep quality. Listen to the differences and repeat.

sabaka, SabaaH, sunbuk, SubH, sarraa' Sarra, siimaa, Siiniyya
daraa, Darra, durr, Durr, dirra, Dirr, dariba, Daraba, daqiiq, SaDiiq
tiik, Tiin, tunn, Tunn, tannuub, Tanna, tumbaak, TamaaTim, talliis, Taliiq
dhalla, DHalla, dhakiyy, DHabiyy, dhull, DHulla, dhiraax, DHirr, dhahaba, DHahara

13H Arabic Script The Letters *miim*, *nuun*, and *haa'*

Now let's focus on the letters *miim*, *nuun*, and *haa'*, which we've been transcribing *m*, *n*, and *h*. All three of these letters are connectors. Notice that there are two main variations on the forms of *miim*—a hook with a tail for the final and isolated forms, and a loop for the initial and medial. The forms of *nuun* are a simple peak with a dot above it in the initial and medial positions, but a dotted open loop that extends below the line for the final and isolated forms. The letter *haa'* has a rather unique form for each of the four positions.

	isolated	initial	medial	final
m	م	مـ	ـمـ	ـم
n	ن	نـ	ـنـ	ـن
h	ه	هـ	ـهـ	ـه

ميم	*miim* (the letter)	سَمِين	*samiin* (fat)
نون	*nuun* (the letter)	نَهْج	*nahj* (street)
مَوْهُوم	*mawhuum* (imagined)	هَذِهِ	*haadhihi* (this)

For more practice, continue reading *Group 10:* ك *k,* ل *l,* م *m and* ن *n*, and also read *Group 11:* ه *h and* ة *a*, reading practice 11, and reading practice 12 of *Part 2: Reading Arabic* in the *Complete Guide to Arabic Script*. You can also practice writing with Groups 10 and 11 and writing practices 24–27 of *Part 3: Writing Arabic*. And finally, you're ready to practice reading Dialogue 1 of *Part 4: Reading Passages*.

13I Cultural Note The Economy and Educational System in the Middle East

The economy of most Middle Eastern countries revolves around the exportation of energy products. The Middle East produces more than 50% of the world's global energy needs, in terms of both oil and natural gas. Saudi Arabia contains more than half of the world's proven oil reserves, and Iraq has the second largest proven oil reserves. As a result, the Middle Eastern business climate, particularly in the Gulf states, is dominated by multinational corporations in the energy sector. Other countries that aren't heavy exporters of oil or natural gas are nevertheless big exporters of other raw materials. Morocco, for instance, is the largest exporter of phosphate in the world.

The educational system is influenced by this economic structure. Most public schools are secular in nature and place a heavy emphasis on math and the sciences, with an additional focus on languages. The educational system is structured similarly to the European or American one, with pre-school, middle school, and high school. Universities offer a wide range of programs of study, some very similar to American or European universities, and others more tailored to the economic and social environment, with degrees in such areas as petrochemical engineering or Islamic clerical law.

Lesson 13 Answer Key

Vocabulary Practice: 1. *xindii xamal jadiid*. 2. *haadhaa huwa al-mudiir al-jadiid*. 3. *daa'irat al-bayx laysat kabiira*. 4. *haadhaa z-zubuun al-muhimm sa–yajii'u 'ilaa l-maktab*. 5. *xamiluu kathiiran*. 6. *katabna l-milaff al-muhimm*. 7. *al-milaff fii l-maktab*. 8. *al-Hasuub/kumbyuutar wa t-taqriir fii l-maktab*. 9. *hiya mashghuula yawm al-khamiis*. 10. *al-'ijtimaax kaana Tawiil*. **Exercise 1:** *Tabakha*: *'aTbukha, taTbukha, taTbukhii, yaTbukha, taTbukha, taTbukhaa, naTbukha, taTbukhuu, taTbukhna, yaTbukhuu, yaTbukhna, yaTbukhaa, taTbukhaa*. *raxaja: 'arjixa, tarjixa, tarjixii, yarjixa, tarjixa, tarjixaa, narjixa, tarjixuu, tarjixna, yarjixuu, yarjixna, yarjixaa, tarjixaa* **Exercise 2:** 1. *tafxalu*; 2. *'adh-habu*; 3. *naftaHu*; 4. *tadrusu;* 5. *yaTbukhu*; 6. *'aqra'u*; 7. *yaktubuuna*; 8. *ta'kuluuna*; 9. *yadh-habna*; 10. *yashrabu* **Exercise 3:** 1. *yadh-haba*; 2. *tadrusa*; 3. *taktubii*; 4. *ta'kuluu*; 5. *narjixa;* 6. *yafxaluu* **Exercise 4:** 1. *'ukhtii dhahabat 'ilaa s-suuq maxa 'ummii*. 2. *kitaabii qadiim*. 3. *haadhaa l-kitaab? qara'tuhu l-baariHa*. 4. *yajibu 'an naktuba t-taqriir*. 5. *Haasuubuhu jadiid*. / *kumbyuutaruhu jadiid*. 6. *bashiir, maktabuka qariib min maktabii*.

LESSON 14

I WOULD LIKE TO CHANGE $100
'uriidu 'an 'aSrifa mi'at duulaar

The dialogue in lesson 14 focuses on an important matter everyone has to deal with—money. So, you'll learn useful vocabulary for banks and other practical situations. You'll also review possessive constructions and negatives, and you'll learn the second important mood or variation of the present tense, the jussive.

14A Dialogue

Mary needs to change some money. Let's listen in as she speaks to the bank teller.

mari	***'uriidu 'an 'aSrifa duulaaraat 'ilaa daraahim.***
'amiin al-maSrif	***kam min duulaar turiidiina 'an tuSarrifii?***
mari	***mi'at duulaar min faDlika.***
'amiin al-maSrif	***hal xindaki jawaaz safariki?***
mari	***naxam. haa huwa.***
'amiin al-maSrif	***shukran. kayfa turiidiina l-fuluus?***
mari	***xashrat 'awraaq min faDlika.***
'amiin al-maSrif	***yajibu l-'imDaa' hunaa min faDliki.***
mari	***tabxan.***
'amiin al-maSrif	***sayyidatii, lam taktubii raqm jawaaz as-safar.***
mari	***xafwan. lam 'arahu fii l-'istimaara. haa huwa.***
'amiin al-maSrif	***shukran. tafaDDalii.***
mari	***shukran jaziilan.***
Mary	I would like to exchange dollars for dirhams.
Teller	How many dollars would you like to change?
Mary	$100, please.
Teller	Do you have your passport?
Mary	Yes. Here it is.
Teller	Thank you. How would you like the money?
Mary	Ten bills, please.
Teller	You need to sign here please.
Mary	Of course.
Teller	Ma'am, you didn't write your passport number.
Mary	I'm sorry. I didn't see it on the form. Here it is.
Teller	Thank you. Here you go.
Mary	Thank you very much.

14B Language Notes

In this dialogue, Mary asks to exchange dollars for dirhams, which are used in both Morocco and the Emirates. Here is a summary of all the currencies found across the Arab world:

Egypt–Egyptian Pound (*junayh miSriyy*)
Saudi Arabia–Saudi riyal (*riyaal saxuudiyy*)
Algeria–Algerian dinar (*diinaar jazaa'iriyy*)
Morocco–Moroccan dirham (*dirham maghribiyy*)
Kuwait–Kuwaiti dinar (*diinaar kuwaytiyy*)
Oman–Omani rial (*riyaal xumaaniyy*)
Bahrain–Bahraini dinar (*diinaar baHrayniyy*)
Qatar–Qatari rial (*riyaal qaTariyy*)
United Arab Emirates–Emirati dirham (*dirham al-imaraat*)
Yemen–Yemeni rial (*riyaal yamaniyy*)
Tunisia–Tunisian dinar (*diinaar tuunisiyy*)
Libya–Libyan dinar (*diinaar liibiyy*)
Syria–Syrian pound (*liira suuriyya*)
Lebanon–Lebanese pound (*liira lubnaaniyya*)
Jordan–Jordanian dinar (*diinaar 'urduniyy*)
Iraq–Iraqi dinar (*diinaar xiraqiyy*)
Palestine–Jordanian dinar, US dollar, Israeli Shekel (*diinaar 'urduniyy, duulaar 'amriikiyy, shakal 'israa'iiliyy*)

Notice the use of the subjunctive forms *'uSarrifa* and *tuSarrifii* in the first two lines of the dialogue. They both follow the expressions meaning "I want to . . . " and "do you want to . . . "

Look at the expression for "passport" in the question *hal xindaki jawaaz safariki* (do you have your passport) and in the phrase *lam taktubii raqm jawaaz as-safar* (you didn't write the number of your passport). Notice that the expression is a possessive noun construction (literally, "permit of the traveling"), so the second noun, *as-safar*, has to be definite. But in the first example, the noun has a possessive suffix on it, *-ki*, which makes it definite without the need for *al-*. Also notice the *-i* in *safariki* in that example. This *-i* is there because it is the second element of a possessive construction—the "possessor" noun. This is another example of the genitive case, which you can read more about in the Grammar Summary.

Take a closer look at the phrase that the teller uses to say "you need to sign." He says *yajibu l-'imDaa'*. As you can see, the second part of the expression is not *'an* + a subjunctive. The word *al-'imDaa'* is a noun. So, you could translate this literally as "it's necessary, the signing." A more literal translation of "you need to sign" is *yajibu 'an tumDii*, but *yajibu l-'imDaa'* is equally correct.

Do you see a connection between the noun *'imDaa'* (signing) and the verb *'amDaa / yumDii* (sign)? Notice that they share the same root consonants. Arabic verbs, like English verbs, can be made into nouns and used in cases such as the example in this dialogue For instance, you know that *yadhhabu* means "he goes," but *adh-dhahaab* means "the act of going." Similarly, *yadrusu* (study) can become *ad-diraasa* (studying) and *yaktubu* (write) can become *al-kitaaba* (writing). Don't worry about the particulars now, but as you advance in your studies of Arabic you'll come across these forms. For now, just remember to look out for familiar consonant roots of verbs that you know. There is a section on verbal nouns in the Grammar Summary if you'd like to read more about them, though.

The phrase *lam taktubii* is a negative in the past tense, meaning "you didn't sign." Arabic negatives take different forms depending on their tense. In this case, a negative past verb is in a form called the jussive, which is the second important variation on the present tense. The *'anti* form of the jussive is identical to the subjunctive form, but there are other differences that you'll learn in this lesson. The present tense form of this verb would be *taktubiina*, as you know.

14C Vocabulary

xumla	money
fuluus	money, physical currency
maal	money, wealth
naqd / nuquud	coin
waraqa / 'awraaq	bill, paper money, sheet of paper
biTaaqat al-'istilaaf	credit card
bitaaqaat al-'istilaaf	credit cards
shiik	check
maSrif / maSaarif	bank

Hisaab maSrifiyy	bank account
'amiin al-maSrif	bank teller
'istimaara / –aat	form
raqm sirriyy	PIN number
jawaaz as-safar	passport
rukhSa	license
Sarf	exchange
waSl	receipt
'imDaa'	signing, signature
'amDaa / yumDii	sign
'awdaxa / yuudixu	deposit
saHaba / yasHabu	withdraw
'iddakhara / yaddakhiru	save
rabaHa / yarbaHu	earn money
Sarafa / yaSrifu	exchange (currency)
'ayDan	too, also, as well
maktab al-bariid	post office
risaala / rasaa'il	letter
xunwaan	address
bariid	mail
bariid jawwiyy	air mail
DHarf	envelope
Taabix / Tawaabix	stamp
biTaaqa baariidiyya	post card
wazn	weight
raqm / 'arqaam	number
raqm al-madiina	ZIP code, city postal code
barada / yabridu	to mail
kayyala /yukayyilu	to weigh
'arsala / yursilu	to send
qabala / yaqbalu	to receive/to accept
bariid 'iliktruuniyy	e-mail
xunwaan 'iliktruuniyy	e-mail address
risaala 'iliktruuniyya	(e-mail) message
'intarnat	internet

14D Vocabulary Practice

Translate the following sentences.

1. This is a long form.
2. This is not my signature.

3. I don't know her address.
4. This bank is not close to my house.
5. I have a bank account in this bank.
6. I want a stamp and an envelope.
7. Does she have a credit card?
8. Your check, sir
9. I wrote a short letter.
10. The receipt is in the car.
11. Where is the post office?
12. She wrote a letter.
13. This is his signature.

14E Grammar and Usage

1 Review of Possessive Noun Constructions

Take a look at the following examples of possessive constructions that appear in this lesson.

biTaaqat l-'istilaaf	credit card (card of credit)
maktab al-bariid	post office (office of the mail)
raqm al-madiina	postal code (number of the city)

Don't forget that possessive noun constructions are formed simply by placing nouns together, first the thing that is possessed, and then the possessor, with an "invisible of" between them. The second noun, the possessor, is prefixed with the definite article. This can translate as an apostrophe-s construction or a phrase with "of," as in: *maktab ar-rajul*, "the man's office" or "the office of the man."

This construction can also be used for phrases that denote quantities or portions of something.

ka's al-maa'	the glass of water
qaaruurat al-khamr	the bottle of wine

Don't forget to use a definite adjective after the entire possessive phrase to describe either of the nouns. Grammar or context will usually tell you which noun the adjective is describing.

sayyaaratu l-mudiir al-jadiid	the new director's car
sayyaaratu l-mudiir al-jadiida	the director's new car

An indefinite adjective after a possessive noun phrase will create a sentence.

sayyaaratu l-mudiir jadiida.	The director's car is new.
kitaab at-tilmiidha jadiid.	The student's book is new.

Finally, don't forget that there are a few changes nouns may undergo in possessive constructions. The "hidden *t*" is pronounced in nouns that end with the feminine ending *–a* when they're in the position of what is possessed, the first noun. This is the case with the noun *sayyaara* (*sayyaarat*) in the examples above. That *–t* may be followed by a *–u* if the noun is the subject of a sentence, or an *–i* after a preposition, or an *–a* if it's the direct object.

sayyaaratu l-mudiir kabiira.	The director's car is big. (subject)
maHmuud fii sayyaarati l-mudiir.	Mahmoud is in the director's car. (after a preposition)
laa 'araa sayyaarata l-mudiir.	I don't see the director's car. (direct object)

If the possessor (second noun) is a masculine sound plural, the *–uun* ending will be replaced by *–iin.*

haadhihi hiya sayyaaraatu l-mudiiriin.	These are the directors' cars.
haadhaa huwa bayt al-miSriyyiin.	This is the Egyptians' house.

If that second noun has a possessive suffix on it, there will be an *–i–* between the noun and the suffix.

baab baytinaa 'azraq.	The door of our house is blue.
xaa'ilat Sadiiqatihaa taskunu fii l-qaahira.	The family of her friend lives in Cairo.

2 The Jussive

In lesson 13 you learned the subjunctive, which is a variation or "mood" of the present tense. Its most important use is after the particle *'an*, which means "to" after verbs like *yuriidu* (want), *yuHibbu* (like, love), *yajibu* (must, have to, it's necessary), *yumkin* / *mumkin* (can, is possible), and *yastaTi-*

ixu (can, able to). The subjunctive is also used after *lan* (will not), *'allaa* (not to), *Hattaa* (so that) and *likay* (in order to).

The jussive, like the subjunctive, is another important mood of the present tense with a few common uses. Its formation is very simple; its greatest difference is that it has no vowel ending where the present ends in *–u* and the subjunctive in *–a*. But again, remember that since the *–u* and *–a* endings are often not pronounced in informal spoken Arabic, the present, the subjunctive, and the jussive may sound alike in the *'anaa, 'anta, huwa, hiya,* and *naHnu* forms. Like the subjunctive, the *–na / –ni* ending of *'anti*, *'antum*, *hum* and the dual forms is dropped. Take a look at this table, which compares the present, subjunctive, and jussive of *faxala / yafxalu,* to do.

	present tense	**subjunctive**	**jussive**
'anaa	*'afxalu*	*'afxala*	*'afxal*
'anta	*tafxalu*	*tafxala*	*tafxal*
'anti	*tafxaliina*	*tafxalii*	*tafxalii*
huwa	*yafxalu*	*yafxala*	*yafxal*
hiya	*tafxalu*	*tafxala*	*tafxal*
'antumaa	*tafxalaani*	*tafxalaa*	*tafxalaa*
naHnu	*nafxalu*	*nafxala*	*nafxal*
'antum	*tafxaluuna*	*tafxaluu*	*tafxaluu*
'antunna	*tafxalna*	*tafxalna*	*tafxalna*
hum	*yafxaluuna*	*yafxaluu*	*yafxaluu*
hunna	*yafxalna*	*yafxalna*	*yafxalna*
humaa (m.)	*yafxalaani*	*yafxalaa*	*yafxalaa*
humaa (f.)	*tafxalaani*	*tafxalaa*	*tafxalaa*

As you can see, with the exception of the missing ending *–a*, the jussive is identical to the subjunctive in most cases.

There are, however, a few differences to note when it comes to "hollow" verbs (verbs with a missing *y* or *w* in the second root consonant position) and doubled verbs (verbs with the same second and third root consonants). (Turn back to lesson 12 to review these types of irregular verbs.) In hollow verbs, a short vowel often replaces the long vowel of the present tense. In doubled verbs, the double root consonants are often separated where they would be next to each other in the present tense. The following table compares these two cases to the present tense of two model verbs, *zaara / yazuuru*, visit, and *radda /yaruddu*, reply.

	present: hollow	jussive: hollow	present: doubled	jussive: doubled
'anaa	*'azuuru*	*'azur*	*'aruddu*	*'ardud*
'anta	*tazuuru*	*tazur*	*taruddu*	*tardud*
'anti	*tazuuriina*	*tazuurii*	*taruddiina*	*taruddii*
huwa	*yazuuru*	*yazur*	*yaruddu*	*yardud*
hiya	*tazuuru*	*tazur*	*taruddu*	*tardud*
'antumaa	*tazuuraani*	*tazuuraa*	*taruddaani*	*taruddaa*
naHnu	*nazuuru*	*nazur*	*naruddu*	*nardud*
'antum	*tazuuruuna*	*tazuuruu*	*tarudduuna*	*tarudduu*
'antunna	*tazurna*	*tazurna*	*tardudna*	*tardudna*
hum	*yazuuruuna*	*yazuuruu*	*yarudduuna*	*yarudduu*
hunna	*yazurna*	*yazurna*	*yardudna*	*yardudna*
humaa (m.)	*yazuuraani*	*yazuuraa*	*yaruddaani*	*yaruddaa*
humaa (f.)	*tazuuraani*	*tazuuraa*	*taruddaani*	*taruddaa*

If you think back to lesson 12 and the fact that doubled consonants occur only in positions right before a vowel, this makes more sense. Since the jussive doesn't have a final *–u* or *–a* in the *'anaa, 'anta, huwa, hiya* and *naHnu* forms, the doubled consonants cannot be written together. These are the same places where the present tense *–uu–* in *zaara / yazuuru* becomes *–u–* in the jussive.

❸ The Negative Past Tense

The most important use of the jussive is to form negative statements in the past tense. To make a negative past statement, such as "he didn't write," simply add *lam* before the jussive form of the verb.

kataba al-kitaab.	He wrote the book.
lam yaktub al-kitaab.	He didn't write the book.
dhahabtu 'ilaa l-maktaba l-'ams.	I went to the library yesterday.
lam 'adh-hab 'ilaa l-maktaba l-'ams.	I didn't go to the library yesterday.
lam yazuuruunii fii miSr.	They didn't visit me in Egypt.
lam tardud.	She didn't reply. / She hasn't replied.

❹ Summary of Negatives

As you've seen, forming negative sentences in Arabic is not necessarily as straightforward as it is in many other languages. Different verb forms are used depending on the tense of the negative, and there are special forms of the verb "to be." Let's take a moment to summarize negative sentences, reviewing what you've learned as well as filling in the gaps.

Present Tense: *laa* + Present Tense

'adrusu fii l-jaamixa. I study at the university.	*laa 'adrusu fii l-jaamixa.* I don't study at the university.
naHnu nashrabu sh-shaay. We are drinking tea.	*naHnu laa nashrabu sh-shaay.* We are not drinking tea.

Present Tense "To Be:" Special Verb *lastu*

al-'imra'a fii l-maktab. The woman is in the office.	*al-'imra'a laysat fii l-maktab.* The woman is not in the office.
'anaa bijaanibi Sadiiqii. I am next to my friend.	*'anaa lastu bijaanibi Sadiiqii.* I am not next to my friend.

If you'd like to review all of the negative forms of "to be," turn back to lesson 5.

Past Tense: *lam* + Jussive

aT-Tullaab qara'uu l-kutub. The students read the books.	*aT-Tullaab lam yaqra'uu l-kutub.* The students didn't read the books.
al-kuumbyuutar al-jadiid waSala al-'ams. The new computer arrived yesterday.	*al-kuumbyuutar al-jadiid lam yaSil al-'ams.* The new computer didn't arrive yesterday.

Past Tense "To Be:" *lam* + *yakun*

The verb *yakun* is a jussive form of the verb *yakuunu* (be) that you learned in lesson 12. The full conjugation is: *'anaa 'akun, 'anta takun, 'anti takuunii, hiya takun, huwa yakun, 'antumaa takuunaa, naHnu nakun, 'antum takuunuu, 'antunna takunna, hum yakuunuu, hunna yakunna, humaa* (m.) *yakuunaa, humaa* (f.) *takuunaa*

'anaa kuntu fii l-maktab. I was in the office.	*'anaa lam 'akun fii l-maktab.* I was not in the office.
naHnu kunnaa maxa l-mudiir. We were with the director.	*naHnu lam nakun maxa l-mudiir.* We were not with the director.

Future Tense: *lan* + Subjunctive (without *sa–* or *sawfa*)

al-'awlaad sa-yadrusuuna l-xarabiyya.	*al-'awlaad lan yadrusuu l-xarabiyya.*
The boys will study Arabic.	The boys will not study Arabic.
zamiilii sa-yafxalu haadhaa.	*zamiilii lan yafxala haadhaa.*
My colleague will do this.	My colleague will not do this.

Future Tense "To Be:" *lan* + *yakuuna*

The verb *yakuuna* is a subjunctive form of the verb *yakuunu* (be) that you learned in lesson 12. The full conjugation is: *'anaa 'akuuna, 'anta takuuna, 'anti takuunii, hiya takuuna, huwa yakuuna, 'antumaa takuunaa, naHnu nakuuna, 'antum takuunuu, 'antunna takunna, hum yakuunuu, hunna yakunna, humaa* (m.) *yakuunaa, humaa* (f.) *takuunaa*

naHnu sa-nakuunu maxa Sadiiqinaa.	*naHnu lan nakuuna maxa Sadiiqinaa.*
We will be with our friend.	We will not be with our friend.
ar-rijaal sawfa yakuunuuna fii tuunis ghadan.	*ar-rijaal lan yakuunuu fii tuunis ghadan.*
The men will be in Tunisia tomorrow.	The men won't be in Tunisia tomorrow.

14F Grammar and Usage Exercises

Exercise 1 Combine the following nouns and adjectives to form possessive noun phrases or sentences, and then translate your answers.

1. *qalam / tilmiidh / 'azraq* (sentence)
2. *kalb / 'imra'a / laTiif* (phrase)
3. *kalb / 'imra'a / laTiifa* (phrase)
4. *Haasuub / mudiir / baahiDH* (phrase)
5. *Suura / 'umm / jamiila* (sentence)
6. *kitaab / tilmiidha / jadiid* (phrase)

Exercise 2 Fill in the missing forms of the verb *dakhala / yadkhulu*—to enter.

	present tense	subjunctive	jussive
'anaa	*'adkhulu*	*'adkhula*	1.
'anta	2.	tadkhula	3.
'anti	tadkhuliina	4.	tadkhulii
huwa	5.	6.	yadkhul
hiya	tadkhulu	7.	8.
'antumaa	tadkhulaani	tadkhulaa	tadkhulaa
naHnu	9.	10.	11.
'antum	tadkhuluuna	tadkhuluu	12.
'antunna	13.	tadkhulna	14.
hum	15.	16.	17.
hunna	yadkhulna	yadkhulna	18.
humaa (m.)	19.	*yadkhulaa*	*yadkhulaa*
humaa (f.)	*tadkhulaani*	20.	tadkhulaa

Exercise 3 Make each of the following sentences negative.

1. *naHnu fii maktab al-mudiir al-jadiid.*
2. *al-mudarrisa dakhalat 'ilaa l-madrasa xalaa s-saaxa at-taasixa.*
3. *al-walad sa-yadkhulu 'ilaa l-madrasa xalaa s-saaxa at-taasixa wa n-niSf.*
4. *'anaa 'aktubu risaala.*

Exercise 4 Translate each of the following sentences into Arabic.

1. The (male) journalist bought a new computer.
2. My office is close to the director's office.
3. I have to go to the bank tomorrow.
4. Do you have money?
5. My sister hasn't come back from Morocco.
6. We will study Arabic at the university.
7. I didn't open the letter.

14G Pronunciation Practice *H* and *x*

Let's focus once again on the two sounds that are uniquely Arabic—the emphatic *H* sound of the Arabic letter *Haa'* and the *x* of the letter *xayn*. You've read a few times that the sound of *H* is similar to the sound you make when you blow on eye glasses or when you eat spicy food—*Haa*! The important thing that distinguishes *H* from *h* (as in the Arabic word *hiya* or the English word "house") is that *h* doesn't require any constriction at the back of your throat, but *H* does. Put your finger on your adam's apple to feel the muscles at work. They're the same muscles you use when you gag.

The Arabic sound that we transcribe as *x* is related to *H*. If you make the *H* sound and get a good sense of where the necessary muscles are located, you'll have an easier time sliding into *x*. The difference is that *x* is "voiced," meaning that it's produced with vibration that you can feel coming from your adam's apple. If you say the English sounds "k" and "g" or "t" and "d" you'll hear that "k" and "t" don't make your adam's apple vibrate, but "g" and "d" do. In other words, "g" and "d" are the voiced (or vibrating) equivalents of "k" and "t", just like the Arabic sound *x* is the voiced equivalent of *H*. If you say the pairs "k-g" and "t-d" together several times, it should help you make the transition from *H* to *x*. But of course, a lot of practice and repetition will help, too. Try it with these pairs:

naHnu, naxam, maHaa, maxa, Halam, xalaa, Halabiyy, xarabiyy, saHb, saxb, Hadiid, xaDHiim, Hammaam, xaamil, Hindis, xindii

14H Arabic Script The Consonants *waaw* and *yaa'*

You've already seen that the letters *waaw* and *yaa'* can be long vowels, transcribed as *uu* and *ii*. They can also serve as consonants, pronounced *w*– and *y*–. Remember that *waaw* is a non-connector, so its isolated and initial forms are the same, and its final and medial forms are also the same.

	isolated	initial	medial	final
waaw	و	و	ـو	ـو
yaa'	ي	يـ	ـيـ	ـي

كُومْبيُوتَر	*kuumbyuutar* (computer)	العَرَبِيَّة	*al-xarabiyya* (Arabic)
يَابَان	*yaabaan* (Japan)	واحِد	*waaHid* (one)

For more practice, try the general review reading practices 13 and 14 of *Part 2: Reading Arabic* in the *Complete Guide to Arabic Script*. You can also tackle Dialogues 2–3 of *Part 4: Reading Passages*.

141 **Cultural Note** Television and Internet in the Middle East

Over the last decade, there has been an explosion in media usage across the Arab world. Today, satellite dishes dot the landscape of any major Arab city, bringing networks such as CNN, the BBC, and other prominent international media sources into Middle Eastern homes. Local news channels have also taken advantage of this new medium to launch their own stations. *Al-jaziira* ("The Island") is one of the better known Arabic language networks. It follows a format very similar to that of other 24-hour news networks, such as CNN or Fox News, although it is naturally adapted for local consumption. Viewers can tune in and listen to politicians, academics, and theologians debating the important issues of the day. With the popularity of the medium, it is not suprising that advertisers, too, have tapped in and begun to reach out to the Arab market.

Internet use in most Arab countries is not regulated. However, there are countries, such as Saudi Arabia, that ban access to certain websites with content considered to be objectionable. Still, most Arab internet users, who tend to be under the age of 35, can access the internet on a daily basis with the same freedoms and opportunities as Western web surfers. Some of the more popular websites and portals in Arabic or related to Arabic are:

http://english.ajeeb.com/
http://www.aljazeera.net/ or http://english.aljazeera.net
http://news.bbc.co.uk/hi/arabic/news/
http://arabic.cnn.com/

A little bit of exploration of these and other internet resources will enhance your learning and give you a great opportunity to learn more about the Arabic language and the Arab world.

Lesson 14 Answer Key

Vocabulary Practice: 1. *haadhihi 'istimaara Tawiila*. 2. *haadhaa laysa 'imDaa'ii*. 3. *laa 'axrifu xunwaanahaa*. 4. *haadhaa l-maSrif laysa qariib(an) min baytii*. 5. *xindii Hisaab maS-rifiyy fii haadhaa l-maSrif*. 6. *'uriidu Taabix wa Dharf*. 7. *hal xindahaa biTaaqatu l-'istilaaf?* 8. *shii-kuka, ya sayyidii*; 9. *katabtu risaala qaSiira*. 10. *al-waSl fii s-sayyaara*. 11. *'ayna maktab al-bariid?* 12. *katabat risaala*. 13. *haadhaa 'imDaa'uhu*. **Exercise 1:** 1. *qalam at-tilmiidh 'azraq*. (The student's pen is blue.); 2. *kalb al-'imra'a l-laTiif* (the woman's friendly dog); 3. *kalb al-'imra'a l-laTiifa* (the friendly woman's dog); 4. *Haasuub al-mudiir al-baahiDH* (the director's expensive computer); 5. *Suurat al-'umm jamiila*. (The mother's picture is beautiful.); 6. *kitaab at-tilmiidha al-jadiid* (the student's new book) **Exercise 2:** 1. *'adkhul*; 2. *tad-khulu*; 3. *tadkhul*; 4. *tadkhulii*; 5. *yadkhulu*; 6. *yadkhula*; 7. tadkhula; 8. *tadkhul*; 9. *nadkhulu*; 10. *nadkhula*; 11. nadkhul; 12. *tadkhuluu*; 13. *tadkhulna*; 14. *tadkhulna*; 15. *yad-khuluuna*; 16. *yadkhuluu*; 17. *yadkhuluu*; 18. *yadkhulna*; 19. *yadkhulaani*; 20. *tadkhulaa* **Exercise 3:** 1. *naHnu lasnaa fii maktab al-mudiir al-jadiid*. 2. *al-mudarrisa lam tadkhul al-madrasa xalaa s-saaxa at-taasixa.*; 3. *al-walad lan yadkhula al-madrasa xalaa s-saaxa at-taasixa wa n-niSf.*; 4. *'anaa laa 'aktubu risaala*. **Exercise 4:** 1. *aS-SaHaafiyy 'ishtaraa Haasuub/kuumbyuutar jadiid*. 2. *maktabii qariib min maktab al-mudiir*. 3. *yajibu 'an adh-haba 'ilaa l-maSrif ghadan*. 4. *hal xindaka/xindaki nuquud/maal?* 5. *'ukhtii lam tarjax min al-maghrib*. 6. *sawfa / sa-nadrusu al-xarabiyya fii l-jaamixa*. 7. *lam 'aftaH ar-risaala*

LESSON 15

LET'S GO TO THE BEACH! *hayyaa binaa 'ilaa sh-shaaTi'!*

In this last lesson you'll learn how to talk about free time, leisure activities, socializing, and having fun. Then you'll learn how to suggest activities and how to use the pronoun suffixes such as *–nii* or *–ki* with prepositions. Finally, you'll learn how to express "more" and "most" with adjectives.

15A Dialogue

Let's listen as Miriam and Ahmed plan their weekend together.

maryam	***maadhaa turiidu 'an tafxala haadhaa s-sabt?***
'aHmad	***'innahu yawm jamiil, wa faaTima wa kariim sawfa yadh-habaani 'ilaa sh-shaaTi'. hayyaa binaa maxahumaa.***
maryam	***mumtaaz! 'anaa 'uHibbu s-slbaaHa.***
'aHmad	***laa, 'anaa 'uHibbu s-sibaaHa. 'anti tuHibbiina an-nawm taHta sh-shams!***
maryam	***jayyid. 'anta wa kariim sawfa tasbaHaani wa 'anaa wa faaTima sawfa nastamtixu taHta sh-shams. hal turiidu 'an nadh-haba 'ilaa s-sinimaa 'ayDan?***
'aHmad	***lan nastaTiixa 'an nadh-haba fii l-layl li'annanaa yajibu 'an nadh-haba 'ilaa Haflati 'akhii.***
maryam	***naxam—'inna xiida miilaadihi yawm as-sabt.***
'aHmad	***hayyaa binaa 'ilaa s-sinimaa yawm al-'aHad.***
maryam	***laa . hayyaa binaa 'ilaa l-masraH. al-masraH 'aHsan mina s-sinimaa.***
'aHmad	***wa 'aghlaa 'ayDan. wa laakin lan nas-hara kathiiran. xindii madrasa al-'ithnayn.***
maryam	***jayyid.***
Miriam	What do you want to do this Saturday?
Ahmed	It's a beautiful day, and Fatima and Karim are going to the beach. Let's go with them.
Miriam	Great! I love swimming.
Ahmed	No, I love swimming. You love to sleep under the sun!

Miriam	Good. You and Karim will swim, and Fatima and I will enjoy ourselves under the sun. Do you want to go to the movies, too?
Ahmed	We can't go at night, because we have to go to my brother's party.
Miriam	Right—it's his birthday Saturday.
Ahmed	Let's go to the movies on Sunday.
Miriam	No, let's go to the theater. The theater is better than a movie.
Ahmed	And more expensive, too. But we can't stay out too late! I have school on Monday.
Miriam	That's fine.

15B Language Notes

Remember that *'inna* is used with personal pronoun suffixes sometimes in place of independent personal pronouns. So, in the second line of the dialogue, *'innahu* simply means *huwa*, and refers to the masculine noun *yawm*.

Later in the dialogue you saw *li'annanaa*, which means "because we . . ." The conjunction *li'anna* functions just like *'inna* in that you add suffixes to show the subject if it is a pronoun. So, you'd say *li'anna T-Taqs* . . . (because the weather is . . .) but *li'annahu* . . . (because it/he is . . .), *li'annanii* . . . (because I . . .), *li'annaka* . . . (because you . . .) and so on.

Notice that the personal pronoun suffix *–humaa* (them, two people) is attached to *maxa* (with) in the phrase *hayyaa binaa maxahumaa* (let's go with the two of them). You'll see more about this in this lesson.

When Miriam says that she loves to swim, she uses the phrase *'anaa 'uHibbu s-sibaaHa*. As you can see from the definite article preceding it, *sibaaHa* is another example of a verbal noun, meaning "swimming." It's related to the verb *sabaHa* (to swim). Another verbal noun right after it is *an-nawm* (sleeping). You saw this first in the last lesson with *yajibu l-'imDaa'* ("the signing is necessary.") Where English generally adds –ing to a verb to produce a noun (also called a gerund,) Arabic verbs can undergo various pattern changes. But you'll always be able to pick out the root consonants, in this case *s-b-H* or *n-w-m*. You can read more about verbal nouns and their use in the Grammar Summary.

Take a look at the root consonants of that verb again: *s-b-H*, to swim. And now look at the word for "swimming pool"—*masbaH*. Do you recognize any pattern that you've seen in other words? The prefix *ma–* in many Arabic words means "place of X" or "place where X happens." It's attached to the root consonants of a verb (meaning "X") in the pattern *ma//a/(a)*. So, from *sabaHa* (swim) you get *masbaH* (swimming pool). From *darasa* (study) you get *madrasa* (school). From *kataba* (write) you get *maktab* (office) or *maktaba* (library). From *Tabakha* (cook) you get *maTbakh* (kitchen) and from *Taxima* (eat) you get *maTxam* (restaurant). This prefix and pattern appear again and again in Arabic.

15C Vocabulary

riyaaDa	sports
kura / kuraat	ball
kurat al-qadam	soccer
darraaja / darraajaat	bicycle
qaarib / qawaarib	boat
shaaTi'	beach
shaaTi' khaas	private beach
raml	sand
baHr	sea
samak	fish
Sayd as-samak	fishing
mubaara	game
Hakam	referee
an-natiija, al-muHraza	score
fawz	win (noun)
khasar	loss
'inTilaaq	start
fariiq	team
karTa, al-waraq	cards
shaTranj	chess
tazalluj	skating
tazaHluq	skiing
faras / furuus, khayl	horse
furuusiyya	horseback riding
sibaaq al-khayl	horse racing
sibaaHa	swimming
masbaH	swimming pool
sinimaa	movies

fiilm / 'aflaam	film, movie
Hafla	party
laxiba / yalxabu	play (sports/games)
qafaza / yaqfizu	jump
ramaa / yarmii	throw
masaka / yamsiku	catch
rabiHa / yarbaHu	win
khasira / yakhsaru	lose
sabaHa / yasbaHu	swim
DaHika / yaD-Haku	laugh
lahw	fun
jayyid, mumtaaz	great, excellent
rahiib	terrible
mumtix	interesting
muqliq	boring
aT-Taqs	weather
al-jaww	weather
al-jaww mumTir.	It's raining. The weather is rainy.
al-jaww ghaa'im.	It's cloudy.
al-jaww mushmis.	It's sunny.
al-jaww muthlij.	It's snowing.
'anaa bardaan (a)	I'm cold.
'anaa Haarraan (a)	I'm hot.

15D Vocabulary Practice

Translate the following sentences into Arabic.

1. I like skiing.
2. The sea is cold.
3. Soccer is interesting.
4. That referee is thirsty.
5. Our big boat is new.
6. Their team lost.
7. The boy's bicycle is beautiful.
8. This is fun!
9. We won.
10. She caught the ball.
11. They lost the game.

12. The horse jumps.
13. The party was great.
14. Her female friend is nice and interesting.
15. The beach is far from their house. (use an *-i-* in "their")

15E Grammar and Usage

❶ Suggestions with "Let's . . . "

In the dialogue you listened to Miriam and Ahmed suggest several different activities. In English, this is done with the expression "let's," as in "let's go" or "let's eat" or "let's sit down." In Arabic, use *hayyaa* with the *naHnu* form of the verb:

hayyaa nadh-habu 'ilaa l-masraH.	Let's go to the theater.
hayyaa nadrusu.	Let's study.
hayyaa na'kulu fii s-saaxa s-saadisa.	Let's eat at 6:00.
hayyaa nashrabu qahwa.	Let's drink coffee.
hayyaa nafxalu haadhaa.	Let's do this.
hayyaa nashtarii kuumbyuutar jadiid.	Let's buy a new computer.

The expression *hayyaa binaa* uses the preposition *bi* (by, with, in) attached to the personal pronoun suffix *–naa* (us, our). It's difficult to literally translate this expression, but it is a common way of agreeing to a suggestion, meaning something along the lines of "let's do that!"

hayyaa binaa!	Let's do it! Let's do that! Let's go!
hayyaa binaa 'ilaa l-maktaba.	Let's (go) to the bookstore.

Notice that *hayyaa binaa* can be used alone, or it can be used to mean any activity, as long as that verb has already been mentioned or is clear from context. This is the case in the second example, where the verb *nadh-habu* (we go) is understood.

❷ Personal Pronoun Suffixes on Prepositions

You've seen the personal pronoun suffixes *–(n)ii, –ka, –ki, –hu, –haa, –kumaa, –naa, –kum, –kunna, –hum, –hunna, –humaa* used with both nouns and verbs. When attached to a noun, they show possession, where English would use a possessive adjective such as "my," "his", "our," "their," etc.

When attached to a verb, they are translated as direct object pronouns, such as "me," "her", "him", "us," etc.

hal djiinzuki jadiid?	Are your jeans new?
'anaa 'araahum.	I see them.

These suffixes can also be used with prepositions, and they are then translated as the object pronouns "me," "you," "him," "them," etc. The expression *hayyaa binaa*, which you just learned, is an example of this construction. Note that *–nii* is used with verbs, but *–ii* is used with nouns and prepositions.

jaa'uu maxahaa.	They came with her.
'anaa bijaanibiki.	I am next to you.
kaanuu waraa'ii.	They were behind me.

Recall that you've also seen an example of this in lesson 11, when you learned how to say "have" or "has" with the preposition *xinda* (with).

xindii 'ukht.	I have a sister.
hal xindakum kumbyuutaraat?	Do you have computers?

3 Degrees of Adjectives

You've already learned how to say that something is "big" or "expensive." In this last lesson you're going to learn how to say that something is "bigger," "biggest," "more expensive" or "most expensive." These are called degrees of adjectives. The comparative degree, where you compare two things, is expressed in English by adding *–er* to shorter adjectives, or by using "more" with longer adjectives. The superlative degree, which is used when comparing something to two or more other things, is expressed by adding *–est* or using "most."

In Arabic, the comparative and superlative are formed by manipulating the consonant root of the adjective. But don't worry—it's much easier than forming plurals or conjugating verbs. In fact, there's only one simple pattern to remember. Let's take *kabiir* (big) as an example. First, strip out the vowels and find the root consonants: *k-b-r*. Now, use the pattern *'a//a/*, meaning, add *'a–* at the beginning, and *–a–* between the second and third consonants. That changes *kabiir* (big) into *'akbar* (bigger). Here are two more examples:

Saghiir (small)	*'aSghar* (smaller)
jamiil (pretty)	*'ajmal* (prettier)

To say that something is bigger than something else, use the word *min* (than).

al-walad 'akbar min al-bint.	The boy is bigger than the girl.
al-maktaba 'aqrab min as-suuq.	The library is nearer than the market.
haadhaa l-kumbyuutar 'ajadd min dhaalika l-kumbyuutar.	This computer is newer than that computer.

Notice that the comparative form of the adjective does not change regardless of the gender of the noun it's describing. For example, *'akbar* in the first example is describing the masculine *walad*, and *'aqrab* (without an *–a*)in the second example is describing the feminine *maktaba*.

Also notice the adjective in the third sentence, *'ajadd*. The word *jadiid* (new) became *'ajadd* (newer), even though this is not what you would expect from the pattern *a//a/*. The reason is that the root *j-d-d* contains a double letter. In such cases, those letters remain "stuck" together at the end of the word, and the pattern is then *a/a//*. There is one other slight variation on the pattern for comparatives, and that is when an adjective ends in a so-called "weak" letter *–w* or *–y* (either single or double). In these cases, the *w* or *y* drops out, and the comparative form ends in a long *–aa*.

qawiyy (strong)	*'aqwaa* (stronger)
dhakiyy (smart, clever)	*'adhkaa* (smarter, cleverer)

The superlative (biggest) is actually the same form, but the word order is different. You know that adjectives in Arabic usually come after the noun that they modify. But superlatives come before nouns.

haadhaa 'ajadd kumbyuutar fii l-maktab.	This is the newest computer in the office.
hiya 'aTwal bint fii l-madrasa.	She is the tallest girl in the school.

Notice that both noun and adjective in each of the examples above are indefinite, even though the English translation uses "the." But a second way to form the superlative uses the definite article *al* with the superlative form of the adjective.

haadhihii s-sayyaara hiya al-'asrax.	This car is the fastest.
'ukhtii hiya al-'aTwal fii l-xaa'ila.	My sister is the tallest in the family.

Finally, there are adjectives in Arabic that are just too long or complex for this kind of consonant root change. Remember that the same is true of many nouns, which take a "sound" plural ending instead of a "broken" plural. Longer adjectives are followed by the word *'akthar* (more, most), which is itself the comparative/superlative form of *kathiir* (a lot).

mashghuul	busy
mashghuul 'akthar	busier
mutashaabik	twisted, tangled
mushtabak 'akthar	more twisted, tangled

15F Grammar and Usage Exercises

Exercise 1 Translate each of the following suggestions.

1. Let's go to the museum.
2. Let's eat in this restaurant.
3. Let's buy new shirts.
4. Let's walk to the office.
5. Let's watch an Egyptian film.

Exercise 2 Translate each of the following sentences using personal pronoun suffixes with prepositions.

1. My sister is next to me.
2. His office is behind you.
3. I have a small car.
4. The boys were with us.
5. She studied at the university with me.
6. We are next to you (singular).

Exercise 3 Change the following adjectives into their comparative forms.

1. *Tawiil*
2. *qaSiir*
3. *qadiim*
4. *jadiid*
5. *xaDHiim*
6. *qawiyy*
7. *Saghiir*
8. *jamiil*

Exercise 4 Translate the following sentences into Arabic.

1. The beach is prettier than the garden.
2. Let's go to the biggest museum in the city.
3. The director is the friendliest man in the office.
4. My brother is the tallest boy in the school.
5. This book is the greatest.
6. My computer is faster than her computer.
7. The library is smaller than the theater.

15G Pronunciation Practice Review of *hamza*, x, and *H*

In this last lesson we're going to review what are probably the three most distinctively Arabic sounds, the glottal stop ' *(hamza)*, the emphatic *H*, and the deep, "throaty" *x*. Listen and repeat each of the words.

'anaa, Haarr, xarabiyy, 'ustaadh, Hadiid, xindii, 'antum, Hayra, xayn, su'aal, SaHaafiyy, saaxa, Taa'ira, TaHiin, Taxaam, maa', miSbaaH, sariix

15H Arabic Script Important Symbols that are not Letters

You've now become aquainted with all of the letters of the Arabic alphabet, including consonants, long vowels, and short vowels. There are a few other symbols you'll see in Arabic, including pronunciation markers, special letter combinations, and symbols to show certain typical grammatical endings. We won't cover all of them, but we'll focus on the three most important ones.

The *shadda* is a symbol that looks like a small "w" that is put on top of consonants to show that they should be pronounced as double letters. Remember that in Arabic it's important to distinguish between single and double letters in pronounciation, because failing to hold a consonant long enough can completely change the meaning of a word.

سَيَّارَة	*sayyaara* (car)	مُدَرِّس	*mudarris* (teacher)

You've seen the feminine ending *–a* many times throughout this course. There is a special letter that is used to indicate this ending, called a *taa' marbuuTa*, or a "tied *taa'*," which makes sense if you think about all the times when the "hidden t" of this ending is pronounced. In writing the feminine ending looks a bit like an *o* with two dots over it, or if it follows a connecting letter, its shape is slightly modified.

سَيَّارَة	*sayyaara* (car)	أُسْتَاذَة	*'ustaadha* (professor)
مَكْتَبَة	*maktaba* (library)	رِسَالَة	*risaala* (letter)

The last special letter we'll focus on is called *laam-'alif*. As you can guess, it's a special combination that is used when an *'alif* follows a *laam*. If you think of the shapes of these two letters, they're both basically straight lines. Writing these two together normally was not considered very pretty, so a special combination was developped.

لا	*laa* (no)	سَلام	*salaam* (peace)

For more practice, read *Group 12: shadda, laam-'alif, and the definite article* and reading practice 15 of *Part 2: Reading Arabic* in the *Complete Guide to Arabic Script*. You can also round off your knowledge of reading with *13: hamza*, *14: 'alif maqSuura*, *15: Grammatical endings with -n*, *16: other symbols*, and reading practices 16–21. You can practice writing the same material with Groups 12–14 and writing practices 28–36 of *Part 3: Writing Arabic*. And finally, you're ready for Dialogue 4 of *Part 4: Reading Passages*.

151 **Cultural Note** Sports and Recreation in the Middle East

The most popular sport in the Middle East is soccer. As is the case in many regions throughout the world, there are different kinds of leagues that attract a very strong and very loyal viewership. Games are usually held on Sundays between local clubs and attract corporate sponsors and large audiences to the stadiums. But there are of course many leisure activities other than soccer. Leisure time is very often considered time to spend with the family, either going to the beach, on picnics, or visiting relatives; so, many activities center around the family.

Night life in most cities is very lively and very active. There are many night clubs and crowded, popular restaurants. Despite religious restrictions in some places, most Middle Eastern cities find a way to accommodate young people's desire to spend time much in the same ways that young people spend time anywhere in the world—meeting with friends, going dancing, driving, or just "hanging out."

Lesson 15 Answer Key

Vocabulary Pratice: 1. *'anaa 'uHibbu al-tazaHluq*; 2. *al-baHr baarid*. 3. *kurat al-qadam mumtixa*. 4. *dhaalika l-Hakam xaTshaan*. 5. *qaaribunaa l-kabiir jadiid*. 6. fariiquhum khasira. 7. *darraajat l-walad jamiila*. 8. *haadhaa lahw*! 9. *rabiHnaa*. 10. *masakat al-kura*. 11. *khasiruu l-mubaara*. 12. *al-faras yaqfizu*. 13. *al-Hafla kaanat mumtaaza*. 14. *Sadiiqatuhaa laTiifa wa mumtixa* 15. *ash-shaaTi' baxiid min baytihim*. **Exercise 1:** 1. *hayyaa nadh-habu 'ilaa l-matHaf*. 2. *hayyaa na'kulu fii haadhaa l-maTxam*. 3. *hayyaa nashtarii 'aqmiSa jadiida*. 4. *hayyaa namshii 'ilaa l-maktab*. 5. *hayyaa nushaahid fiilm miSriyy*. **Exercise 2:** 1. *'ukhtii bijaanibii*. 2. *maktabuhu waraa'aka/-ki*. 3. *xindii sayyaara Saghiira*. 4. *al-'awlaad kaanuu maxanaa*. 5. *darasat fii l-jaamixa maxii*. 6. *naHnu bijaanibika/-ki*. **Exercise 3:** 1. *'aTwal; 2. 'aqSar*; 3. *'aqdam*; 4. *'ajadd*; 5, *'axDHam*; 6. *'aqwaa*; 7. *'aSghar*; 8. *'ajmal* **Exercise 4:** 1. *ash-shaaTi' 'ajmal min al-bustaan*. 2. *hayyaa nadh-habu 'ilaa 'akbar matHaf fii l-madiina*. 3. *al-mudiir 'alTaf rajul fii l-maktab*. 4. *'akhii 'aTwal walad fii l-madrasa*. 5. *haadhaa l-kitaab huwa al-'axDHam*. 6. *Haasuubii 'asrax min Haasuubihaa*. 7. *al-maktaba 'aSghar min al-masraH*.

GRAMMAR SUMMARY

1. Nouns

1A. Gender

Nouns that have natural gender (man, woman, boy, girl, bull, cow) have logical grammatical gender. Masculine nouns that denote professions (*'ustaadh*, male professor) can be made feminine by adding the feminine endings *–a* (*'ustaadha*, female professor). Inanimate nouns are generally masculine if they end in a consonant, and generally feminine if they end in *–a*. However, there are some irregular inanimate nouns that end in consonants but are feminine, such as *shams* (sun). Also, nouns denoting parts of the body that exist in pairs (*xayn*, eye) are feminine.

1B. Articles

The indefinite article is implied in Arabic, so *kitaab* can mean "book" or "a book." The definite article is *al*, attached to a noun, so *al-kitaab* is "the book." The *l* in the definite article is assimilated (made the same as the following consonant) before the "sun" consonants *t–, th–, d–, dh–, r–, z–, sh–, S–, D–, T–, DH–,* and *n–*. So, *ar-rajul* means "the man" and *aT-Taawila* means "the table."

The short *a* vowel of the definite article is elided (dropped) in pronunciation when it follows a word that ends in a vowel: *al-ghurfa* (the room) but *fii l-ghurfa* (in the room). The long vowels of prepositions are shortened before this elision (*fii* is pronounced as *fi*, *'ilaa* is pronounced as *'ila*, etc.). For simplicity's sake, this pronunciation change isn't shown in the transcription in this course.

1C. Plurals

Nouns form their plurals in one of two ways. The first type of plural is called a "sound" plural and involves adding an ending to the singular form. Sound plurals are reserved mainly for nouns that denote human profession or nationalities, or inanimate nouns that are too long to follow the system of manipulating root consonants. The human masculine sound plural ending is *–uun* (see 1E for an alternate ending), and the human feminine sound plural ending is *–at* (added to the singular *–a* ending to produce *–aat*). Non-human sound plurals have the same ending as the feminine, *–aat*.

miSriyy	Egyptian man	*miSriyyuun*	Egyptian men
miSriyya	Egyptian woman	*miSriyyaat*	Egyptian women
mudarris	male teacher	*mudarrisuun*	male teachers
mudarrisa	female teacher	*mudarrisaat*	female teachers
'ijtimaax	meeting	*'ijtimaaxaat*	meetings
tiqniyya	technique	*tiqniyyaat*	techniques
tilifizyuun	television	*tilifizyuunaat*	televisions

Most nouns take "broken" plurals, which involve altering the vowels before, after, or between their root consonants. Broken plurals follow general patterns, but they must be memorized. The following are the most common patterns for forming broken plurals. A slash (/) indicates a root consonant.

Pattern	Singular Examples	Plural Examples
'a//aa/	*walad* (boy)	*'awlaad* (boys)
	qalam (pen)	*'aqlaam* (pens)
	waqt (time)	*'awqaat* (times)
/u/uu/	*bayt* (house)	*buyuut* (houses)
	fann (art)	*funuun* (arts)
	malik (king)	*muluuk* (kings)
/i/aa/	*jabal* (mountain)	*jibaal* (mountains)
	kalb (dog)	*kilaab* (dogs)
	rajul (man)	*rijaal* (men)
/u/u/	*madiina* (city)	*mudun* (cities)
	kitaab (book)	*kutub* (books)
	Tariiq (main street)	*Turuq* (main streets)
/u/a/	*ghurfa* (room)	*ghuraf* (rooms)
	dawla (country)	*duwal* (countries)
	Suura (picture, copy)	*Suwar* (pictures, copies)
'a//u/	*shahr* (month)	*'ashhur* (months)
	nahr (river)	*'anhur* (rivers)
	rijl (foot)	*'arjul* (feet)
/u/a/aa'	*xaalim* (scholar)	*xulamaa'* (scholars)
	waziir (minister)	*wuzaraa'* (ministers)
	'amiir (prince)	*'umaraa'* (princes)
'a//i/aa'	*Sadiiq* (friend)	*'aSdiqaa'* (friends)
	qariib (relative)	*'aqribaa'* (relatives)
	ghaniyy (rich man)	*'aghniyaa'* (rich men)

1D. The Dual Form

Nouns also have a dual form, denoting two or a pair, which is regular in all cases and involves the ending *-aani/-ayni,* or *-taani/-tayni* for feminine nouns ending in *-a.*

kitaab	a book	*kitaabaani* *kitaabayni*	two books, a pair of books
bint	a girl	*bintaani* *bintayni*	two girls, a pair of girls
mudarris	a male teacher	*mudarrisaani* *mudarrisayni*	two male teachers
mudarrisa	a female teacher	*mudarrisataani* *mudarrisatayni*	two female teachers

1E. Noun Cases

A case is a grammatical term that refers to how a noun functions in a sentence. In many languages, nouns change form in some way—often by adding or changing an ending—depending on how they are used in a sentence. This shows what case they are in, and therefore what role they are playing in a sentence. For example, the subject of a sentence will be in one case, the direct object in another, possessives in another, and so on. English is not a language that shows case endings on nouns (with the exception of the apostrophe-*s* in a possessive such as *Gary's . . .* or *the woman's . . .*) but English pronouns do show cases. For example, *I* is used for the subject of a sentence, *me* for the object, and *mine* shows possession. Arabic nouns have case endings, but they are used only in certain situations, such as very formal or academic discourse, recitations of religious texts, or in "high brow" language. It's not usually necessary to use them, but there are limited circumstances where they can be heard following prepositions or in possessive constructions.

There are three cases in Arabic, called the nominative, the accusative, and the genitive. These labels only correspond roughly to the equivalent cases in Western languages, but the most important uses are similar. In sentences beginning with a subject (noun or pronoun), subjects are in the nominative case, direct objects are in the accusative case, and nouns after prepositions or nouns in the second or possessor position in possessive constructions are in the genitive case. In sentences beginning with a verb (see section 7B) or an introductory word such as *‘inna* (emphasis), *‘anna* (that . . .), *laakinna* (but . . .), *li’anna* (because), or *ka’anna* (as if) the subject is in the accusative case. The endings are:

	Nominative	**Accusative**	**Genitive**
Definite	*al-kitaabu* (the book)	*al-kitaaba* (the book)	*al-kitaabi* (of, for the book)
Indefinite	*kitaabun* (a book)	*kitaaban* (a book)	*kitaabin* (of, for a book)

It's important to note that the masculine sound plural ending *–uun* changes to *–iin* in the accusative and genitive. Another important thing to keep in mind about case endings is that while the endings themselves aren't typically used in spoken Arabic, there are instances when the vowel of a case, especially the *–i* of the genitive, will be pronounced before suffixes, or when it will show up in the *–at(u)* ending of feminine nouns as *–ati*.

For example, *fii l-bayt* means "in the house," and the *–i* ending on *bayt* (since it follows a preposition) isn't typically pronounced. However, if a suffix is attached, it will be pronounced. So, *fii baytinaa* (instead of *fii baytunaa*) means "in our house." The same is true of the *–at(u)* ending on feminine nouns. The *–a* on *sayyaara* is pronounced *–at(u)* in certain cases, such as in the first position of a possessive construction or before a possessive suffix. But that *–u* will become an *–i* after prepositions: *sayyaaratuka kabiira* (your car is big) or *sayyaarat al-mudiir* (the director's car) but *fii sayyaaratika* (in your car). The other instance where this will occur is in the second position in possessive noun constructions: *baab al-bayt* (the door of the house) but *baab baytinaa* (the door of our house). Masculine sound plurals in the same position will take the ending *–iin* instead of *–uun*: *makaatib al-mudiiriin* (the directors' offices).

2. Pronouns and Personal Suffixes

The subject pronouns are used as the subject of a sentence, but they may be omitted, since the verb form generally makes the subject clear. The personal suffixes, when added to nouns, are translated as possessive adjectives (my, your, his, her, etc.). When added to verbs or prepositions, they are translated as object pronouns (me, you, him, her, etc.). The forms are identical except in the first person singular, which is *–nii* when used with verbs (me) and *–ii* with nouns and prepositions (my/me). A *–u–* can be inserted before the other endings to aid pronunciation, but this *–u* will change to an *–i* or an *–a* in the genitive or accusative (see section 1E).

Subject Pronouns		**Personal Suffixes**	
I	*'anaa*	me, my	*–nii / –ii*
you, m.	*'anta*	you, your, m.	–(u)ka
you, f.	*'anti*	you, your, f.	–(u)ki
he, it	*huwa*	him, it, his, its	–(u)hu
she, it, they*	*hiya*	her, it, them, its, their*	–(u)haa
you two	*'antumaa*	you, belonging to the two of you	-(u)kumaa
we	*naHnu*	us, our	-(u)naa
you, pl., m.	*'antum*	you, your, pl., m.	-(u)kum
you, pl., f.	*'antunna*	you, your, pl., f.	-(u)kunna
they, m.	*hum*	them, their, m.	-(u)hum
they, f.	*hunna*	them, their, f.	-(u)hunna
the two of them	*humaa*	them, their, belonging to the two of them	-(u)humaa

*Plural nouns denoting nonhuman objects are treated as feminine singulars. Therefore, the pronoun *hiya* or the suffix *–haa* may refer to singular feminine nouns, or also to plural nonhuman nouns, such as cities, books, cars, etc. The plural forms in the table above, then, are only used to refer to human beings.

3. Adjectives

3A. Position and Agreement

Adjectives in Arabic come after the noun they modify (*kitaab jayyid*, a good book). They must agree with the nouns they modify in gender, definiteness, and number. To make a masculine adjective feminine, an *-a* is added: *walad Tawiil* (a tall boy) but *bint Tawiila* (a tall girl). To make an indefinite adjective definite, the same article *al-* is used, with the same rules for "sun" letters: *al-walad aT-Tawiil* (the tall boy), *al-bint al-laTiifa* (the friendly girl). In the plural, masculine human adjectives take either a broken or a sound plural form, and feminine human adjectives take the sound plural *-aat*. Non-human plurals all take the feminine singular ending *-a*.

Singular		Plural	
walad Tawiil	a tall boy	*'awlaad Tiwaal*	tall boys
rajul 'amriikiyy	an American man	rijaal 'amriikiyyuun	American men
bint Tawiila	a tall girl	banaat Tawiilaat	tall girls
kitaab jayyid	a good book	kutub jayyida	good books
sayyaara kabiira	a big car	sayyaaraat kabiira	big cars

All dual form masculine adjectives end in *-aani*: *waladaani Tawiilaani* (a pair of tall boys), *kitaabaani jayyidaani* (a pair of good books). Dual form feminine adjectives end in *-taani*: *bintaani Tawiilataani* (two tall girls), *miSriyyataani laTiifataani* (a pair of friendly Egyptian women).

3B. Irregular Adjectives

Many common adjectives denoting colors have irregular feminine forms. In the following list, the masculine is given first, followed by the feminine: red—*'aHmar, Hamraa'*; blue—*'azraq, zarqaa'*; yellow—*'aSfar, Safraa'*; black—*'aswad, sawdaa'*; white—*'abyaD, bayDaa'*; green—*'akhDar, khaDraa'*; brown (skin)—*'asmar, samraa'*.

3C. Degrees of Adjectives

The comparative and superlative degrees of adjectives are formed following the pattern *'a//a/*. So, *kabiir* becomes *'akbar* (bigger, biggest), and *Saghiir* become *'aSghar* (smaller, smallest). If an adjective has a double consonant in its root (*jadiid*, with the root *j-d-d*, for example) the double consonants will remain next to each other: *jadiid* becomes *'ajadd* (newer, newest). If an adjective ends in a *–w* or a *–y*, this consonant will drop out, and the comparative/superlative form will end in *–aa*: *qawiyy* becomes *'aqwaa* (stronger, strongest). The word *'akthar* (more) is used with longer adjectives: *mashghuul 'akthar* (busier/busiest).

The comparative and superlative share one form in Arabic, which remains the same regardless of the gender, definiteness, or number of the noun it modifies. These two forms are distinguished either by word order, comparatives coming after nouns and superalatives before them, or by the use of the definite article.

ar-rajul 'aTwal min al-'imra'a.	The man is taller than the woman.
haadhihi s-sayyaara 'ajadd min tilka s-sayyaara.	This car is newer than that car.
haadha 'aTwal rajul fii l-maktab.	This is the tallest man in the office.
haadhihi 'ajadd sayyaara.	This is the newest car.
al-'imra'a hiya l-'aqSar.	The woman is the shortest.
al-rajul huwa l-'aTwal.	The man is the tallest.

4. Demonstratives

The forms of the demonstratives in Arabic are:

haadhaa	this, masc.	*dhaalika*	that, masc.
haadhihi	this, fem.	*tilka*	that, fem.
haa'ulaa'i	these	*'uulaa'ika*	those

The plural forms *haa'ulaa'i* and *ulaa'ika* are used for both masculine and feminine people. Nonhuman plurals use the feminine singular forms *haadhihi* or *tilka*. Demonstratives can be translated as adjectives (this book) when used with a definite noun or as pronouns (this is a book) when used with an indefinite noun.

haadhaa l-kitaab	this book	*haadhaa kitaab.*	This is a book.
haadhihi l-'imra'a	this woman	haadhihi 'imra'a	This is a woman.
haa'ulaa'i r-rijaal	these men	haa'ulaa'i rijaal.	These are men.
haadhihi s-sayyaaraat	these cars	haadhihi sayyaaraat.	These are cars.

If a pronoun and a definite noun follow a demonstrative, this translates as "this/that is the . . . " So, *haadhihi hiya al-'ustaadha l-jadiida* means "this is the new professor."

5. Numbers

5A. Cardinal

0	*Sifr*
1	*waaHid*
2	*'ithnayn, ithnaan*
3	*thalaatha*
4	*'arbaxa*
5	*khamsa*
6	*sitta*
7	*sabxa*
8	*thamaaniya*
9	*tisxa*
10	*xashara*
11	*'aHada xashar*
12	*'ithnay xashar, ithnaa xashar*
13	*thalaathata xashar*
14	*'arbaxata xashar*
15	*khamsata xashar*
16	*sittata xashar*
17	*sabxata xashar*
18	*thamaaniyyata xashar*
19	*tisxata xashar*
20	*xishruun, -iin*

21	*waaHid wa xishruun, -iin*
22	*'ithnaan wa xishruun, -iin*
23	*thalaatha wa xishruun, -iin*
30	*thalaathuun, -iin*
40	*'arbaxuun, -iin*
50	*khamsuun, -iin*
60	*sittuun, -iin*
70	*sabxuun, -iin*
80	*thamaanuun, -iin*
90	*tisxuun, -iin*
100	*mi'a*
1,000	*'alf*
1,000,000	*milyuun*

5B. Ordinal

'awwal, 'uulaa	first
thaanii, thaaniya	second
thaalith, thaalitha	third
raabix, raabixa	fourth
khaamis, khaamisa	fifth
saadis, saadisa	sixth
saabix, saabixa	seventh
thaamin, thaamina	eighth
taasix, taasixa	ninth
xaashir, xaashira	tenth
Haadii xashar, Haadia xashra	eleventh
thaanii xashar, thaania xashra	twelfth

6. Verbs

6A. Regular Verbs

There are two main tenses in Arabic, the past and the present. The past tense is conjugated with a short *–a–* between the root consonants (and rarely an *–i-* between the second and third) and a set of endings that change depending on the person. The present tense is conjugated with both prefixes and endings, and a vowel between the second and third root consonant that must be memorized for each verb. Dictionaries will indicate this present tense vowel. There is no infinitive form in Arabic, so the third person singular of the past tense is usually used as the "basic" form of the verb in dictionaries, as it is the simplest form.

faxala (a)—to do				
	Past Tense		**Present Tense**	
	conjugation pattern	***example***	***conjugation pattern***	***example***
'anaa	*/a/a/tu*	*faxaltu*	*'a//*/u*	*'afxalu*
'anta	*/a/a/ta*	*faxalta*	*ta//*/u*	*tafxalu*
'anti	*/a/a/ti*	*faxalti*	*ta//*/iina*	*tafxaliina*
huwa	*/a/a/a*	*faxala*	*ya//*/u*	*yafxalu*
hiya	*/a/a/at*	*faxalat*	*ta//*/u*	*tafxalu*
'antumaa	*/a/a/tumaa*	*faxaltumaa*	*ta//*/aani*	*tafxalaani*
naHnu	*/a/a/naa*	*faxalnaa*	*na//*/u*	*nafxalu*
'antum	*/a/a/tum*	*faxaltum*	*ta//*/uuna*	*tafxaluuna*
'antunna	*/a/a/tunna*	*faxaltunna*	*ta//*/na*	*tafxalna*
hum	*/a/a/uu*	*faxaluu*	*ya//*/uuna*	*yafxaluuna*
hunna	*/a/a/na*	*faxalna*	*ya//*/na*	*yafxalna*
humaa (m.)	*/a/a/aa*	*faxalaa*	*ya//*/aani*	*yafxalaani*
humaa (f.)	*/a/a/ataa*	*faxalataa*	*ta//*/aani*	*tafxalaani*

The *–u* suffix of the *'anaa, 'anta, huwa, hiya,* and *naHnu* forms is often not pronounced in informal spoken Arabic, so the forms *'afxal, tafxal, yafxal*, and *nafxal* are also correct.

There are also certain types of verbs that take a *–u* in the present tense prefixes (*'u–, tu–, yu–,* etc.). and *–i* as the inserted vowel marked as * above. These are the derived forms II, III, and IV (see section 6D) and they're easy to spot because they have either a doubled second root consonant (*faxxala*) or a long *aa* (*faaxala*) or begin with *'a* (*'afxala*) in the past *huwa* form.

On top of the past and present tense, there are also two principle variations (or moods) of the present tense used in particular cases—the subjunctive and the jussive. Their forms are very similar to the present tense with two main exceptions. The final vowel in the subjunctive is *–a*, and there is no final vowel in the jussive. The *–na/ –ni* endings of the *'anti*, *'antum*, *hum*, and dual forms are also missing in both moods.

	Subjunctive Mood		**Jussive Mood**	
	conjugation pattern	**example**	**conjugation pattern**	**example**
'anaa	*'a//*/a*	*'afxala*	*'a//*/*	*'afxal*
'anta	*ta//*/a*	*tafxala*	*ta//*/*	*tafxal*
'anti	*ta//*/ii*	*tafxalii*	*ta//*/ii*	*tafxalii*
huwa	*ya//*/a*	*yafxala*	*ya//*/*	*yafxal*
hiya	*ta//*/a*	*tafxala*	*ta//*/*	*tafxal*
'antumaa	*ta//*/aa*	*tafxalaa*	*ta//*/aa*	*tafxalaa*
naHnu	*na//*/a*	*nafxala*	*na//*/*	*nafxal*
'antum	*ta//*/uu*	*tafxaluu*	*ta//*/uu*	*tafxaluu*
'antunna	*ta//*/na*	*tafxalna*	*ta//*/na*	*tafxalna*
hum	*ya//*/uu*	*yafxaluu*	*ya//*/uu*	*yafxaluu*
hunna	*ya//*/na*	*yafxalna*	*ya//*/na*	*yafxalna*
humaa (m.)	*ya//*/aa*	*yafxalaa*	*ya//*/aa*	*yafxalaa*
humaa (f.)	*ta//*/aa*	*tafxalaa*	*ta//*/aa*	*tafxalaa*

6B. Irregular Verbs

There are four main categories of irregular verbs in Arabic, called in traditional grammars assimilated, hollow, defective, and doubled. The first three categories can be grouped together as "weak" verbs, because their roots contain a so-called weak letter, *w* or *y*. Assimilated verbs have a *w* or (much less frequently) *y* in the first root consonant position, hollow verbs have a *w* or *y* (appearing as a vowel) in the middle root consonant position, and defective verbs have a *w* or *y* in the final root consonant position. These weak letters may drop out of conjugation, or they may be pronounced as, or replaced by, a vowel. Doubled verbs are verbs that have doubled root consonants.

Assimilated verbs are generally regular in the past tense, but lose the weak consonant in the present tense.

waSala / yaSilu--arrive			
Past		**Present**	
'anaa waSaltu	*naHnu waSalnaa*	*'anaa 'aSilu*	*naHnu naSilu*
'anta waSalta	*'antum waSaltum*	*'anta taSilu*	*'antum taSiluuna*
'anti waSalti	*'antunna waSaltunna*	*'anti taSiliina*	*'antunna taSilna*
huwa waSala	*hum waSaluu*	*huwa yaSilu*	*hum yaSiluuna*
hiya waSalat	*hunna waSalna*	*hiya taSilu*	*hunna yaSilna*
	humaa (m.) *waSalaa*		*humaa (m.) yaSilaani*
'antumaa waSaltumaa	*humaa* (f.) *waSalataa*	*'antumaa taSilaani*	*humaa* (f.) *taSilaani*

In hollow verbs, the weak consonant will often be replaced by a long or short vowel. In the past tense, this replacement vowel will be a long *–aa–* in the *huwa*, *hiya*, *hum*, and *humaa* forms. In the other past forms, a *–y–* will usually be replaced by *–i–*, and *–w–* will usually be replaced by *–u–*. In the present tense, hollow verbs have long replacement vowels (*-uu–* for *–w–* and *–ii–* for *–y-*) in all forms except the feminine plurals *'antunna* and *hunna*, where these vowels are short.

zaara / yazuuru– visit			
Past		**Present**	
'anaa zurtu	*naHnu zurnaa*	*'anaa 'azuuru*	*naHnu nazuuru*
'anta zurta	*'antum zurtum*	*'anta tazuuru*	*'antum tazuuruuna*
'anti zurti	*'antunna zurtunna*	*'anti tazuuriina*	*'antunna tazurna*
huwa zaara	*hum zaaruu*	*huwa yazuuru*	*hum yazuuruuna*
hiya zaarat	*hunna zurna*	*hiya tazuuru*	*hunna yazurna*
	humaa (m.) *zaaraa*		*humaa (m.) yazuuraani*
'antumaa zurtumaa	*humaa* (f.) *zaarataa*	*'antumaa tazuuraani*	*humaa* (f.) *tazuuraani*

baaxa / yabiixu—sell			
Past		**Present**	
'anaa bixtu	*naHnu bixnaa*	*'anaa 'abiixu*	*naHnu nabiixu*
'anta bixta	*'antum bixtum*	*'anta tabiixu*	*'antum tabiixuuna*
'anti bixti	*'antunna bixtunna*	*'anti tabiixiina*	*'antunna tabixna*
huwa baaxa	*hum baaxuu*	*huwa yabiixu*	*hum yabiixuuna*
hiya baaxat	*hunna bixna*	*hiya tabiixu*	*hunna yabixna*
	humaa (m.) *baaxaa*		*humaa (m.) yabiixaani*
'antumaa bixtumaa	*humaa* (f.) *baaxataa*	*'antumaa tabiixaani*	*humaa* (f.) *tabiixaani*

Defective verbs will be regular in most forms of the past tense, except for the *huwa*, *hiya*, and *hum* forms, which will drop the final weak consonant. The past *humaa* forms may insert a *–y* before their endings. In the present tense the weak consonant will drop out and be replaced by either *–aa–*, *–ii–*, *–uu–*, *–ay–*, or *–aw–*. The dual forms will insert a *–y–* before the endings. There are rules for determining which long vowel or diphthong will appear in the present tense, but it's best to memorize each defective verb individually.

mashaa / yamshii—walk			
Past		**Present**	
'anaa mashaytu	*naHnu mashaynaa*	*'anaa 'amshii*	*naHnu namshii*
'anta mashayta	*'antum mashaytum*	*'anta tamshii*	*'antum tamshuuna*
'anti mashayti	*'antunna mashaytunna*	*'anti tamshiina*	*'antunna tamshiina*
huwa mashaa	*hum mashaw*	*huwa yamshii*	*hum yamshuuna*
hiya mashat	*hunna mashayna*	*hiya tamshii*	*hunna yamshiina*
	humaa (m.) *mashayaa*		*humaa (m.) yamshiyaani*
'antumaa mashaytumaa	*humaa* (f.) *mashayataa*	*'antumaa tamshiyaani*	*humaa* (f.) *tamshiyaani*

Doubled verbs have the same root consonants in the second and third positions. These doubled consonants remain together before vowels, and they are separated before consonants. In the present tense, the vowel is inserted before the doubled consonants, rather than after them.

radda / yaruddu–**answer**			
Past		**Present**	
'anaa radadtu	*naHnu radadnaa*	*'anaa 'aruddu*	*naHnu naruddu*
'anta radadta	*'antum radadtum*	*'anta taruddu*	*'antum tarudduuna*
'anti radadti	*'antunna radadtunna*	*'anti taruddiina*	*'antunna tardudna*
huwa radda	*hum radduu*	*huwa yaruddu*	*hum yarudduuna*
hiya raddat	*hunna radadna*	*hiya taruddu*	*hunna yardudna*
	humaa (m.) *raddaa*		*humaa (m.) yaruddaani*
'antumaa radadtumaa	*humaa* (f.) *raddataa*	*'antumaa taruddaani*	*humaa* (f.) *taruddaani*

There are certain principal irregularities to watch out for in the subjunctive and jussive. Defective verbs that end in *–ii* or *–uu* in the present take *–iya* or *–uwa* in the subjunctive, and long vowels at the end of present forms change to short vowels in the jussive.

daxaa / yadxuu–**call**			
	Present	**Subjunctive**	**Jussive**
'anaa	*'adxuu*	*'adxuwa*	*'adxu*
'anta	*tadxuu*	*tadxuwa*	*tadxu*
'anti	*tadxiina*	*tadxii*	*tadxii*
huwa	*yadxuu*	*yadxuwa*	*yadxu*
hiya	*tadxuu*	*tadxuwa*	*tadxu*
'antumaa	*tadxuwaani*	*tadxuwaa*	*tadxuwaa*
naHnu	*nadxuu*	*nadxuwa*	*nadxu*
'antum	*tadxuuna*	*tadxuu*	*tadxuu*
'antunna	*tadxuuna*	*tadxuuna*	*tadxuuna*
hum	*yadxuuna*	*yadxuu*	*yadxuu*
hunna	*yadxuuna*	*yadxuuna*	*yadxuuna*
humaa (m.)	*yadxuwaani*	*yadxuwaa*	*yadxuwaa*
humaa (f.)	*tadxuwaani*	*tadxuwaa*	*tadxuwaa*

Hollow verbs with long vowels in the present and subjunctive take short vowels in the jussive before consonants.

qaama / yaquumu—rise			
	Present	**Subjunctive**	**Jussive**
'anaa	*'aquumu*	*'aquuma*	*'aqum*
'anta	*taquumu*	*taquuma*	*taqum*
'anti	*taquumiina*	*taquumii*	*taquumii*
huwa	*yaquumu*	*yaquuma*	*yaqum*
hiya	*taquumu*	*taquuma*	*taqum*
'antumaa	*taquumaani*	*taquumaa*	*taquumaa*
naHnu	*naquumu*	*naquuma*	*naqum*
'antum	*taquumuuna*	*taquumuu*	*taquumuu*
'antunna	*taqumna*	*taqumna*	*taqumna*
hum	*yaquumuuna*	*yaquumuu*	*yaquumuu*
hunna	*yaqumna*	*yaqumna*	*yaqumna*
humaa (m.)	*yaquumaani*	*yaquumaa*	*yaquumaa*
humaa (f.)	*taquumaani*	*taquumaa*	*taquumaa*

The most important rule of thumb to keep in mind with doubled verbs in the jussive is that double consonants will remain together if a vowel follows the third root consonant directly. If there is no vowel, or no letter at all, right after the third root consonant, they will be separate.

radda (u)—to answer		
	Present	**Jussive**
'anaa	*'aruddu*	*'ardud*
'anta	*taruddu*	*tardud*
'anti	*taruddiina*	*taruddii*
huwa	*yaruddu*	*yardud*
hiya	*taruddu*	*tardud*
'antumaa	*taruddaani*	*taruddaa*
naHnu	*naruddu*	*nardud*
'antum	*tarudduuna*	*tarudduu*
'antunna	*tardudna*	*tardudna*
hum	*yarudduuna*	*yarudduu*
hunna	*yardudna*	*yardudna*
humaa (m.)	*yaruddaani*	*yaruddaa*
humaa (f.)	*taruddaani*	*taruddaa*

6C. Negation

Verbs are made negative in Arabic in different ways, depending on tense. For each tense, a different negative word ("not") must be used with a particular tense or mood.

To negate the . . .	Use . . .	Before the . . .
present tense	*laa*	present tense
past tense	*lam*	jussive mood
	maa	past tense (mostly spoken)
future	*lan*	subjunctive

6D. Derived Forms of Verbs

On top of the basic tenses in Arabic—past and present—and the moods of the present—subjunctive and jussive—there are also a number of derived forms in which a basic verb is changed by adding a consonant or syllable, by adding a long *-aa-*, by doubling one of the root consonants, or by a combination of these things. These changes lead to new verbs with new meanings, often, but not always, related to the basic meaning of the root verb through some predictable extension. For example, doubling the second root consonant of a basic verb can mean causing someone to do the action of the basic verb. So, if *darasa* means "he studied," then *darrasa* means "he caused to study," or, more simply, "he taught."

There are ten main patterns that derived verbs follow, although no one verb in Arabic has all ten forms. The table below summarizes these forms and their possible meanings and use. The verb *faxala* (to do) is used as a model to show how the changes affect the shape of a basic verb.

Form	Past	Present	Changes Made to Root	Meaning
I	*faxala*	*yafxalu*	Basic root form	"X"
II	*faxxala*	*yufaxxilu*	Double second root, present tense with *–u* and *–i*.	To cause X to be done, sometimes to do X intensely or repeatedly.
III	*faaxala*	*yufaaxilu*	Add *–aa–* after second root, present tense with *–u* and *–i*.	To do X to, with, or for someone else, or to attempt to do X.

Form	Past	Present	Changes Made to Root	Meaning
IV	*'afxala*	*yufxilu*	Add a– to beginning, remove vowel between first and second root, present tense with –*u* and –*i*.	To cause X to be done.
V	*tafaxxala*	*yatafaxxalu*	Add *ta*– before Form II.	To do X to oneself, reflexive form of II.
VI	*tafaaxala*	*yatafaaxalu*	Add *ta*– before Form III.	To do the action of III collectively or reciprocally.
VII	*'infaxala*	*yanfaxilu*	Add *'in*– before basic verb	Passive or intranstive form.
VIII	*'iftaxala*	*yaftaxilu*	Add *'i*– before first root, and –*ta*– between first and second.	Various meanings, may be reflexive, may mean to do an action for one's own benefit.
IX	*'ifxalla*	*yafxallu*	Add *'i*– before first root, remove vowel between first and second roots, double third root.	Used only with adjectives such as colors, meaning "to turn or become."
X	*'istafxala*	*yastafxilu*	Add *'ista*– before root, and remove vowel between first and second roots.	To ask or desire the action of X, to find or believe the action of X to be true.

6E. Verbal Nouns

There is one last important verb form used often in Arabic—the verbal noun, which is very similar to the gerund (swimming, talking) and the infinitive (to swim, to talk) in English. To form verbal nouns, the verb root undergoes certain changes, such as the addition of a prefix, suffix, or vowel, etc. The changes for the derived forms are predictable, but the changes for the first (and most basic) form I must be memorized individually. Some common examples are:

Verb	Meaning	Verbal Noun	Meaning
kataba / yaktubu	write	*al-kitaaba*	to write, writing, the act of writing
xamila / yaxmalu	work	*al-xamal*	to work, working, the act of working
sakana / yaskunu	live	*as-sakan*	to live, living, the act of living
shaahada / yushaahidu	watch	*al-mushaahada*	to watch, watching, the act of watching
takallama / yatakallamu	talk	*at-takallum*	to talk, talking, the act of talking

Verb	Meaning	Verbal Noun	Meaning
darasa / yadrusu	study	*ad-diraasa*	to study, studying, the act of studying
darrasa / yudarrisu	teach	*at-tadriis*	to teach, teaching, the act of teaching

Verbal nouns in Arabic are used much as gerunds or infinitives are used in English: *ad-diraasa muhimma* can be translated as "studying is important" or "it's important to study." They can also often be used after such verbs as "want" or "like" where English would use infinitives: *'uHibbu diraasat al-lugha l-xarabiyya*, "I like to study the Arabic language." (The subjunctive can also be used after such verbs: *'uHibbu an 'adrusa al-lugha l-xarabiyya.*)

7. Arabic Sentences

7A. Sentences Without Verbs

Since the present tense of the verb "to be" is understood in Arabic, it is possible to have sentences that lack verbs.

baytii kabiir.	My house is big.
huwa Taalib fii l-jaamixa.	He is a student at the university.

It is important to distinguish between sentences and phrases in these cases.

indefinite noun + indefinite adjective	*bayt qariib*	phrase	a near-by house
definite noun + indefinite adjective	*al-bayt qariib.*	sentence	The house is near-by.
definite noun + definite adjective	*al-bayt al-qariib*	phrase	the near-by house
pronoun + noun	*hiya Taaliba.*	sentence	She is a student.
noun/pronoun + adjective	*hiya laTiifa.*	sentence	She is nice.
noun/pronoun + prepositional phrase	*hiya min lubnaan.*	sentence	She is from Lebanon.
noun + definite noun	*bayt al-'imra'a*	possessive phrase	the house of the woman / the woman's house

7B. Word Order

Arabic verbs may come before or after the subject of a sentence. Verb-first word order is more common in higher levels of formality, or it may show emphasis. In spoken Modern Standard Arabic, it is increasingly common for sentences to begin with subjects, followed by verbs.

Sentences in Arabic may begin with the word *'inna*, which is used to show emphasis. If *'inna* is followed by a noun subject in formal Arabic where case endings are used, that subject will be in the accusative case (see section 1E on Noun Cases). If it is followed by a pronoun subject, the pronoun will be in the form of the personal pronoun suffixes, attached to the *word 'inna*, such as *'innaka* (you) or *'innahu* (he).

If a sentence begins with a verb, that verb will agree with its subject only in gender. In other words, if the subject is *nisaa'* (women), the verb will be feminine but singular if it comes before that subject.

Subject is first, verb agrees in both gender and number:

an-nisaa' qara'na al-jariida.	The women read the newspaper.

Verb is first, verb agrees in gender only:

qara'at an-nisaa' al-jariida.	The women read the newspaper.

It is also important to remember that non-human plurals are treated as feminine singulars. So, a plural non-human noun will take a feminine singular verb form, be modified by an adjective in the feminine singular form, and be replaced by the pronoun *hiya* or the pronoun suffix *-haa*. This means that the plural forms of verbs, plural adjective endings, plural pronouns and pronoun suffixes are used only for human beings in Arabic.

GLOSSARY OF GRAMMATICAL TERMS

Accusative A grammatical case, or category. In many European languages, the accusative is the case of the direct object. In Arabic, the direct object of sentences beginning with a subject is in the accusative, and the subject of sentences beginning with certain introductory words is in the accusative. Case endings are not normally pronounced in spoken Arabic.

Adjective A word that describes or modifies a noun or pronoun in some way. Examples of adjectives are *important*, *beautiful*, and *big*. Adjectives answer the question "What is X like?"

Adverb A word that describes or modifies a verb, an adjective, or even another adverb. Many adverbs (but not all) in English end in *-ly*: *happily*, *quickly*, *wonderfully*. Other examples are *very*, *well*, *almost*, and *often*. Adverbs answer the question "How is X done" or "To what degree X?"

Agreement The modification of a word, such as a verb or adjective, to match another word it is linked to in some way. Verbs in English must agree with their subjects (*I go* but *she goes*). In many other languages adjectives must agree with the nouns or pronouns that they describe.

Article A word that introduces a noun and indicates whether it is particular and defined (definite) or non-specific and general (indefinite). There are two articles in English, the definite article is *the*, and the indefinite article is *a*.

Cardinal number A number used in counting, such as *one*, *two*, *three*, or *four*, as opposed to numbers used to order things, such as *first*, *second*, *third*, or *fourth*.

Case A grammatical category that a noun or pronoun falls into based on how it is used in a sentence, for example whether it is the subject, the direct object, an indirect object, a possessive, etc. Some languages show case by certain endings or other changes to a noun. Some languages show case by word order in a sentence. Particular cases may vary from language to language.

Comparative A degree of an adjective used to compare one item to one other. In English, comparative adjectives end in *-er*, or they are introduced by the word *more*.

Conjunction A word that links parts of a sentence, such as *and*, *or*, *although*, *because*, etc. Conjunctions may link two complete, independent thoughts, or they may link an incomplete "dependent" thought to a complete one.

Consonant Sounds that are produced by using the tongue, lips, teeth, or parts of the throat to change the way air passes through the mouth. Examples of consonants are the sounds of *b, k, s, l, m, th, sh, ch,* etc. Consonants vary greatly from language to language. Some are very common and are heard in many languages, and others may be very rare or even limited to one language or related language group.

Definite Defined and specific, referred to previously in conversation. Describes a type of article that can introduce a noun (or an adjective in Arabic).

Degree (of adjective) The forms of an adjective used to make comparisons. The comparative degree compares one item to one other (*more, -er*) and the superlative degree compares one item to two or more others (*most, -est*).

Demonstrative An adjective or pronoun that "points to" something. The demonstratives in English are *this*, *that*, *these*, and *those*.

Diphthong A sound produced by two or more vowel sounds acting together and gliding into one another. The sound *ay* in *say* is a diphthong made of the "pure" vowels *eh* and *ee*.

Direct object The "receiver of the action" in a sentence. The noun or pronoun that the verb happens to. In the sentence, *The director handed Greg the report*, the direct object is *the report*.

Dual Describes a pair or two of an item. Neither singular (one) nor plural (more than two).

Gender Natural gender describes the "sex" of a person or animal—male (masculine) or female (feminine). In some languages, such as English, there is only natural gender, and all inanimate objects, ideas, etc., are considered "neuter," *he* for a *man*, *she* for a *woman*, but *it* for a *car*, a *city*, a *rock*, or an *idea*. However, in some languages, all nouns have gender. Animate nouns with natural gender may or may not follow their logical gender, and other nouns have grammatical gender, which may be related to the ending of the noun, or which may follow no obvious logic.

Genitive A grammatical case, or category. In many European languages, the genitive is the case of possession. In Arabic, nouns that follow prepositions and nouns that are in the second (or possessor) position of possessive constructions are in the genitive. Case endings are not normally pronounced in spoken Arabic.

Indefinite Undefined and non-specific, not previously referred to in conversation. Describes a type of article that can introduce a noun in English. In Arabic, the indefinite article is implied but not overt.

Indirect object The "beneficiary of the action" in a sentence. The noun or pronoun that benefits or is affected by the verb and/or the direct object. In the sentence, *The director handed Greg the report*, the indirect object is *Greg*.

Jussive A mood of the present tense in Arabic. The jussive is used after *lam* (not) to show negatives in the past tense, after *laa* in negative commands, after *fal* and *li* to mean "let's" and also as the base for forming commands.

Mood A variation of the present tense in Arabic. There are two moods in Arabic—the subjunctive and the jussive.

Negation The act of making a verb negative. The most common negative in English is *not*. In Arabic, there are different ways to form negatives depending on the tense.

Nominative A grammatical case, or category. In many European languages and in Arabic as well, the nominative is the case of the subject of a sentence. Case endings are not normally pronounced in spoken Arabic.

Noun A grammatical category of words that name items—people, things, animals, places, concepts, ideas, etc.

Ordinal number A number used to order things, such as *first*, *second*, *third*, or *fourth*, as opposed to numbers used in counting, such as *one*, *two*, *three*, or *four*.

Past tense The tense, or time, of verbs that indicate actions that happened before the present or actions that are complete. In English, the simple past tense is indicated by the ending *-ed* on regular verbs (*walked*, *discussed*) but may also be indicated irregularly (*was, were, spoke, got, saw*).

Phrase A group of words that form one unit of thought, but that do not express a complete idea or constitute a complete sentence. Phrases form around a main word, such as a noun or preposition. Examples of phrases are *the big red car*, *a very original idea*, *in the house, to the office*, etc.

Plural A number of items that is neither singular (*one*) nor—if it exists in the language—dual (*two*).

Plural, broken The most common type of plural found in Arabic. Broken plurals are formed by changing the pattern of vowels occurring before, after, or between the root consonants of a word. For example, the plural of *rajul* (man) is *rijaal*, the plural of *kitaab* (book) is *kutub*, and the plural of *Sadiiq* (friend) is *'aSdiqaa'*.

Plural, sound The less common type of plural in Arabic, used mostly for nationalities, professions, or inanimate nouns that are too long to be changed into broken plurals. Examples of sound plurals are *miSriyyuun* (Egyptians, from *miSriyy*) *mudarrisaat* (teachers, from *mudarrisa*) and *tilifizyuunaat* (televisions, from *tilifizyuun*).

Possessive Indicating ownership or temporary possession.

Prefix A syllable that is added to the beginning of a word. Examples of English prefixes are *re-*, *pre-*, *post-*, *un-*, and *over-* in the words *remake*, *prefabricated*, *postsecondary*, *untold*, and *overweight*.

Preposition A word that describes some kind of relationship between two other words. Prepositions may describe location (*in*, *on*, *under*), motion or movement (*to*, *from*, *toward*), time (*after*, *before*, *during*) or other types of relationships (*for*, *without*, *because of*, *despite*).

Prepositional phrase A phrase that is introduced by a preposition. Examples of prepositional phrases are *to the beach, after school, for the new neighbors*, etc.

Present tense The tense, or time, of verbs that indicate actions that are happening now, that are unfinished, or that happen in general.

Pronoun A word that can replace a noun in a sentence. For example, *he* can replace *the man*, *she* can replace *Dr. Janet Harris*, *they* can replace *the children in the car*, and *it* can replace *liberty*.

Pronoun, personal The pronouns that are used to refer to people. *I, you, he, she, we,* and *they* are personal pronouns that can be used as subjects in English.

Root consonant In Arabic, one of the consonants that make up the "skeleton" of a word. There are generally three root consonants in verbs, nouns, and adjectives. For example, in the noun *rajul* (man) the root consonants are *r-j-l*. In the adjective *kabiir* (big) the root consonants are *k-b-r*. In the verb *waSala* (arrive) the root consonants are *w-S-l*.

Sentence A group of words that expresses a complete thought with a verb and usually a subject. A sentence makes a complete logical statement and can be agreed or disagreed with. Commands are considered complete sentences, too. Sentences are different from phrases in that they are considered complete thoughts.

Singular One of something. A number of items that is neither plural (more than two) or—if it exists in the language—dual (two).

Subject The "doer of the action" in a sentence or the person/thing/topic being spoken about in a sentence without a verb. The noun or pronoun that carries out the action expressed by the verb. In the sentence, *The director handed Greg the report*, the subject is *The director*.

Subjunctive A mood of the present tense in Arabic. The subjunctive is used after such words as *'an* (to, used after modals such as *must*, *want*, and *can*) *'allaa* (not to), *li* (in order to) *likay* (in order to) and *Hattaa* (so that). It is also used to make negative future statements after *lan*.

Suffix A syllable added to the end of a word. Examples of English suffixes are *-er, -ness, -tion, and -est* in the words *writer, darkness, liberation*, and *biggest.*

Superlative A degree of an adjective used to compare three or more items. In English, superlative adjectives end in *-est*, or they are introduced by the word *most*.

Syllable A division of a word that is centered around a vowel and that may or may not include consonants before or after that vowel. In the word *educate*, there are three syllables, *e—du—cate*, pronounced *eh-joo-kate*. The first syllabe *eh* receives the stress; it is pronounced with more emphasis than the others.

Tense The time of a verb. Verb tenses indicate whether an action happened in the past, is happening now, or will happen in the future.

Verb A word that expresses an action or a state of being. Verbs undergo different changes to agree with subjects and to show tense. Examples of verbs are *go, took, sing, jumps, is, are, were, seem, appeared,* etc.

Verb, assimilated Arabic verbs that have either *w* or *y* as their first root consonant. This so-called weak letter drops out of conjugation in the present tense.

Verb, defective Arabic verbs that have either *w* or *y* as their final root consonant. This so-called weak consonant changes into a vowel or a diphthong in conjugation.

Verb, doubled Arabic verbs with the same root consonant in the second and third positions.

Verb, hollow Arabic verbs that have either *w* or *y* as their middle root consonant. This so-called weak consonant changes into a vowel in conjugation.

Vowel A sound produced by only slightly modifying the shape of the mouth as air passes through it. Vowels can be held or sung, as opposed to consonants, which cannot. Examples of vowels are the sounds *ah*, *eh*, *ay*, *ee*, *oh*, *uh*, etc.

ARABIC-ENGLISH GLOSSARY

The words in this glossary are arranged alphabetically in the order of transcription letters in English. The transcription letters *D, dh, DH, gh, H, kh, sh, S, T,* and *th* appear as separate, distinct letters. Plural forms appear after slashes, and feminine forms if irregular appear after commas. The abbreviations m., f., and pl. mean "masculine," "feminine," and "plural" respectively. In the case of verbs, the past tense *huwa* form is given, followed by the present tense *huwa* form.

a

'ab / 'aabaa' father
'abadan never
'abriil April
'abyaD, bayDaa' / biiD white
'aDH-DHuhr noon
'adwiya medication, drugs
'afghaanistaan Afghanistan
'afghaaniyy, 'afghaaniyya Afghani
'afriil April
'aghusTus August
'aHad someone, one (person)
'aHad xashar eleven
'aHad, al- Sunday
'aHmar, Hamraa' / Humr red
'aHsan . . . the best . . .
'aHyaanaan sometimes
'ajaaba / yujiibu answer (to)
'akala / ya'kulu eat (to)
'akh / 'ikhwa brother
'akhadha / ya'khudhu take (to)
'akhDar, khaDraa' / khuDr green
'alf mabruuk! Congratulations!
al-'aan now
al-ghad tomorrow
al-Hamdu lillaah I'm fine, I'm doing well.
'allaa not to (+subjunctive)
'almaaniyy, 'ammaaniyya German
'almaanyaa Germany

'amiin al-maSrif bank teller
'amriikaa America
'amriikiyy, 'amriikiyya American
'ams yesterday
'ams al-'awwal the day before yesterday
'amtixa baggage
'an to (+ subjunctive)
'anaa I
'anna . . . that . . .
'anf nose
'anta you (m.)
'anti you (f.)
'antum you (m. plural)
'antumaa the two of you (m. or f.)
'antunna you (f. plural)
'arbaxa four
'arbaxata xashar fourteen
'arbaxiin / 'arbaxuun forty
'arsala / yursilu send (to)
'aruzz rice
'asbiriin aspirin
'aSfar, Safraa' / Sufr yellow
'asmar, samraa' / sumr brown (skin)
as-salaamu xalaykum hello, good day
'aswad, sawdaa' / suud black
'awdaxa / yuudixu deposit (to)
'awwal first
'axid Repeat.
'axTinii Give me . . .
'ayDan also, too, as well
'ayna where?
'azraq, zarqaa' / zurq blue

b

baa'ix / –uun salesman
baab / 'abwaab door
baahiDH expensive
baar / –aat bar
baarid / –uun cold

baariHa, al- yesterday
bada'a / yabda'u begin, start (to)
baHr sea
baHrayniyy, baHrayniyya Bahraini
baHrayn, al Bahrain
balgha / –aat slippers
balligh taHiyyaatii. Give my greetings/regards.
banyuu bathtub
baqshiish tip
barada / yabridu mail (to)
bard cold
bariid mail
bariid 'iliktruuniyy e-mail
bariid jawwiyy air mail
baSala / baSlaat onion
baTii' / –uun slow
baTTaniiya / –aat blanket
bawwaab / –uun concierge
baxda after
baxda aDH-DHuhr afternoon
baxda l-ghad the day after tomorrow
baxiid / –uun far
bayDa / –aat egg
bayt / buyuut house
bi with, in
biduuni without
bijaanibi next to
binaaya / –aat building
binaayat al-xamal office building
binaayat as-sakan apartment building
bint / banaat daughter, girl
bint khaal(a) cousin, maternal side, female
bint xamm(a) cousin, paternal side, female
biira beer
biTaaqa bariidiyya / –aat post card
biTaaqat al-'istilaaf / biTaaqaat l-'istilaaf credit card
biTaaqat ar-rukuub boarding pass
burtuqaala / burtuqaal orange
bustaan garden

d

daa'Iman always
daa'ira / dawaa'ir department
daa'irat al-bayx sales department
daar house (feminine)
dajaaj chicken
dakhala / yadkhulu enter, go in (to)
daliil al-haatif / 'adillat al-haatif telephone book
dam blood
daqiiqa minute
darasa / yadrusu study (to)
darraaja / –aat bicycle
darrasa / yudarrisu teach
diiviidii / –yaat DVD
diiwaana customs
dimaagh brain
disambar December
djiinz / djiinzaat jeans
dukkaan / dakaakiin store
dukkaan al-aHdhia shoe store
dukkaan al-'iliktruuniyaat electronics store
dukkaan al-baqqaal grocery store
dukkaan al-fawaakih fruit store
dukkaan al-Halwaani pastry shop
dukkaan al-malaabis clothing store
dukkaan as-samak fish store
dushsh shower

D

Daa'ix / –uun lost
DaHika / yaD-Haku laugh (to)
Daxiif / Duxafaa' weak

dh

dhaalika that (masculine)
dhahaba / yadh-habu go (to)
dhakiyy / 'adhkiyaa' smart, intelligent
dhiraax / dhiraaxaan arm (feminine)

DH

DHanna / yaDHunnu think (to)
DHarf envelope

f

faaDii free, available
faakiha / fawaakih fruit
faaks fax
fahima / yafhamu understand (to)
fam mouth
fann / funuun art
fannaan / fannaanuun artist
faqiir / fuqaraa' poor
faransaa France
faransiyy, faransiyya French
faras / furuus horse
farHaan / –uun happy
fariiq team
farraqa / yufarriqu give out, distribute (to)
fataHa / yaftaHu open (to)
fawz win (noun)
faxala / yafxalu do (to)
fibraayir February
fii in
filisTiin Palestine
filisTiiniyy, filisTiiniyya Palestinian
fiilm / 'aflaam film, movie
fulful pepper
fuluus money, physical currency
funduq hotel
furuusiyya horseback riding
fustaan / fasaatiin dress
fuTuur / fuTuuraat, wajabaat al-fuTuur breakfast
fuul beans
fuuTa towel

gh

ghaa'im, al-jaww ghaa'im it's cloudy
ghaalii expensive
ghad, al- tomorrow

ghadan tomorrow
ghariib / ghurabaa' stranger
ghadaa' / 'aghdia, wajabaat al-gadaa' lunch
ghurfa / ghuraf room
ghurfa li-ithnayn double room
ghurfa li-waaHid single room
ghurfat al-haatif phone booth
ghurfat al-juluus livingroom, sitting room
ghurfat an-nawm bedroom

h

haa'ulaa'i these (gender neutral)
haadhaa this (masculine)
haadhihi this (feminine)
haadi' quiet
haatif / hawaatif telephone
haatif mutajawwil cell phone
haatif xumuumiyy public phone, payphone
haram / 'ahraam pyramid
hind, al- India
hindiyy, hindiyya Indian
hiya she, it, they (non-human)
hum they (m. plural)
humaa the two of them (m. or f.)
hunaa here
hunaaka there
hunna they (f. plural)
huwa he, it

H

Haadii xashar eleventh
Haafila / –aat bus
Haarr hot
Haasuub / Haasuubaat computer
HaDHDHan saxiidan! Best of luck!
Hafla / –aat party
Hakam referee
Haliib milk
Hallaaq / Hallaaquun barber
Hammaal porter/baggage handler

Hammaam bathroom
Hariir silk
Harq burn
Hasaa' soup
Hattaa so that (+subjunctive)
Haziin / Huzanaa' sad
Hidhaa' / 'aHdhia shoe, pair of shoes
Hajz reservation
Hisaab bill, check
Hisaab maSrifiyy bank account
Hizaam / 'aHzimaa' belt

i

'ibn / 'abnaa' son
'ibn khaal(a) cousin, maternal side, male
'ibn xamm(a) cousin, paternal side, male
'iDaafiyya extra
'iddakhara / yaddakhiru save (to)
'intarnat internet
'ijtimaax / 'ijtimaaxaat meeting
'ilaa to, towards
'ilaa l-ghad. Until tomorrow. See you tomorrow.
'ilaa l-liqaa'. Until next time.
'imDaa' signature
'imra'a / nisaa' woman (irregular singular/plural)
'imra'at 'axmaal businesswoman
'injiltraa England
'injiliiziyy, 'injiliiziyya English
'inTilaaq departure
'arbixaa', al- Wednesday
'isbaaniyaa Spain
'isbaaniyy, 'isbaaniyya Spanish
'iSbax / 'aSaabix finger
'iSbax al-qadam / 'aSaabix . . . toe
'ishtaraa / yashtarii buy (to)
'ism / 'asmaa' name
'ismii my name
'ismuka, 'ismuki your name (masculine, feminine)
'istimaara / –aat form
'iiTaaliyy, iiTaaliyaa Italian

'iiTaaliyaa Italy
'ithnaa xashar twelve
'ithnayn two
'ithnayn wa xishruun twenty two
'ithnayn, al-' Monday
'ixtiyaadiyyan usually

j

jaa'ix / –uun hungry
jaahil / juhalaa' foolish, ignorant
jaamix / jawaamix mosque
jaamixa / –aat university
jadd / juduud grandfather
jadda / –aat grandmother
jadiid / judud new
jadwal / jadaawil schedule
jadwal al-'awqaat, jadaawil al-'awqaat schedule
jalasa / yajlisu sit (to)
jallaabiyya / –aat traditional Arab robe
jamiil pretty, beautiful
jariida / jaraa'id newspaper
jarraaH surgeon
jasad / 'ajsaad body
jawaarib socks
jawaaz as-safar passport
jawharjiyy / –yuun jeweler
jaww weather
jayyid good
jazaa'ir, al- Algeria
jazaa'iriyy, jazaa'iriyya Algerian
jazzaar/-uun butcher shop
jiddan very
jild leather, skin
jisr / jusuur bridge
jubn cheese
jumuxa, al- Friday

k

ka's / ku'uus glass, cup (feminine)
kaatib clerk, writer, secretary

kaatiba / –aat receptionist, secretary
kabiir / kibaar big, great, old
kadhaalika as well, also, equally
kahrabaa'iyy electrician
kalb / kilaab dog
kallafa / yukallifu cost (to)
kallama / yukallimu call (to)
kam (min) how much (of)? / how many (of)?
kammala / yukammilu finish, complete (to)
kanadaa Canada
kanadiyy, kanadiyya Canadian
kaniisa / kanaa'is church, synagogue
karaaj garage (less standard)
karTa cards (game)
kasuul / –uun lazy
kataba / yaktubu write (to)
kathiira(n) a lot, much
katif / katifaan shoulder (feminine)
kayfa how?
kayfa l-Haal How are you?
kayyala / yukayyilu weigh (to)
kiiniyy, kiiniyya Kenyan
kiinyaa Kenya
kitaab / kutub book
kulliyya / –aat college, school in a university
kura / kuraat ball
kurat al-qadam soccer
kursiyy chair
kuskus couscous
kuub / 'akwaab glass
kuumbyuutar / kuumbyuutaraat computer
kuuriyy, kuuriyya Korean
kuuriyaa Korea
kuwayt Kuwait
kuwaytiyy, kuwaytiyya Kuwaiti

kh

khaadima / –aat cleaning woman
khaal / 'akhwaal uncle (maternal side)

khaala / khaalaat aunt (maternal side)
khaamis fifth
khaatim / khawaatim ring
khafiif light
khajuul / –uun shy
khalaxa / yakhlaxu take off (clothes) (to)
khallaSa / yukhalliSu pay (to)
khamiis, al- Thursday
khamr wine
khamsa five
khamsata xashar fifteen
khamsiin / khamsuun fifty
khariif, al- autumn
khariiTa / kharaa'iT map
khasar loss
khasira / yakhsiru lose (to)
khaTa' wrong
khayl horses
khinziir pork
khiyaar cucumber
khizaana safe (n.)
khubz bread
khuDar vegetable
khudhnii . . . Take/Drive me . . .

l

laa no
laaxib ad-diiviidii DVD player
laaxib as-siidii CD player
labisa / yalbasu put on (clothes) (to)
ladhiidh delicious
laHm al-baqar beef
lahw fun
lan will not (+subjunctive)
laTiif / liTaaf nice, friendly
lawn / 'alwaan color
laxiba / yalxabu play (sports/games) (to)
layla /layl / layaal night
li for, in order to
liibiyy, liibiyya Libyan

liibiyaa Libya
likay in order to (+subjunctive)
lisaan tongue
lubnaan Lebanon
lubnaaniyy, lubnaaniyya Lebanese

m

ma'waa as-sayyaara garage
maa what? (used with nouns and pronouns)
maa' water
maadhaa what? (used with verbs)
maal money
maaris March
maay May
maayuu May
madiina / mudun city
madrasa / madaaris school
maghrib, al- Morocco
maghribiyy, maghribiyya Morrocan
maghsala / –aat sink
maHall store
maHaTTat al-Haafila bus station
maHaTTat al-qiTaar train station
makhbaz / makhaabiz bakery
maktab / makaatib office, counter
maktab al-bariid post office
maktaba / –aat library, bookstore
maktab al-'istiqbaal reception desk
maktab as-siyaaHa travel agency
malhaa / malaahii discotheque
man who?
mandiil / manaadil napkin
manzil home, residence
maraD sickness
maraD al-Hasaasiyya allergy
marHaban bika/biki welcome
mariiD / marDaa sick, ill
marratan 'ukhra again, another time
masaa', al- evening, afternoon
masaka / yamsiku catch (to)

masbaH swimming pool
mashaa / yamshii walk (to)
mashghuul / –uun busy, booked
masjid / masaajid mosque
masraH / masaariH theater
maSrif / maSaarif bank
mataa when?
maTaar airport
maTbakh kitchen
maTbaxa printer
matHaf / mataaHif museum
matjar kabiir department store, mall
maTxam / maTaaxim restaurant
mawxid / mawaaxiid appointment
mawxid al-wuSuul time of arrival
mawza / mawz banana
maxa with
maxa s-salaama. Good bye.
maxaa 'aTyab al-'umniyaat. With best wishes.
maxida belly, abdomen
maxluuma / –aat information
maxmal factory
mi'a hundred
miftaaH key
miftaaH al-kahrabaa' light switch
mihna / mihan profession, work
mikwaa(t) iron (clothes)
milaff / milaffaat file
milH salt
milxaqa / malaaxiq spoon
min from
mir'aa(t) mirror
mirHaaD toilet
miSbaaH lamp
miSr Egypt
miSriyy, miSriiyya Egyptian
miSxad elevator
mixTaf / maxaaTif coat
mubaara(t) game
mudarris / –uun teacher

muDHiif / –uun flight attendant
mudiir / –uun director
mughannii / –uun singer
muHaamii / muHaamuun lawyer
muHaasib / –uun accountant, bookkeeper
muhandis / –uun architect, engineer
muHarrir / –uun editor
muhimm important
muHraza score
mujaawara / –aat neighborhood
mukaalama / –aat call, phone call
mukaalama duwaliyya international call
mukaalama haatifiyya phone call
mukaalama maHalliyya domestic call
mukaalama xalaa Hisaabi l-mutalaqqii collect call
mumarriDa / –aat nurse
mumaththil / –uun actor
mumkin possible
mumtaaz wonderful, amazing; excellent
mumTir, al-jaww mumTir it's raining
mumtix interesting; enjoyable
munaaqasha/ –aat discussion
muntazah / muntazahaat park
muqabbilaat appetizers
muqliq boring; worrisome
muSawwira / –aat camera
mushmis, al-jaww mushmis it's sunny
mustashfaa / mustashfayaat hospital
mutarjim / –uun translator
muthaabir / –uun hard-working
muthlij, al-jaww muthlij it's snowing
muusiiqiyy / –uun musician
muwaDHDHaf / –uun employee
muxallim / –uun teacher

n

naama / yanaamu sleep (to)
naDHiif / niDHaaf clean
nafas breath
naHiif thin, slim

nahj / 'anhuj street
naHnu we
najjaar carpenter
naqd / nuquud coin
naxam yes
nisaa' women
nufambar November
nuzl / nuzul hotel

q

qaamuus dictionary
qaarib / qawaarib boat
qaaxat aT-Taxaam dining room
qabala / yaqbalu receive, accept (to)
qabl before
qadam / qadamaan foot (feminine)
qadiim / qudamaa' old (things)
qafaza / yaqfizu jump (to)
qahwa coffee
qalb / quluub heart
qaliil(an) a little
qamiiS / 'aqmiSa shirt
qara'a / yaqra'u read (to)
qariib (min) near (to)
qarya / quraa village
qaSiir / qiSaar short, brief
qatar Qatar
qatariyy, qatariyya Qatari
qawiyy / 'aqwiyaa' strong
qif Stop.
qilaada / –aat necklace
qiTaar train
qubbaxa / –aat hat
qul-lii Tell me . . .
qutn cotton

r

ra'aa / yaraa see (to)
ra'iis / ru'asaa' manager, boss, chief, president
ra's / ru'uus head

raabix fourth
raadyuu radio
raakib passenger
rabaHa / yarbaHu earn money (to)
rabaHa / yarbiHu win (to)
rabiix, ar– spring
raDDa bruise
rad-ha lobby
radii' bad
rafaxa / yarfaxu lift, raise (to)
rahiib terrible
rajaxa / yarjixu come back, return (to)
rajul / rijaal man
rajul 'axmaal businessman
rakhiiS inexpensive, cheap
rakkaba r-raqm dial
ramaa / yarmii throw (to)
raml sand
raqm / 'arqaam number
raqm al-haatif telephone number
raqm sirriyy PIN number
raqm al-madiina ZIP code, city postal code
rasm / rusuum fee
ri'a / ri'ataan lung
riHla / –aat flight
riHla dawliyya international flight
rijl / rijlaan leg (feminine)
risaala / rasaa'il letter
risaala 'iliktruuniyya (e-mail) message
riyaaDa sports
rukba / rukbataan knee
rukhSa license

S

sa'ala / yas'alu ask (to)
saa'iH / suwwaaH tourist
saa'iq driver
saabix seventh
saadis sixth
saaxa / –aat watch, clock, hour

saafara / yusaafiru travel (to)
sabaHa / yasbaHu swim (to)
sabt, as– Saturday
sabxa seven
sabxata xashar seventeen
sabxiin / sabxuun seventy
safaran saxiidan. Have a good trip.
saHaba / yasHabu withdraw (to)
sakana / yaskunu live (to)
saliim healthy
samak fish
samaka / samak fish
samiin / simaan fat
sana / sanawaat year
sariir / 'asirra bed
sariix fast
saxala / yasxulu cough (to)
saxuudiyy, saxuudiyya Saudi
saxuudiyya, as– Saudi Arabia
sayyaara / –aat car
sibaaHa swimming
siidii / –yaat CD
sikkiin / sakaakiin knife
simsaar broker
sinighaal, as- Senegal
sinighaaliyy, sinighaaliyya Senegalese
sinimaa movies
sinn / 'asnaan tooth
sibtambar September
sirwaal / saraawiil pants
sitta six
sittata xashar sixteen
sittiin / sittuun sixty
su'aal / 'as'ila question
sukkar sugar
suudaan, as– Sudan
suudaaniyy, suudaaniyya Sudanese
suuq / 'aswaaq market
suuriyy, suuriyya Syrian

suuriyaa Syria
suxaal cough

S

SabaaH, aS– morning
Sadiiq / 'aSdiqaa' friend (m.)
Sadiiqa / Sadiiqaat friend (f.)
Sadr chest
Saghiir / Sighaar small, young
SaHaafiyy / –uun journalist
SaHiiH right
Sarf exchange
Sarrafa / yuSarrifu exchange (currency) (to)
Sawwara / yuSawwiru copy (to)
Sayd as-samak fishing
Sayf, aS– summer
Sibaaq al-khayl horse racing
Sifr zero
Siin, aS– China
Siiniyy, Siiniyya Chinese
SubH, aS– morning
Suura / Suwar copy, picture, photograph
Suurat ashixxa x-ray

sh

shaahada / yushaahidu watch (to)
shaarix / shawaarix avenue
shaaTi' beach
shaaTi' khaaS private beach
shaay tea
shahr / 'ash-hur month
shakhS / 'ashkhaaS person
sharaab / mashruubaat drink/beverage
sharaab as-suxaal cough syrup
shariba / yashrabu drink (to)
sharika / –aat company
shaTranj chess
shawka / –aat fork
shaxara / yashxuru feel (to)
shaxr hair

shiik check
shitaa', ash– winter
shubbaak window
shukran (jaziilan) thank you (very much)
shuqqa / shuqaq apartment
shurTiyy policeman

t

taabiliyy spicy
taajir merchant, trader
taaksii taxi
taasix ninth
tadhakkara / yatadhakkaru remember (to)
tadhkira / tadhaakir ticket
tafaDDal, tafaDDalii come in, welcome, please
taHta under
takallam bi buT'in Speak slowly.
takallama / yatakallamu speak (to)
tamra / tamr date
taqriir report
tasliim al-'amtixa baggage claim area
taxbaan tired, sleepy
tayland Thailand
taylandiyy, taylandiyya Thai
tazaHluq skiing
tazalluj skating
tilifizyuun / –aat television
tilka that (feminine)
tilmiidh / talaamiidh high school student, pupil
timthaal / tamaathiil statue
tisxa nine
tisxata xashar nineteen
tisxiin / tisxuun ninety
tuffaaHa / tuffaH apple
tuunis Tunisia
tuunisiyy, tuunisiyya Tunisian

T

Taa'ira / –aat airplane
Taabix / Tawaabix stamp

Taabiq floor
Taabiq al-'awwal, al- first floor
Taalib / Tullaab student
Taazaj fresh
Tabbaakh cook, chef
Tabakha / yaTbukhu cook (to)
Tabaq / 'aTbaaq plate
Tabiib / 'aTibbaa' doctor
Tabiib l-'asnaan / 'aTibbaa' . . . dentist
Tabxan of course
TamaaTima / TamaaTim tomato
Taqs weather
Tariiq / Turuq main street
Tawiil / Tiwaal tall, long, lengthy
Taxaam / 'aTxima food

th

thaalith third
thaamin eighth
thaanii xashar twelfth
thaanii second
thalaatha three
thalaatha wa xishruun twenty three
thalaathata xashar thirteen
thalaathiin / thalaathuun thirty
thamaaniin / thamaanuun eighty
thamaaniya eight
thamaaniyata xashar eighteen
thaqiil heavy
thulaathaa', ath– Tuesday
thuum garlic

u

'udhun / 'udhunaan ear (feminine)
'ukht / 'akhawaat sister
'uktub Write. (command)
'uktuubar October
'umm / 'ummahaat mother
'urdun, al- Jordan
'urduniyy, 'urduniyya Jordanian

'ustaadh / 'asaatidha professor
'usbuux / 'asaabiix week
'uulaa'ika those (gender neutral)

W

wa and
waHiid alone, lonely
wa xalaykum as-salaam response to 'assalamu xalaykum
waaHid one
waaHid wa xishruun twenty one
wajax aDH-DHahr backache
wajh / wujuuh face
walad / 'awlaad son, boy
waqafa / yaqifu stand (to)
waqt faarigh free time
waqtan mumtixan. Have a good time.
waraq, al- cards (game)
waraqa / 'awraaq bill, paper money
warda / wuruud rose
waSala / yaSilu arrive (to)
wasikh dirty
waSl receipt
wazn weight
wilaayaat al-muttaHida, al- The United States
wisaada pillow
wuSuul arrival

X

xaa'ila / xaa'ilaat family
xaalii loud
xaamil / xummaal worker
xaamil al-maktab desk clerk
xaamil bi l-maTxam waiter
xaamil haatifiyy / xummaal haatifiyyiin operator
xaashir tenth
xadad / 'axdaad number
xaDHiim / xuDHamaa' great, powerful
xaDHm / xiDHaam bone
xafwan I'm sorry/Pardon me. / Excuse me.
xalaa on
xallama / yuxallimu teach (to)

xamal job
xamila / yaxmalu work (to)
xamm / 'axmaam uncle (paternal side)
xamma / –aat aunt (paternal side)
xarafa / yaxrifu know (to)
xashaa' / –aat dinner
xashara ten
xaSiir juice
xaSr, al- late afternoon
xaTafa / yaxTufu turn (to)
xaTshaan / xaTishuun thirsty
xayn / xuyuun eye (feminine)
xiid miilaad saxiid Happy birthday!
xilaaj remedy
xindii al-'anfiluwanza I have the flu.
xindii bard I have a cold.
xindii Haraara I have a temperature.
xindii Hajz I have a reservation.
xindii Sudaax I have a headache.
xiraaq, al- Iraq
xiraaqiyy, xiraaqiyya Iraqi
xishruun twenty
xiyaada clinic
xumla money; currency
xumaan Oman
xumaaniyy, xumaaniyya Omani
xunwaan address
xunwaan 'iliktruuniyy e-mail address

y

yaabaan, al- Japan
yaabaaniyy, yaabaaniyya Japanese
yad / yadaan / 'ayd hand (feminine), (s., dual, pl.)
yaman, al- Yemen
yamaniyy, yamaniyya Yemeni
yamiin right, on the right
yanaayir January
yasaar left, on the left
yawm / 'ayyaam day
yawm, al- today

yuulyuu July
yuunyuu June

Z

zaara / yazuuru visit (to)
zaawiya / zawaayaa corner (of a room)
zabuun client
zahra / –aat flower
zamiil / zumalaa' colleague
zanqa / –aat little street, especially in older part of town
zawj / 'azwaaj husband
zawja / –aat wife
zubda butter

ENGLISH-ARABIC GLOSSARY

A

a little qaliil(an)
a lot kathiir(an)
abdomen maxida
accept (to) qabala / yaqbalu
accountant muHaasib / –uun
actor mumaththil / –uun
address xunwaan
Afghani 'afghaaniyy, 'afghaaniyya
Afghanistan 'afghaanistaan
after baxda
afternoon baxda aDH-DHuhr, al-masaa'
again, another time marratan 'ukhra
air mail bariid jawwiyy
airplane Taa'ira / –aat
airport maTaar
Algeria jazaa'ir, al-
Algerian jazaa'iriyy, jazaa'iriyya
allergy maraD al-Hasaasiyya
alone waHiid
also 'ayDan
always daa'iman
amazing mumtaaz
America 'amriikaa
American 'amriikiyy, 'amriikiyya
and wa
answer (to) 'ajaaba / yujiibu
apartment building binaayat as-sakan
apartment shuqqa / shuqaq
appetizers muqabbilaat
apple tuffaaHa / tuffaH
appointment mawxid / mawaaxiid
April 'abriil
architect muhandis / –uun
arm dhiraax / dhiraaxaan
arrival wuSuul
arrive (to) waSala / yaSilu

art fann / funuun
artist fannaan / fannaanuun
as well, equally kadhaalika
ask (to) sa'ala / yas'alu
aspirin 'asbiriin
August 'aghusTus
aunt (maternal side) khaala / –aat
aunt (paternal side) xamma / –aat
autumn khariif, al-
available faaDii
avenue shaarix / shawaarix

B

backache wajax aDH-DHahr
bad radii'
baggage 'amtixa
baggage claim area tasliim al-'amtixa
baggage handler Hammaal
Bahrain al-baHrayn
Bahraini baHrayniyy, baHrayniyya
bakery makhbaz / makhaabiz
ball kura / kuraat
banana mawza / mawz
bank account Hisaab maSrifiyy
bank teller 'amiin al-maSrif
bank maSrif / maSaarif
bar baar / –aat, Haana / -aat
barber Hallaaq / Hallaaquun
bathroom Hammaam
bathtub banyuu
beach shaaTi'
beach, private shaaTi' khaaS
beans fuul
beautiful jamiil
bed sariir / 'asirra
bedroom ghurfat an-nawm
beef laHm al-baqar
beer biira
before qabl
begin (to) bada'a / yabda'u

belly maxida
belt Hizaam / 'aHzimaa'
beverage sharaab / mashruubaat
Best of luck! HaDHDHan saxiidan!
bicycle darraaja / –aat
big kabiir / kibaar
bill Hisaab
bill (money) waraqa / 'awraaq
black 'aswad, sawdaa' / suud
blanket baTTaniyya / –aat
blood dam
blue 'azraq, zarqaa' / zurq
boarding pass biTaaqat ar-rukuub
boat qaarib / qawaarib
body jasad / 'ajsaad
bone xaDHm / xiDHaam
book kitaab / kutub
bookkeeper muHaasib / –uun
bookstore maktaba / –aat
booked mashguul / –uun
boring muqliq; mumill
boy walad, 'awlaad
brain dimaagh
brief qaSiir / qiSaar
bread khubz
breakfast fuTuur / fuTuuraat, wajabaat al-fuTuur
breath nafas
bridge jisr / jusuur
broker simsaar
brother 'akh / 'ikhwa
brown (skin) 'asmar, samraa' / sumr
bruise raDDa
building binaaya / –aat
burn Harq
bus station maHaTTat al-Haafila
bus Haafila / –aat
businessman rajul 'axmaal
businesswoman 'imra'at 'axmaal
busy mashghuul / –uun
butcher shop jazzaar / jazzaaruun

butter zubda
buy (to) 'ishtaraa / yashtarii

C

call (to) kallama / yukallimu
call, phone call mukaalama / –aat
call, collect mukaalama xalaa Hisaabi l-mutalaqqii
call, domestic mukaalama maHaliyya
call, international mukaalama duwaliyya
camera muSawwira / –aat
Canada kanadaa
Canadian kanadiyy, kanadiyya
car sayyaara / –aat
cards (game) karTa, al-waraq
carpenter najjaar
catch (to) masaka / yamsiku
CD player laaxib as-siidii
CD siidii / –yaat
cell phone haatif mutajawwil
chair kursiyy
cheap rakhiiS
check shiik, Hisaab, Sakk
cheese jubn
chef Tabbaakh
chess shaTranj
chest Sadr
chicken dajaaj
China Siin, aS-
Chinese Siiniyy, Siiniyya
church kaniisa / kanaa'is
city madiina / mudun
clean naDHiif / niDHaaf
cleaning woman khaadima / –aat
clerk kaatib
client zubuun
clinic xiyaada
clock saaxa / –aat
clothes iron mikwaa(t)
clothing store dukkaan al-malaabis

cloudy, it's al-jaww ghaa'im
coat mixTaf / maxaaTif
coffee qahwa
coin naqd / nuquud
cold baarid / –uun
cold, a bard
colleague zamiil / zumalaa'
collect call mukaalama xalaa Hisaabi l-mutalaqqii
college kulliyya / –aat
color lawn / 'alwaan
come back (to) rajaxa / yarjixu
come in tafaDDal, tafaDDalii
company sharika / –aat
complete (to) kammala / yukammilu
computer Haasuub, kumbyuutar / kumbyuutaraat
concierge bawwaab / –uun
Congratulations! 'alf mabruuk!
cook (to) Tabakha / yaTbukhu
cook Tabbaakh
copy (to) nasakha / yansakhu
copy nuskha / -aat
correct SaHiiH
corner (of a room) zaawiya / zawaaya
corner (of a street) maqtax; taqaaTux; naaSiya
cost (to) kallafa / yukallifu
cotton qutn
cough (to) saxala / yasxulu
cough syrup sharaab as-suxaal
cough suxaal
counter maktab / makaatib
couscous kuskus
cousin, maternal side, female bint khaal(a)
cousin, maternal side, male 'ibn khaal(a)
cousin, paternal side, female bint xamm(a)
cousin, paternal side, male 'ibn xamm(a)
credit card biTaaqat al-'istilaaf, biTaaqaat l-'istilaaf
cucumber khiyaar
cup ka's / ku'uus (f.)
customs diiwaana; jumruk/jamaarik

D

date tamra / tamr
daughter bint / banaat
day yawm / 'ayyaam
December disambar
delicious ladhiidh
dentist Tabiib l-'asnaan / 'aTibbaa' . . .
department store matjar kabiir
department daa'ira / dawaa'ir
departure 'inTilaaq
deposit (to) 'awdaxa / yuudixu
desk clerk xaamil al-maktab
dial rakkaba r-raqm
dictionary qaamuus
dining room qaaxat aT-Taxaam
dinner xashaa' / –aat, wajabaat al xashaa'
director mudiir / –uun
dirty wasikh
discotheque malhaa / malaahii
discussion munaaqasha/ –aat
distribute (to) farraqa / yufarriqu
do (to) faxala / yafxalu
doctor Tabiib / 'aTibbaa'
dog kalb / kilaab
domestic call mukaalama maHaliyya
door baab / 'abwaab
double room ghurfa li-'ithnayn
dress fustaan / fasaatiin
drink (to) shariba / yashrabu
drink sharaab / mashruubaat
Drive me . . . khudhnii . . .
driver saa'iq
drug 'adwiya
DVD player laaxib ad-diiviidii
DVD diiviidii / –yaat

E

ear 'udhun / 'udhunaan (f.)
earn money (to) rabiHa / yarbaHu
eat (to) 'akala / ya'kulu
editor muHarrir / –uun

egg bayDa / –aat
Egypt miSr
Egyptian miSriyy, miSriiyya
eight thamaaniya
eighteen thamaaniyyata xashar
eighth thaamin
eighty thamaaniin / thamaanuun
electrician kahrabaa'iyy
electronics store dukkaan al-iliktruuniyaat
elevator miSxad
eleven 'aHad xashar
eleventh Haadii xashar
e-mail bariid 'iliktruuniyy
e-mail address xunwaan 'iliktruuniyy
e-mail message risaala 'iliktruuniyya
employee muwaDHDHaf / –uun
England 'injiltraa
English 'injiliiziyy, 'injiliiziyya
enter (to) dakhala / yadkhulu
envelope DHarf
evening masaa', al-
exchange (currency) (to) Sarrafa / yuSarrifu
exchange Sarf
Excuse me. xafwan.
expensive baahiDH, ghaalii
extra 'iDaafiyy
eye (feminine) xayn / xuyuun

F

face wajh / wujuuh
factory maxmal, maSnax
family xaa'ila / xaa'ilaat
far baxiid / –uun
fast sariix
fat samiin / simaan
father 'ab / 'aabaa'
fax faaks
February fibraayir
fee rasm / rusuum
feel (to) shaxara / yashxuru

fifteen khamsata xashar
fifth khaamis
fifty khamsiin / khamsuun
file milaff / milaffaat
film, movie fiilm / 'aflaam
finger 'iSbax / 'aSaabix
finish (to) kammala / yukammilu
first 'awwal
first floor aT-Taabiq al-'awwal
fish samak, samaka / samak
fish store dukkaan as-samak
fishing Sayd as-samak
five khamsa
flight riHla / –aat
flight attendant muDHiif / –uun
flight, international riHla dawliyya
floor Taabiq
flower zahra / –aat
food Taxaam / 'aTxima
foolish jaahil / juhalaa'
foot qadam / qadamaan (f.)
for li
fork shawka / –aat
form 'istimaara / –aat
forty 'arbaxiin / 'arbaxuun
four 'arbaxa
fourteen 'arbaxata xashar
fourth raabix
France faransaa
free faaDii
free time waqt faarigh
French faransiyy, faransiyya
fresh Taazaj
Friday jumuxa, al-
friend (f.) Sadiiqa / Sadiiqaat
friend (m.) Sadiiq / 'aSdiqaa'
friendly laTiif / liTaaf
from min
fruit faakiha / fawaakih

fruit store dukkaan al-fawaakih
fun lahw

G

game mubaaraa(t)
garage ma'waa as-sayyaara, karaaj
garden bustaan
garlic thuum
German 'almaaniyy, 'almaaniyya
Germany 'almaanyaa
girl bint / banaat
Give me . . . 'axTinii
Give my greetings/regards. balligh taHiyyaatii.
give out (to) farraqa / yufarriqu
glass kuub / 'akwaab
glass ka's / ku'uus (f.)
go (to) dhahaba / yadh-habu
go in (to) dakhala / yadkhulu
Good bye. maxa s-salaama.
good jayyid
grandfather jadd / juduud
grandmother jadda / –aat
great xaDHiim / xuDHamaa', kabiir / kibaar
green 'akhDar, khaDraa' / khuDr
grocery store dukkaan al-baqqaal

H

hair shaxr
hand yad / yadaan / 'ayd (f.), (s., dual, pl.)
Happy birthday! xiid miilaad saxiid
happy farHaan / –uun
hard-working muthaabir / –uun
hat qubbaxa / –aat
Have a good time. waqtan mumtixan.
Have a good trip. safaran saxiidan.
he huwa
head ra's / ru'uus
healthy saliim
heart qalb / quluub
heavy thaqiil
hello, good day as-salaamu xalaykum

here hunaa
high school student tilmiidh / talaamiidh
home manzil
horse racing sibaaq al-khayl
horse faras / furuus, khayl
horseback riding furuusiyya
hospital mustashfaa / mustashfayaat
hot Haarr
hotel funduq, nuzl
hour saaxa / –aat
house daar (feminine)
house bayt / buyuut
How are you? kayfa l-Haal?
how many (of)? kam (min)
how much (of)? kam (min)
how? kayfa
hundred mi'a
hungry jaa'ix / –uun
husband zawj / 'azwaaj

I

I 'anaa
I have a cold. xindii bard
I have a headache. xindii Sudaax
I have a reservation. xindii Hajz
I have a temperature. xindii Haraara
I have the flu. xindii al-'anfiluwanza
I'm fine, I'm doing well. al-Hamdu lillaah
I'm sorry. xafwan
ignorant jaahil / juhalaa'
ill mariiD / marDaa
important muhimm
in order to (+subjunctive) likay
in fii, bi
in order to li
India al-hind
Indian hindiyy, hindiyya
inexpensive rakhiiS
information maxluuma / –aat

intelligent dhakiyy / 'adhkiyaa'
interesting mumtix, shayyiq
international call mukaalama duwaliyya
international flight riHla dawliyya
internet 'intarnat
Iraq al-xiraaq
Iraqi xiraaqiyy, xiraaqiyya
iron (clothes) mikwaa(t)
it huwa (m.), hiya (f.)
Italian 'iiTaaliyy, iiTaaliyyaa
Italy 'iiTaaliyaa

J

January yanaayir
Japan al-yaabaan
Japanese yaabaaniyy, yaabaaniyya
jeans djiinz / djiinzaat
jeweler jawharjiyy / –yuun
job xamal
Jordan al-'urdun,
Jordanian 'urduniyy, 'urduniyya
journalist SaHaafiyy / –uun
juice xaSiir
July yuulyuu
jump (to) qafaza / yaqfizu
June yuunyuu

K

Kenya kiinyaa
Kenyan kiiniyy, kiiniyya
key miftaaH
kitchen maTbakh
knee rukba / rukbataan
knife sikkiin / sakaakiin
know (to) xarafa / yaxrifu
Korea kuuriyaa
Korean kuuriyy, kuuriyya
Kuwait al-kuwayt
Kuwaiti kuwaytiyy, kuwaytiyya

L

lamp miSbaaH
late afternoon al-xaSr
laugh (to) DaHika / yaD-Haku
lawyer muHaamii / –uun
lazy kasuul / –uun
leather jild
Lebanese lubnaaniyy, lubnaaniyya
Lebanon lubnaan
left, on the left yasaar
leg (feminine) rijl / rijlaan
lengthy Tawiil
letter risaala / rasaa'il
library maktaba / –aat
Libya liibiyaa
Libyan liibiyy, liibiyya
license rukhSa
lift (to) rafaxa / yarfaxu
light switch miftaaH al-kahrabaa'
light khafiif
little Saghiir / Sighaar
live (to) sakana / yaskunu
livingroom ghurfat al-juluus
lobby rad-ha
lonely waHiid
long Tawiil
lose (to) khasira / yakhsiru
loss khasar
lost Daa'ix / –uun; taa'ih/ –uun
loud xaalii
lunch ghadaa' / 'aghdia, wajabaat al-ghadaa'
lung ri'a / ri'ataan

M

mail (to) barada / yabridu
mail bariid
main street Tariiq / Turuq
man rajul / rijaal
manager ra'iis / ru'asaa'
map khariiTa / kharaa'iT

March maaris
market suuq / 'aswaaq
May maayuu
medication 'adwiya
meeting 'ijtimaax / 'ijtimaaxaat
merchant taajir
milk Haliib
minute daqiiqa
mirror mir'aa(t)
Monday al-'ithnayn
money xumla, maal, fuluus
month shahr / 'ash-hur
morning aS-SabaaH
morning aS-SubH
Morocco al-maghrib
Morrocan maghribiyy, maghribiyya
mosque jaamix / jawaamix
mosque masjid / masaajid
mother 'umm / 'ummahaat
mouth fam
movies sinimaa
much kathiiran
museum matHaf / mataaHif
musician muusiiqiyy / –uun
my name 'ismii

N

name 'ism / 'asmaa'
napkin mandiil / manaadil
near (to) qariib (min)
necklace qilaada / –aat
neighborhood mujaawara / –aat
never 'abadan
new jadiid / judud
newspaper jariida / jaraa'id
next to bijaanibi
nice laTiif / liTaaf
night al-layl
nine tisxa
nineteen tisxata xashar

ninety tisxiin / tisxuun
ninth taasix
no laa
noon 'aDH-DHuhr
nose 'anf
not to (+subjunctive) 'allaa
November nufambar
now al-'aan
number raqm / 'arqaam, xadad / 'axdaad
nurse mumarriDa / –aat

O

October 'uktuubar
of course Tabxan
office building binaayat al-xamal
office maktab / makaatib
old (people) kabiir / kibaar
old (things) qadiim / qudamaa'
Oman xumaan
Omani xumaaniyy, xumaaniyya
on xalaa
one waaHid
one (person) 'aHad
onion baSala / baSalaat
open (to) fataHa / yaftaHu
operator xaamil haatifiyy / xummaal haatifiyyiin
orange burtuqaala / burtuqaal

P

Palestine filisTiin
Palestinian filisTiiniyy, filisTiiniyya
pants sirwaal / saraawiil
paper (sheet of) waraqa / 'awraaq
Pardon me. xafwan.
park muntazah / muntazahaat
party Hafla / –aat
passenger raakib
passport jawaaz as-safar
pastry shop dukkaan al-Halwaani
pay (to) khallaSa / yukhalliSu

payphone haatif xumuumiyy
pepper fulful
person shakhS / 'ashkhaaS
phone booth ghurfat al-haatif
phone call mukaalama haatifiyya
photograph Suura / Suwar
picture Suura / Suwar
pillow wisaada
PIN number raqm sirriyy
plate Tabaq / 'aTbaaq
play (sports/games) (to) laxaba / yalxabu
please tafaDDal(ii)
policeman shurTiyy
poor faqiir / fuqaraa'
pork khinziir
porter Hammaal
possible mumkin
post card biTaaqa bariidiyya / –aat
post office maktab al-bariid
powerful xaDHiim / xuDHamaa'
pretty jamiil
printer maTbaxa
private beach shaaTi' khaaS
profession mihna / mihan
professor 'ustaadh / 'asaatidha'
public phone haatif xumuumiyy
put on (clothes) (to) labisa / yalbasu
pyramid haram / 'ahraam

Q

Qatar qatar
Qatari qatariyy, qatariyya
question su'aal / 'as'ila
quiet haadi'

R

radio raadyuu
raise (to) rafaxa / yarfaxu
rain maTar
raining, it's al-jaww mumTir

read (to) qara'a / yaqra'u
receipt waSl
receive (to) qabala / yaqbalu
reception desk maktab al-'istiqbaal
receptionist kaatiba / –aat
red 'aHmar, Hamraa' / Humr
referee Hakam
remedy xilaaj
remember (to) tadhakkara / yatadhakkaru
Repeat. 'axid
report taqriir
reservation Hajz
residence manzil
restaurant maTxam / maTaaxim
return (to) rajaxa / yarjixu
rice 'aruzz
right (correct) SaHiiH
right, on the right yamiin
ring khaatim / khawaatim
robe, traditional Arab jallaabiyya / –aat
room ghurfa / ghuraf
room, double ghurfa li-ithnayn
room, single ghurfa li-waaHid
rose warda / wuruud

S

sad Haziin / Huzanaa'
safe khizaana
sales department daa'irat al-bayx
salesman baa'ix / baaxa(t)
salt milH
sand raml
Saturday as-sabt
Saudi Arabia as-saxuudiyya
Saudi saxuudiyy, saxuudiyya
save (to) 'iddakhara / yaddakhiru
schedule jadwal (al-'awqaat), jadaawil (al-'awqaat)
school madrasa / madaaris
school of a university kulliyya / –aat
score muHraza

sea baHr
second thaanii
secretary kaatiba / –aat, kaatib
see (to) ra'aa / yaraa
See you tomorrow. 'ilaa l-ghad.
send (to) 'arsala / yursilu
Senegal as-sinighaal
Senegalese sinighaaliyy, sinighaaliyya
September sibtambar
seven sabxa
seventeen sabxata xashar
seventh saabix
seventy sabxiin / sabxuun
she hiya
shirt qamiiS / 'aqmiSa
shoe Hidhaa' / 'aHdhia
shoe store dukkaan al-aHdhia
short qaSiir / qiSaar
shoulder (feminine) katif / katifaan
shower dushsh
shy khajuul / –uun
sick mariiD / marDaa
sickness maraD
signature 'imDaa'
silk Hariir
singer mughannii / –iyuun
single room ghurfa li-waaHid
sink maghsala / –aat
sister 'ukht / 'akhawaat
sit (to) jalasa / yajlisu
sitting room ghurfat al-juluus
six sitta
sixteen sittata xashar
sixth saadis
sixty sittiin / sittuun
skating tazalluj
skiing tazaHluq
skin jild
sleep (to) naama / yanaamu
sleepy taxbaan

slim naHiif
slippers balgha / –aat
slow baTii' / –uun
small Saghiir / Sighaar
smart dhakiyy / 'adhkiyaa'
snowing, it's al-jaww muthlij
so that (+subjunctive) Hattaa
soccer kurat al-qadam
socks jawaarib
someone 'aHad
sometimes aHyaanaan
son 'ibn / 'abnaa', walad / 'awlaad
soup Hasaa'
Spain 'isbaaniyaa
Spanish 'isbaaniyy, 'isbaaniyya
speak (to) takallama / yatakallamu
Speak slowly. takallam bi buT'in
spicy taabiliyy; mutabbal
spoon milxaqa / malaaxiq
sports riyaaDa
spring ar-rabiix
stamp Taabix / Tawaabix
stand (to) waqafa / yaqifu
start (to) bada'a / yabda'u
statue timthaal / tamaathiil
Stop. qif
store dukkaan / dakaakiin, maHall
stranger ghariib / ghurabaa'
street nahj / 'anhuj, zanqaa / –aat (small street)
strong qawiyy / 'aqwiyaa'
student (college, grad) Taalib / Tulaab
student (high school) tilmiidh / talaamiidh
study (to) darasa / yadrusu
Sudan as-suudaan
Sudanese suudaaniyy, suudaaniyya
sugar sukkar
summer aS-Sayf
Sunday al-'aHad
sunny, it's al-jaww mushmis
surgeon jarraaH

swim (to) sabaHa / yasbaHu
swimming pool masbaH
swimming sibaaHa
synagogue kaniisa / kanaa'is
Syria suuriyaa
Syrian suuriyy, suuriyya

T

take (to) 'akhadha / ya'khudhu
take off (clothes) (to) khalaxa / yakhlaxu
Take me . . . khudhnii . . .
tall Tawiil / Tiwaal
taxi taaksii
tea shaay
teach (to) xallama / yuxallimu
teach darrasa / yudarrisu
teacher mudarris / –uun
teacher muxallim / –uun
team fariiq
telephone book daliil al-haatif / 'adillat al-haatif
telephone number raqm al-haatif
telephone haatif / hawaatif
television tilifizyuun/ –aat
Tell me . . . qul-lii
ten xashara
tenth xaashir
terrible rahiib
Thai taylandiyy, taylandiyya
Thailand taylaand
thank you (very much) shukran (jaziilan)
that (feminine) tilka
that (masculine) dhaalika
that . . . 'anna . . .
the best . . . 'aHsan . . .
the day after tomorrow baxda l-ghad
the day before yesterday 'ams al-'awwal
the two of them (m. or f.) humaa
the two of you (m. or f.) 'antumaa
The United States al-wilaayaat al-muttaHida
theater masraH / masaariH

there hunaaka
these (gender neutral) haa'ulaa'i
they (f. plural) hunna
they (m. plural) hum
they (non-human) hiya
they (two) humaa
thin naHiif
think (to) DHanna / yaDHunnu
third thaalith
thirsty xaTshaan / xaTishuun
thirteen thalaathata xashar
thirty thalaathiin / thalaathuun
this (feminine) haadhihi
this (masculine) haadhaa
those (gender neutral) 'uulaa'ika
three thalaatha
throw (to) ramaa / yarmii
Thursday khamiis, al-
ticket tadhkira / tadhaakir
time of arrival mawxid al-wuSuul
tip baqshiish
tired taxbaan
to (+ subjunctive) 'an
to 'ilaa
today al-yawm
toe 'iSbax al-qadam / 'aSaabix . . .
toilet mirHaaD
tomato TamaaTima / TamaaTim
tomorrow 'al-ghad, ghadan
tongue lisaan
too (also) 'ayDan
tooth sinn / 'asnaan
tourist saa'iH / suwwaaH
towards 'ilaa
towel fuuTa
traditional Arab robe jallaabiyya / –aat
train station maHaTTat al-qiTaar
train qiTaar
trader taajir
translator mutarjim / –uun

travel (to) saafara / yusaafiru
travel agency maktab as-siyaaHa
Tuesday ath-thulaathaa'
Tunisia tuunis
Tunisian tuunisiyy, tuunisiyya
turn (to) xaTafa / yaxTufu
twelfth thaanii xashar
twelve 'ithnaa xashar
twenty one waaHid wa xishruun
twenty three thalaatha wa xishruun
twenty two 'ithnayn wa xishruun
twenty xishruun
two 'ithnayn

U

uncle (maternal side) khaal / 'akhwaal
uncle (paternal side) xamm / 'axmaam
under taHta
understand (to) fahima / yafhamu
university jaamixa / –aat
Until next time. 'ilaa l-liqaa'.
Until tomorrow. 'ilaa l-ghad.
usually 'ixtiyaadiyyan

V

vegetable khuDar
very jiddan
village qarya / quraa
visit (to) zaara / yazuuru

W

waiter xaamil bi l-maTxam, naadil
walk (to) mashaa / yamshii
watch (to) shaahada / yushaahidu
watch saaxa / –aat
water maa'
we naHnu
weak Daxiif / Duxafaa'
weather jaww
weather Taqs

Wednesday al-'arbixaa'
week 'usbuux / 'asaabiix
weigh (to) kayyala / yukayyilu
weight wazn
welcome marHaban bika/biki, tafaDDal(ii)
what? (used with nouns and pronouns) maa
what? (used with verbs) maadha
when? mataa
where? 'ayna
white 'abyaD, bayDaa' / biiD
who? man
wife zawja / –aat
will not (+subjunctive) lan
win (noun) fawz
win (to) rabaHa / yarbiHu
window shubbaak
wine khamr
winter ash-shitaa'
With best wishes. maxaa 'aTyab al-'umniyyaat.
with maxa
with bi
withdraw (to) saHaba / yasHabu
without biduun
woman (irregular singular/plural) 'imra'a / nisaa'
women nisaa'
wonderful mumtaaz
work xamal, mihna
work (to) xamila / yaxmalu
worker xaamil / xummaal
write (to) kataba / yaktubu
Write. (command) 'uktub
writer kaatib
wrong khata'

X

x-ray Suurat ashixxa

Y

year sana / sanawaat
yellow 'aSfar, Safraa' / Sufr

Yemen al-yaman
Yemeni yamaniyy, yamaniyya
yes naxam
yesterday 'ams
yesterday al-baariHa
you (f. plural) 'antunna
you (f.) 'anti
you (m. plural) 'antum
you (m.) 'anta
you (two) 'antumaa
young Saghiir / Sighaar
your name (masculine, feminine) 'ismuka, 'ismuki

Z

zero Sifr
ZIP code, city postal code raqm al-madiina, tarqiim al-bariid

INDEX